SIGHT WORDS

Puzzles
and
Games

BY SHANNON KEELEY

FlashKids

New York

New York

An Imprint of Sterling Publishing Co., Inc.
1166 Avenue of the Americas
New York, NY 10036

ISBN 978-1-4114-7904-3

Distributed in Canada by Sterling Publishing Co., Inc.
C/o Canadian Manda Group, 664 Annette Street
Toronto, Ontario M6S 2C8, Canada
Distributed in the United Kingdom by GMC Distribution Services
Castle Place, 166 High Street, Lewes, East Sussex BN7 1XU, England
Distributed in Australia by NewSouth Books
University of New South Wales,Sydney,NSW 2052,Australia

For information about custom editions, special sales, and premium and corporate
purchases, please contact Sterling Special Sales at 800-805-5489 or
specialsales@sterlingpublishing.com.

Manufactured in Canada

Lot #:
2 4 6 8 10 9 7 5 3
12/18

flashkids.com

Cover and interior design by Irene Vandervoort

Dear Parent,

This book contains 220 words that are key to your child's reading success. "Sight words" are the most frequently used words in our language. In fact, sight words make up over half of what we read! But even though these words are commonly used, many have uncommon spelling patterns and cannot be sounded out. This is why it's so important that children learn to recognize them immediately—or "on sight."

Memorizing sight words requires time and repetition. This book introduces your child to all 220 sight words, and offers practice tracing, writing, and reading each word. Fun puzzles and games help your child identify each sight word within a larger block of text, recognize correct spelling patterns, and differentiate between words that look similar. The key to making sight words "stick" is to make the practice fun, and these pages will do just that!

This book is divided into five sections of increasing difficulty. Regular review units bring together many sight words and help readers retain what they've learned. Watch your child's fluency and confidence soar as he or she begins reading and making sentences using sight words. Enjoy this special time as your child builds a strong foundation and unlocks the keys to reading!

a	call	funny	just	only	small	use
about	can	gave	keep	open	so	very
after	came	get	kind	or	some	walk
again	carry	give	know	our	soon	want
all	clean	go	laugh	out	start	warm
always	cold	goes	let	over	stop	was
am	come	going	light	own	take	wash
an	could	good	like	pick	tell	we
and	cut	got	little	play	ten	well
any	did	grow	live	please	that	went
are	do	green	long	pretty	thank	were
around	does	had	look	pull	the	what
as	done	has	made	put	their	when
ask	don't	have	make	ran	them	where
at	down	he	many	read	then	which
ate	draw	help	may	red	there	white
away	drink	her	me	ride	these	who
be	eat	here	much	right	they	why
because	eight	him	must	round	think	will
been	every	his	my	run	this	wish
before	fall	hold	myself	said	those	with
best	far	hot	never	saw	three	work
better	fast	how	new	say	to	would
big	find	hurt	no	see	today	write
black	first	I	not	seven	together	yellow
blue	five	if	now	shall	too	yes
both	fly	in	of	she	try	you
bring	for	into	off	show	two	your
brown	found	is	old	sing	under	
but	four	it	on	sit	up	
buy	from	its	once	six	upon	
by	full	jump	one	sleep	us	

Section 1

The sight words included in this section are:

a	funny	make	so
and	go	me	the
away	help	my	three
big	here	not	to
blue	I	on	two
but	in	one	up
can	is	play	we
come	it	red	where
down	jump	run	yellow
find	little	said	yes
for	look	see	you

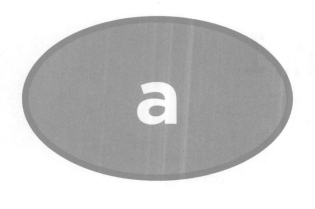

Trace the word a and say it aloud.

a

Practice writing the word a.

I am ____ boy.

Balloon Buddies

Draw a circle around the word a to make a balloon.
Put an X through the other words.

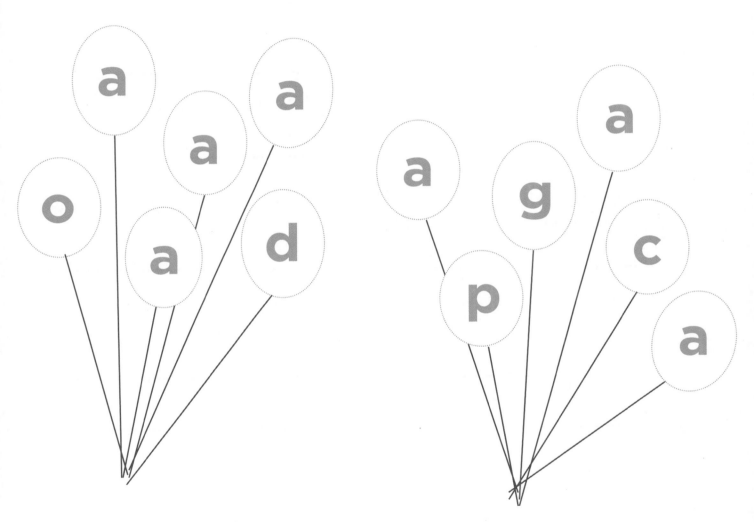

Count the balloons in each bunch.
Circle the bunch that has more balloons.

How many balloons are there altogether? _____

the

Trace the word the and say it aloud.

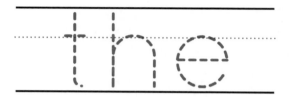

Practice writing the word the.

_____

_____

_____

_____

_____

_____

_____

_____

I see _____ sun.

Made in the Shade

Shade each box that has the word **the**. Then match each number to the corresponding letter to fill in the blanks below.

5	he	hen	thin	the	with
4	the	her	her	why	tee
3	to	tree	to	tee	the
2	this	the	she	that	than
1	it	then	the	his	tea

l   h   C   e   i

What country makes you shiver?

____ ____ ____ ____ ____
 1   2   3   4   5

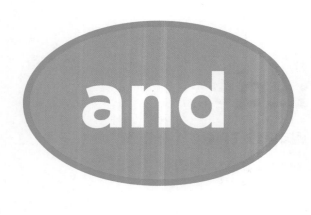
and

Trace the word and and say it aloud.

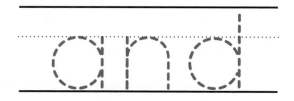

Practice writing the word and.

_____   _____

....

_____   _____

_____   _____

....

_____   _____

I can run _____ jump.

Word Tunnels

Connect the letters of the word **and** to make a tunnel. Use the number at the tunnel exit to complete the fun fact.

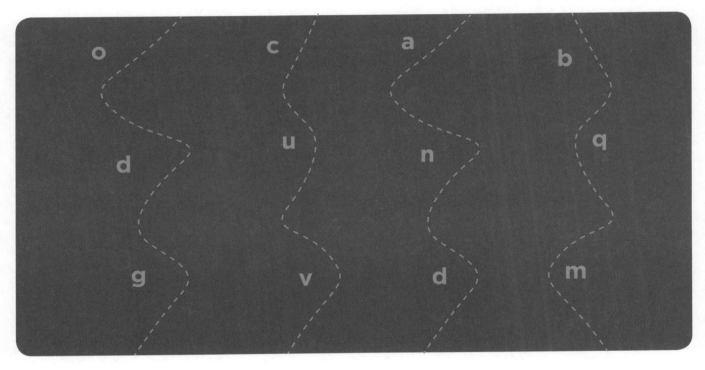

o   c   a   b

d   u   n   q

g   v   d   m

5   100   25   52

There are _____ species of chipmunks!

Circle the nuts that show the word **and**.

and   add   and   and   abd

Trace the word **to** and say it aloud.

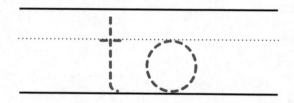

Practice writing the word to.

I go _____ school.

Sight Word Slices

Draw a line from the word **to** in the middle of each pizza to the matching words on the edges of each pizza. See how many slices you make.

Pizza A

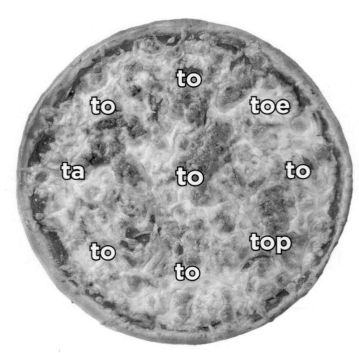

Pizza B

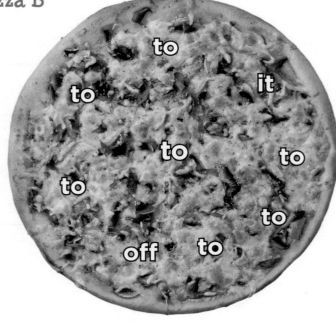

Which pizza has more slices? _____

How many slices in all? _____

Trace the word I and say it aloud.

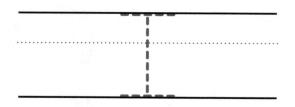

Practice writing the word I.

_____ see you.

Postcard Puzzler

Circle the word I each time it appears on the postcard. Write the number in the stamp in the corner. Find the matching number below to see where the postcard is from.

Dear Kim,

I am having so much fun! It rains a little bit in the morning. I go to the beach every day. Dad and I are visiting a volcano tomorrow. Dad says I have to wear sunblock. I miss you!

Love,

Nora

Kim Smith

47 South Street

Seattle, WA 98101

1. New York City

2. Paris

3. San Diego

4. Boston

5. Hawaii

6. Washington, D.C.

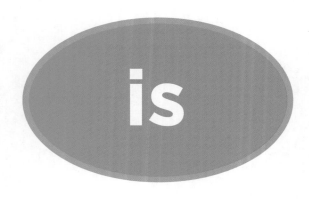**is**

Trace the word is and say it aloud.

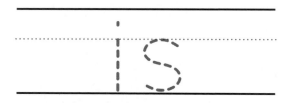

Practice writing the word is.

It _____ hot.

Riddle Row

Circle all rows and columns that have the word is five times. Match the symbols with the letters outside the grid to solve the riddle.

	+	*	<	+	#	
#	is	us	is	is	is	g
+	is	is	if	is	is	i
<	is	is	is	sit	is	e
*	is	is	is	is	is	a
<	in	is	it	its	is	t
	a	n	u	d	o	

Which two days other than Tuesday and Thursday start with a "T"?

t ____ d ____ y   ____ n d   t ____ m ____ r r ____ w
　 #　 *　 　　 *　　　 #　 #　 #

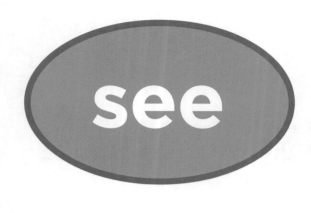

Trace the word **see** and say it aloud.

see

Practice writing the word see.

We _____ the bus.

Ladder Line Up

Underline **see** if it appears within the longer word. Circle the ladder that has an underlined word on the most steps.

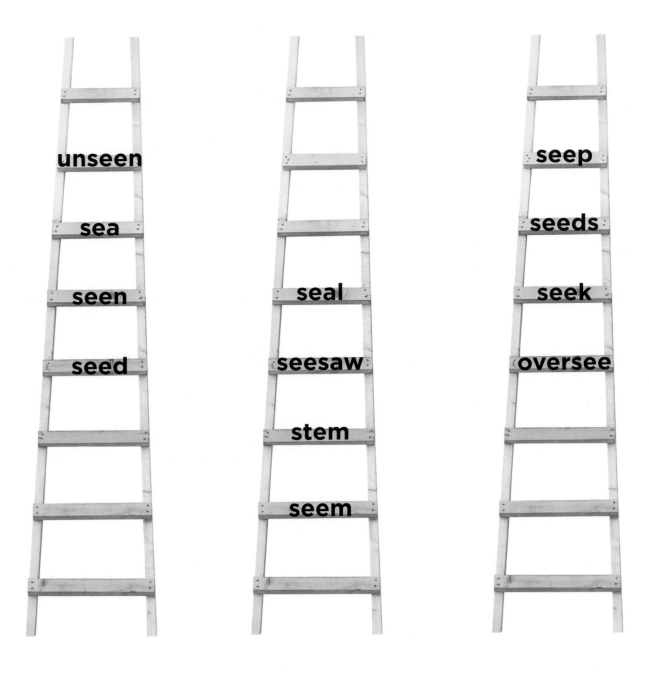

unseen

sea

seen

seed

seep

seeds

seek

oversee

seal

seesaw

stem

seem

Trace the word me and say it aloud.

Practice writing the word me.

Look at _____ !

Follow the Chain

Draw a circle every time you see the word me.
If your circles make a chain, write the number of
times the word me appears.

m e m e m e m e m e m e   _____

m e m e m e m e m e m e m e   _____

m e m e m e e m e m e m e e   _____

m e m e m e m e m e m e m e   _____

m e m e m e m e m e m e m e m e   _____

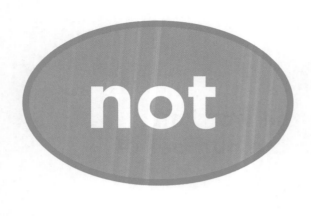

Trace the word not and say it aloud.

not

Practice writing the word not.

I do _____ eat nuts.

Rhyme Score

Circle the word not each time it appears on the field. Underline any words that rhyme with not. Count the total for each and fill in the score board.

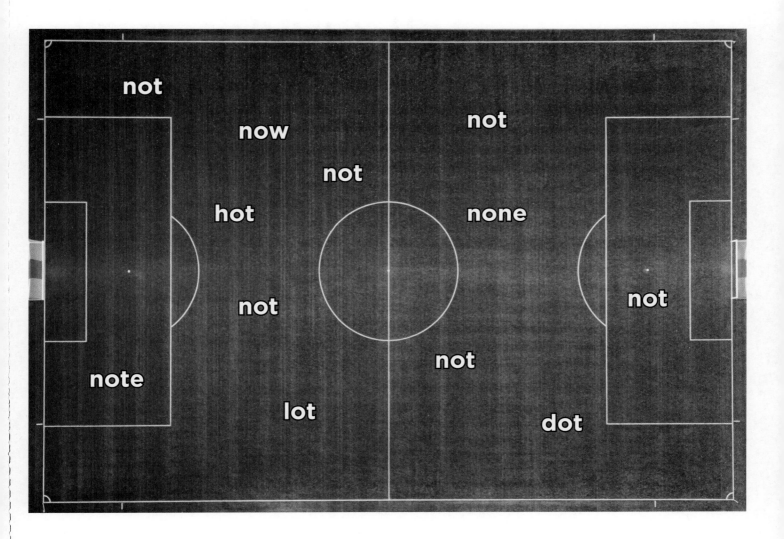

NOT   RHYMES WITH NOT

_____   _____

**can**

Trace the word **can** and say it aloud.

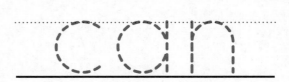

Practice writing the word can.

I _____ help.

Three Ring Circus

Find the word **can** three times inside each ring and circle it.

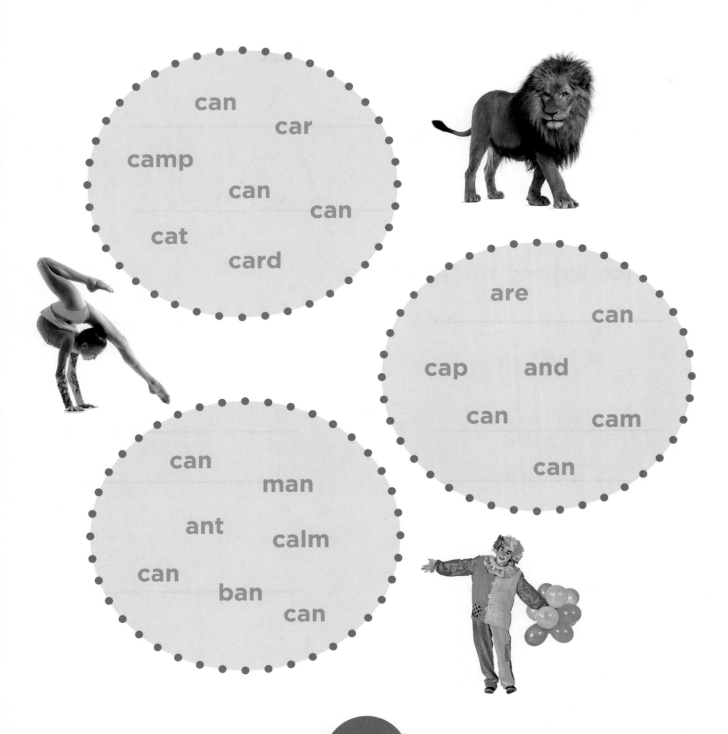

can

car

camp

can

can

cat

card

are

can

cap   and

can   cam

can

can

man

ant

calm

can

ban

can

 **you**

Trace the word you and say it aloud.

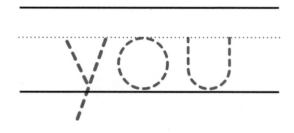

Practice writing the word you.

I like _____.

Play Along

Draw a circle around the word you to make a music note. Follow the code for the circled notes to answer the joke.

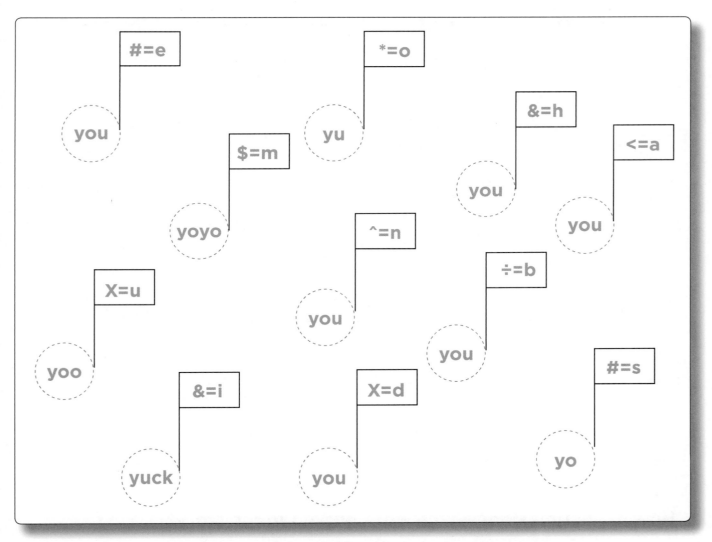

What makes music on your hair?

___ _____ ___

< & # < X ÷ < ^ X

REVIEW: The Bottom Line

Use the codes to help fill in the missing words to the story.

a	the	and	I	to
——	• • • • •	～	═	- - -

_____ went with my dad _____ _____ fair. We saw
(═)   (- - -)   (• • • • •)

pigs _____ horses. _____ played lots of games. We ate hot dogs
      (～)   (═)

_____ popcorn. _____ wanted _____ buy cotton candy too.
(～)   (═)   (- - -)

My dad _____ _____ rode _____ big slide together. It started
        (～)   (═)   (• • • • •)

_____ get dark. Some of _____ rides lit up! _____ stayed up late
(- - -)   (• • • • •)   (═)

_____ watch _____ fireworks. Then it was time _____ go.
(- - -)   (• • • • •)   (- - -)

How many times does each word appear in the story?

a _____   I _____

the _____   to _____

and _____

28

REVIEW: Matching Caps

Draw a line to connect the matching sight words.
Fill in the letter in the blue circle next to each cap to
name the sport below.

1. is

2. see

3. can

4. me

5. not

6. you

you — r

me — c

not — e

can — c

is — s

see — o

The field this sport is played on is called the "pitch."

___ ___ ___ ___ ___ ___
 1   2   3   4   5   6

29

it

Trace the word **it** and say it aloud.

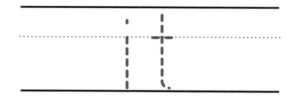

Practice writing the word it.

_____   _____
....

_____   _____

_____   _____
....

_____   _____

Please put _____ away.

Button Up

Draw a circle around the word **it** to make buttons on the sweaters. Circle the sweater with more buttons.

it
it
in
it
is
on

it
if
it
it
it
in

 **my**

Trace the word my and say it aloud.

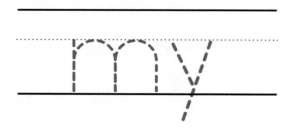

Practice writing the word my.

This is _____ room.

Funny Food

Circle the word my each time you see it. Write the total under each can, and use the code to answer the joke.

my
many
my
may
my
you

_____ = c

my
eye
am
my
fly
ny

_____ = b

my
my
my
may
my
yam

_____ = i

my
by
move
mv
mom
man

_____ = e

my
mv
my
my
my
my

_____ = t

my
my
my
my
my
my

_____ = r

What's a penguin's favorite food?

____ ____ ____ ____ ____ g
 4   3   1   2   1   6

l____ ____ ____ u____ ____
  1   5   5   3   1

33

for

Trace the word for and say it aloud.

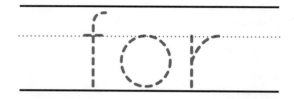

Practice writing the word for.

_____   _____

_____   _____

_____   _____

_____   _____

She made it _____ me.

Check It Out

Put a check mark by the word **for** in the book titles.
If the title does not have the word **for**, leave it blank.

Tricks for Dogs

Food and Fun for Parties

Letters from My Brother

Far and Wide

Two for Tea

Life on the Farm

Searching for Gold

For the Love of Baseball

How many book titles have the word **for**?

_____

 **go**

Trace the word go and say it aloud.

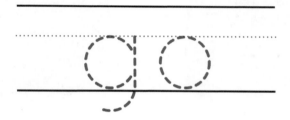

Practice writing the word go.

I _____ to the park.

Prize Tickets

Underline the word **go** each time you see it on the ticket. Write the number on the line.

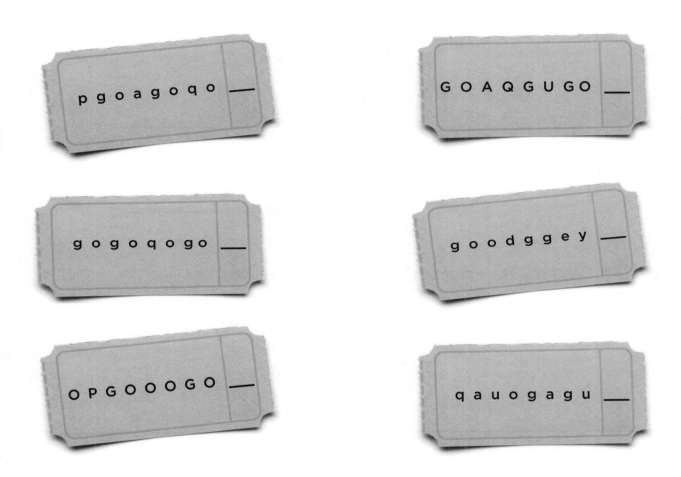

p g o a g o q o ___

G O A Q G U G O ___

g o g o q o g o ___

g o o d g g e y ___

O P G O O O G O ___

q a u o g a g u ___

Add up the numbers on all the tickets. _____

10   2   5   2   1

Circle the prize that equals the number of underlined words.

Trace the word said and say it aloud.

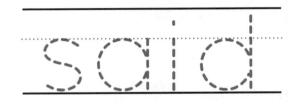

Practice writing the word said.

_____   _____

....

_____   _____

_____   _____

....

_____   _____

"Hello," she _____ .

Candy Code

Look at the letters inside each candy. If you can unscramble the letters to make the word said, then write said on the line and follow the code. If not, leave it blank.

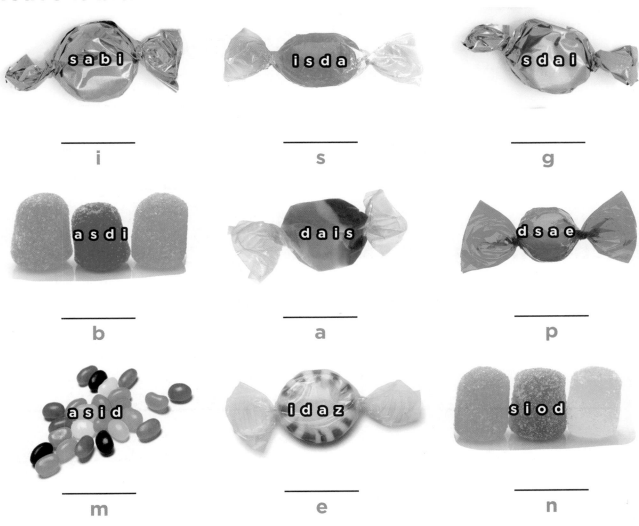

sabi	isda	sdai
_____	_____	_____
i	s	g
asdi	dais	dsae
_____	_____	_____
b	a	p
asid	idaz	siod
_____	_____	_____
m	e	n

What kind of candy do bears eat?

___ u ___ ___ y ___ e ___ r ___

Trace the word up and say it aloud.

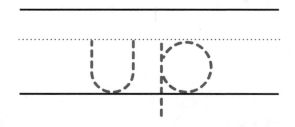

Practice writing the word up.

We go _____ and down.

Boxcar Race

Draw a box around the word up when you see it hiding inside another word. The car with more boxes wins the race.

bug

puppy

upbeat

upside

hop

pull

warmup

ugly

cup

under

rub

backup

pup

push

fun

upset

muddy

upbeat

 **we**

Trace the word **we** and say it aloud.

Practice writing the word we.

Today _____ are at school.

Lucky Card

Color all the shapes that have the word **we** inside.

Circle the card suit that has all the shapes colored.

 **big**

Trace the word big and say it aloud.

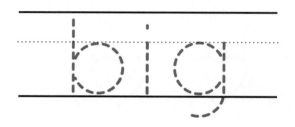

Practice writing the word big.

_____   _____

_____   _____

_____   _____

The box is _____.

Around the Clock

Draw a line from the middle of the clock to the word big. Follow each line to fill in the correct letter below.

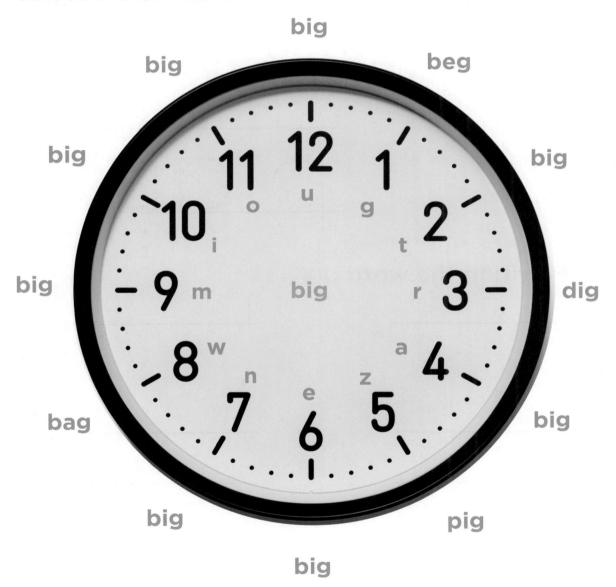

big
big   beg
big   big
              big
big   dig
bag   big
     big   pig
          big

Why was the clock in the corner?

It was ___ ___   ___   ___ ___ ___   ___ ___ ___
       10 7   4   2 10 9   6 11 12 2

play

Trace the word play and say it aloud.

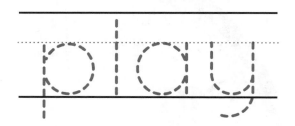

Practice writing the word play.

_____

_____

_____

_____

_____

_____

We _____ outside.

Fishing for Rhymes

Draw a line from each fishing pole to the words that rhyme with play.

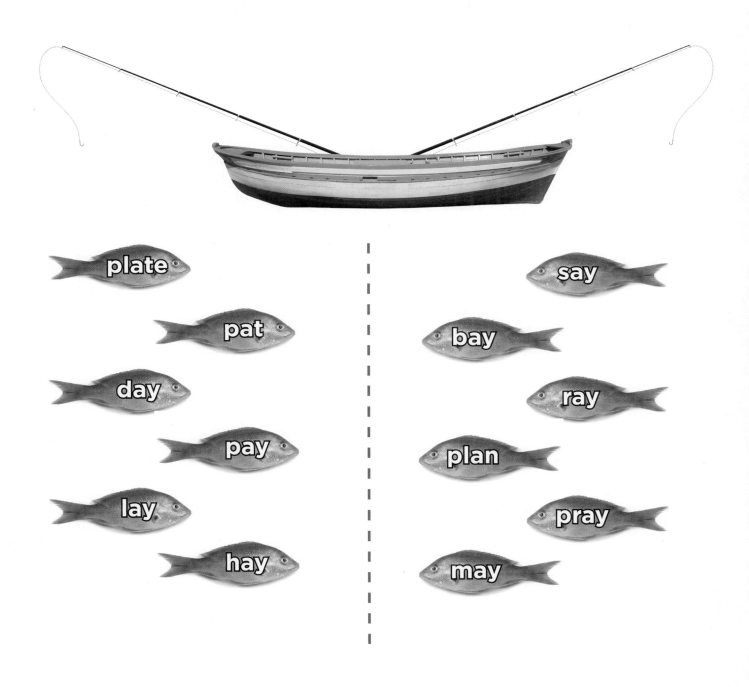

plate

say

pat

bay

day

ray

pay

plan

lay

pray

hay

may

Which side caught more fish? _____

Trace the word **run** and say it aloud.

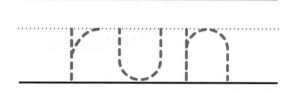

Practice writing the word run.

I _____ fast.

Fun Fact

Ask an adult to read you the paragraph below. Then shade one box from the bottom up every time you see the word **run**.

70	run
60	run
50	run
40	run
30	run
20	run
10	run

Cheetahs can run very fast! How do they run so fast? Their long legs help them run. Cheetah's bodies are light. This helps them run faster than other animals. Their claws grip the ground as they run. Cheetahs like to run away instead of fighting.

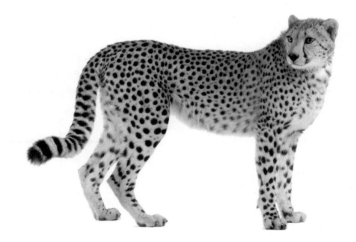

Use the number at the top of your bar to complete this fun fact:

Cheetahs can run about _____ miles per hour.

Trace the word here and say it aloud.

Practice writing the word here.

_____   _____

....

_____   _____

_____   _____

....

_____   _____

We are _____ .

Beautiful Bubbles

Cross out any bubble that does not have the word **here**.

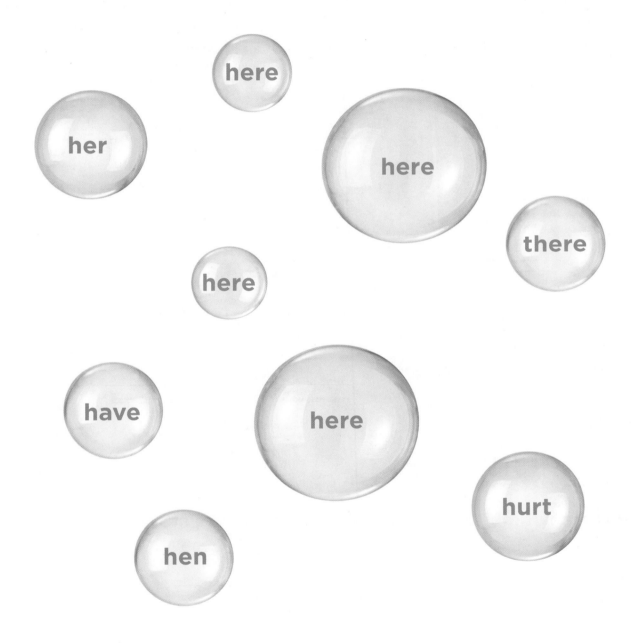

here

her

here

here

there

have

here

hurt

hen

How many bubbles remain? _____

REVIEW: The Bottom Line

Use the codes to help fill in the missing words to the story.

my	big	run	we	play
——	•••••	~~~	══	- - -

_____ dog Sparky is really _____ . Sparky likes to _____

and _____ outside. He can _____ fast and catch a ball in his

mouth. _____ go on walks and _____ at the park. Sometimes,

Sparky chews on _____ shoes. _____ mom doesn't like that.

On weekends, Sparky gets on _____ bed and _____ take a nap.

Sparky is _____ best friend.

How many times does each word appear in the story?

my _____   we _____

big _____   play _____

run _____

REVIEW: Matching Caps

Draw a line to connect the matching sight words. Fill in the letter in the blue circle next to each cap to name the sport below.

1. it

2. go

3. said

4. here

5. for

6. up

 **a**

for **t**

it **k**

go **a**

up **e**

said **r**

In this sport, you wear a colored belt to show what level you are.

___ ___ ___ ___ ___ ___
1   2   3   4   5   6

REVIEW: Word Search

Find the review words in the word search.

is   can   you   me   my   big   and   up   I   a   for

```
C   F   N   M   E   J   F   Y
N   I   D   W   T   A   N   D
O   S   T   U   K   Y   D   T
A   R   V   W   B   O   Q   C
U   C   A   N   T   U   P   X
T   Y   B   U   M   J   K   O
B   I   G   N   Y   T   I   U
X   T   H   D   F   O   R   Y
```

REVIEW: The Lost Word

Look for each review word from page 54 and circle it below. There is one word from the list that is missing.

Stormy is lost!

Can you help me find my cat, Stormy?

She is big and gray.

I have a reward for anyone

who can help!

Which review word is missing? _____

REVIEW: Crossword Clues

Complete each sentence with a review word from the box. Use the words to fill in the puzzle on the next page.

the	to	see	not	it	go
said	we	play	run	here	

ACROSS

2. We live _____ .

5. Please do _____ run.

7. Let's _____ outside.

9. _____ game is today.

10. We _____ to school.

DOWN

1. I _____ a rainbow.

3. We _____ in the race.

4. Today, _____ is sunny.

6. He _____ his name.

8. _____ are at home.

9. You can go _____ the park.

Use the clues on page 56 to fill in the puzzle.

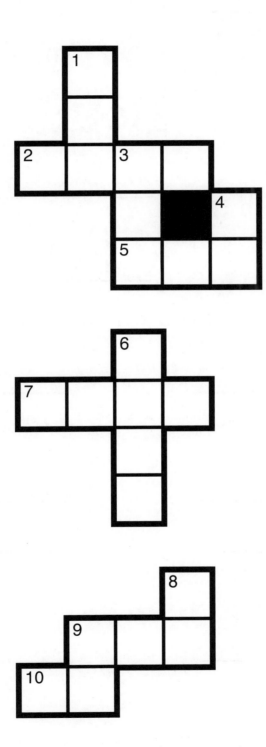

 **away**

Trace the word away and say it aloud.

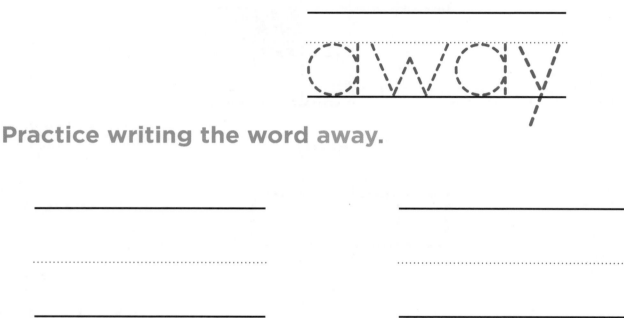

Practice writing the word away.

I live far _____ .

Balloon Buddies

Draw a circle around the word **away** to make a balloon.
Put an X through the other words.

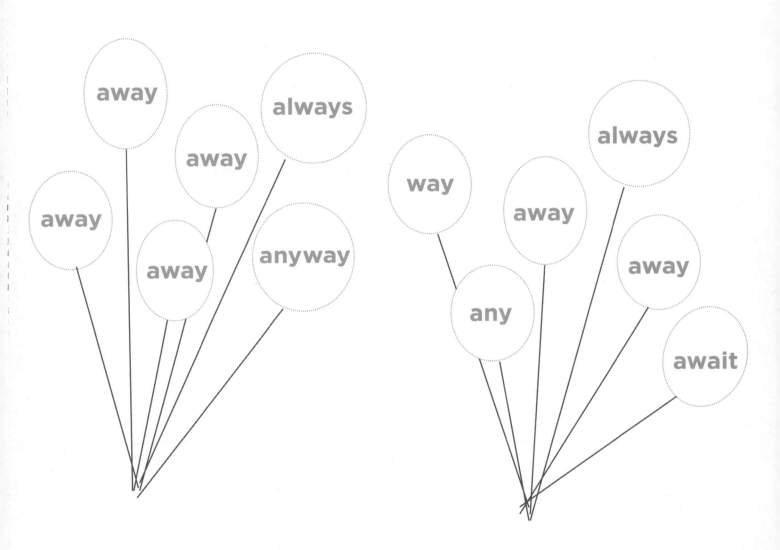

Count the balloons in each bunch.
Circle the bunch that has more balloons.

How many balloons are there altogether? _____

 **down** Trace the word **down** and say it aloud.

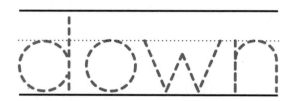

Practice writing the word down.

Go _____ the stairs.

Made in the Shade

Shade each box that has the word **down**.
Then match each number to the corresponding
letter to fill in the blanks below.

5	doubt	bone	down	dawn	done
4	down	door	doll	don't	dawn
3	dawn	done	dud	done	down
2	dent	down	dove	do	bow
1	bows	dot	dog	down	dine

t   a   y   p   r

What kind of tea should you give a large group?

A ____ ____ ____ ____ ____
    1   2   3   4   5

 **Trace the word yellow and say it aloud.**

Practice writing the word yellow.

_____   _____

_____   _____

_____   _____

The banana is _____ .

Word Tunnels

Connect the letters of the word yellow to make a tunnel. Use the number at the tunnel exit to complete the fun fact.

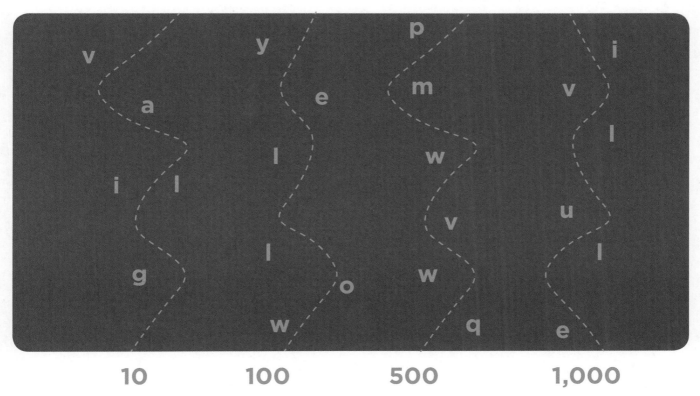

10   100   500   1,000

Chipmunks gather about _____ acorns a day!

Circle the nuts that show the word yellow.

yawn   yellow   yell   yellow   yellow

 **red**

Trace the word red and say it aloud.

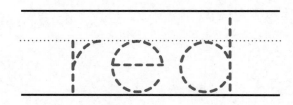

Practice writing the word red.

The stop sign is _____ .

Sight Word Slices

Draw a line from the word red in the middle of each pie to the matching words on the edge of each pie. See how many slices you make.

Pie A

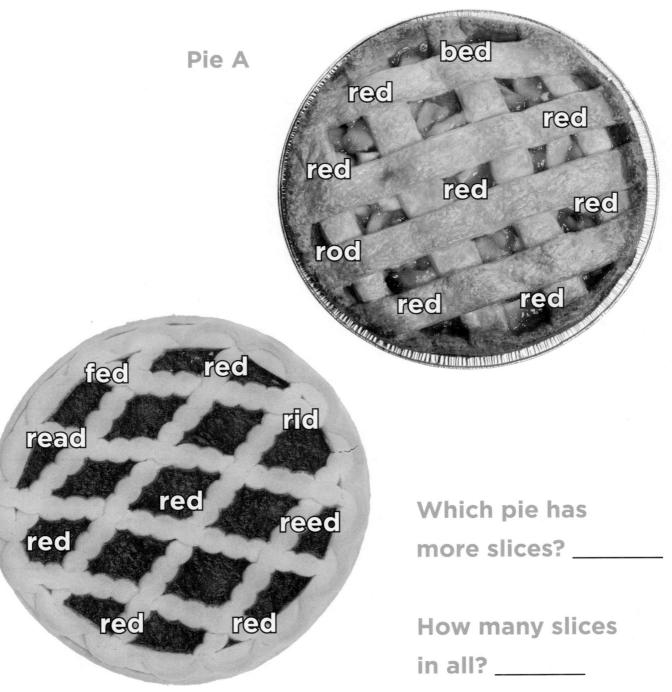

Pie B

Which pie has more slices? _____

How many slices in all? _____

Trace the word **two** and say it aloud.

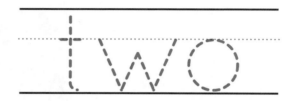

Practice writing the word two.

_____   _____

_____   _____

_____   _____

I have _____ hands.

Postcard Puzzler

Circle the word **two** each time it appears on the postcard. Write the number in the stamp in the corner. Find the matching number below to see where the postcard is from.

Dear Brad,

These have been the best two weeks! We take the subway to all kinds of places. We are only two stops away from a great museum. We are close to Central Park too. I saw two musicals on Broadway. The time is flying by. I will be home in two days. See you soon!

~Peter

Brad Riley

657 Hill Street

Los Angeles, CA 90001

1. Mexico

2. San Francisco

3. Florida

4. New York City

5. Seattle

6. England

 **Trace the word come and say it aloud.**

Practice writing the word come.

_____   _____

....

_____   _____

_____   _____

....

_____   _____

Please _____ here.

Riddle Row

Circle all rows and columns that have the word come five times. Match the symbols with the letters outside the grid to solve the riddle.

	+	<	*	+	<	
*	came	come	come	cone	come	g
+	come	come	come	come	come	c
<	can	come	cold	came	cow	l
+	come	come	come	code	come	t
*	can't	come	cane	come	come	s
	b	d	m	o	r	

What has thirteen hearts?

A __ a r __ __ e __ k.
   +   <   <   +

where

Trace the word where and say it aloud.

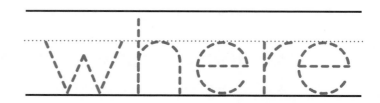

Practice writing the word where.

_____   _____

_____   _____

_____   _____

_____   _____

I know _____ to go.

Ladder Line Up

Underline **where** **if it appears within the longer word. Circle the ladder that has an underlined word on the most steps.**

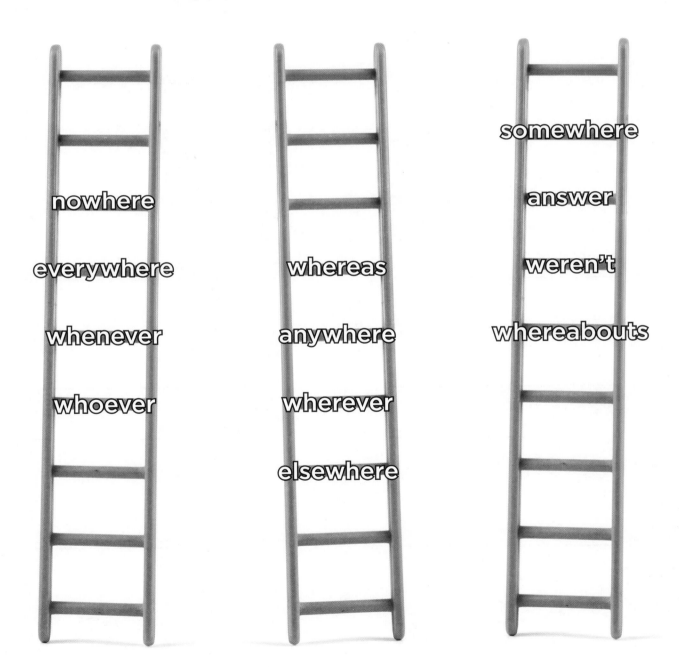

nowhere

everywhere

whenever

whoever

whereas

anywhere

wherever

elsewhere

somewhere

answer

weren't

whereabouts

Trace the word **help** and say it aloud.

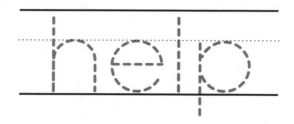

Practice writing the word **help**.

Can you _____ me?

Follow the Chain

Draw a circle every time you see the word **help**. If your circles make a chain write the number of times the word **help** appears.

h e l p h e l p h e l p   _____

h e l p h e l p   _____

h e l p h e l l o h l p   _____

h e l p h e l p h e l p   _____

h e l p h e l p h e l p   _____

find

Trace the word find and say it aloud.

Practice writing the word find.

_____   _____

_____   _____

_____   _____

_____   _____

I can _____ the way.

Rhyme Score

Circle the word find each time it appears on the field. Underline any words that rhyme with find. Count the total for each and fill in the score board.

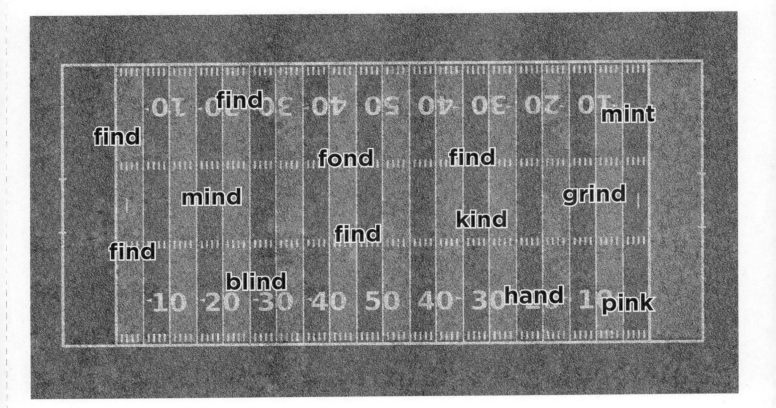

FIND   RHYMES WITH FIND

_____   _____

blue

Trace the word blue and say it aloud.

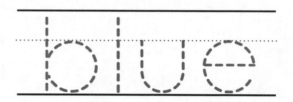

Practice writing the word blue.

_____   _____

_____   _____

_____   _____

The sky is _____.

Three Ring Circus

Find the word **blue** three times inside each ring and circle it.

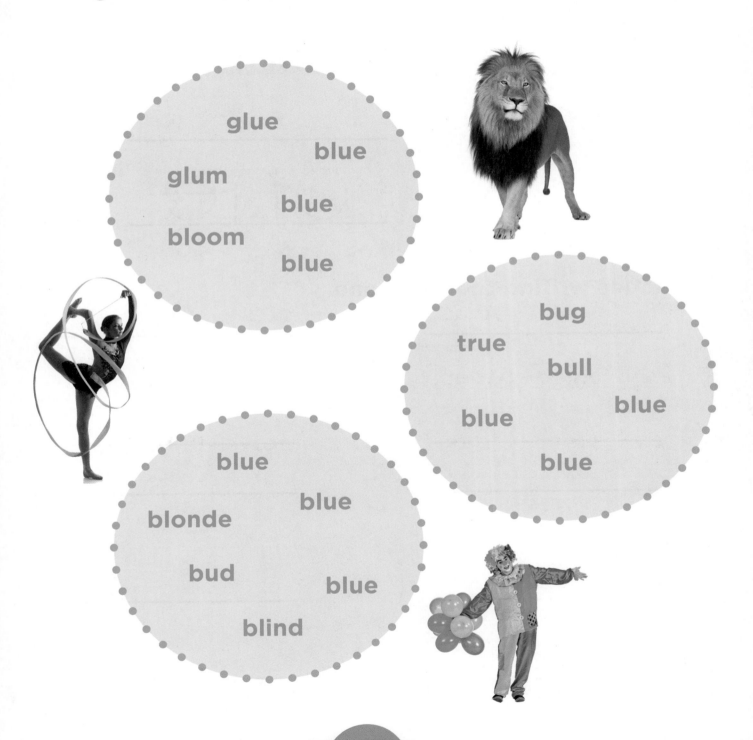

glue

blue

glum

blue

bloom

blue

bug

true

bull

blue

blue

blue

blue

blonde

blue

bud

blue

blind

Trace the word **one** and say it aloud.

one

Practice writing the word one.

I ate _____ cookie.

Play Along

Draw a circle around the word **one** to make a music note. Follow the code for the circled notes to answer the joke.

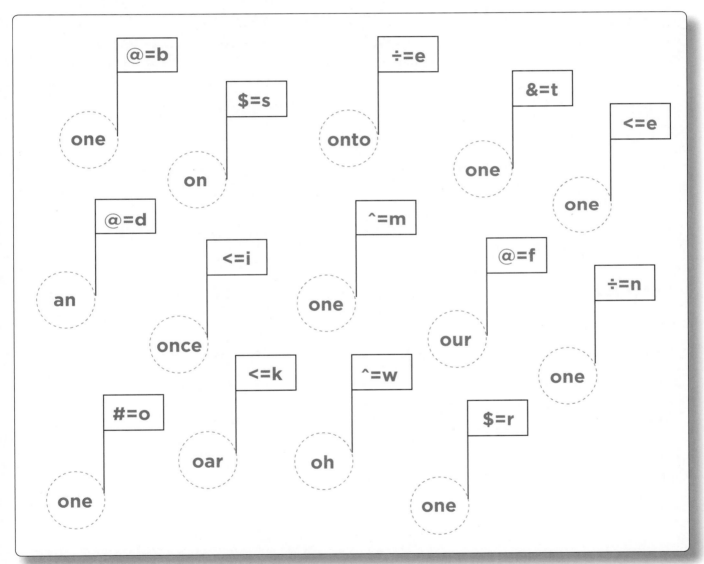

What kind of instrument does a skeleton play?

__ __ __ __ __ __ __ __

& $ # ^ @ # ÷ <

REVIEW: The Bottom Line

Use the codes to help fill in the missing words to the story.

away	help	find	two	red
——	·····	～～	＝＝	- - -

I got _____ _____ balloons at the fair. One balloon
          ＝＝   - - -

blew _____ in the wind. I wanted to _____ my balloon!
        ＝＝   ～～

Far _____, I saw a something_____. But it was just a ball.
      ＝＝   - - -

I saw lots of _____ things, but not my balloon. I needed _____
              - - -   ·····

to _____ my balloon. I asked my _____ friends to _____ me.
   ～～   ＝＝   ·····

We were able to _____ it in a tree. Now, I have _____ _____
                ～～   ＝＝   - - -

balloons again!

How many times does each word appear in the story?

away _____   two _____

help _____   red _____

find _____

REVIEW: Matching Caps

Draw a line to connect the matching sight words.
Fill in the letter in the blue circle next to each cap
to name the sport below.

1. down

2. yellow

3. come

4. where

5. blue

6. one

 where **n**

down **t**

 blue **i**

 yellow **e**

 come **n**

 one **s**

In this sport, the word "love" means no points.

___ ___ ___ ___ ___ ___
1   2   3   4   5   6

**in**

Trace the word in and say it aloud.

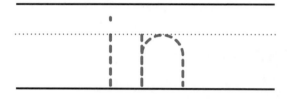

Practice writing the word in.

Let's go _____ the house.

Button Up

Draw a circle around the word **in** to make buttons on the shirt. Circle the shirt with more buttons.

in

I'm

it

in

an

in

in

in

ill

in

in

is

 **make**

Trace the word **make** and say it aloud.

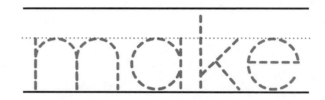

Practice writing the word make.

_____   _____

. . . .

_____   _____

_____   _____

. . . .

_____   _____

Let's _____ a cake.

Funny Food

Circle the word **make** each time you see it. Write the total under each bag, and use the code to answer the joke.

make	make	maid
make	make	make
make	make	made
make	make	make
make	make	make
made	make	map
_____ = d	_____ = o	_____ = s

main	mate	make
mad	make	maze
male	rake	make
make	made	make
maze	make	make
man	mile	mike
_____ = i	_____ = f	_____ = r

What do knights eat for dinner?

___ w ___ ___ ___ ___ ___ h
 3   6   4   5   2   1   3

little

Trace the word little and say it aloud.

Practice writing the word little.

_____   _____

_____   _____

_____   _____

_____   _____

_____   _____

The mouse is _____.

Check It Out

Put a check mark by the word little in the book titles. If the title does not have the word little, leave it blank.

The Little Cabin

Little Boy Blue

The Magic Letter

Projects for Little Hands

No More Litter

A Little Bit of Sunshine

The Light in the Forest

A Little Sugar on Top

How many book titles have the word little?

_____

so

Trace the word so and say it aloud.

Practice writing the word so.

Thank you _____ much.

Prize Tickets

Underline the word so each time you see it on the ticket. Write the number on the line.

z o o s o o s o ___

O O S A S S O O ___

s o s o s o o s ___

c o s u o o s o ___

S O S Q S C O O ___

s o a s o s o u ___

Add up the numbers on all the tickets. _____

10   2   11   2   1

Circle the prize or prizes that equals the number of underlined words.

but

Trace the word **but** and say it aloud.

but

Practice writing the word **but.**

_____   _____

_____   _____

_____   _____

_____   _____

The car is little _____ fast.

Candy Code

Look at the letters inside each candy. If you can unscramble the letters to make the word **but**, then write **but** on the line and follow the code. If not, leave it blank.

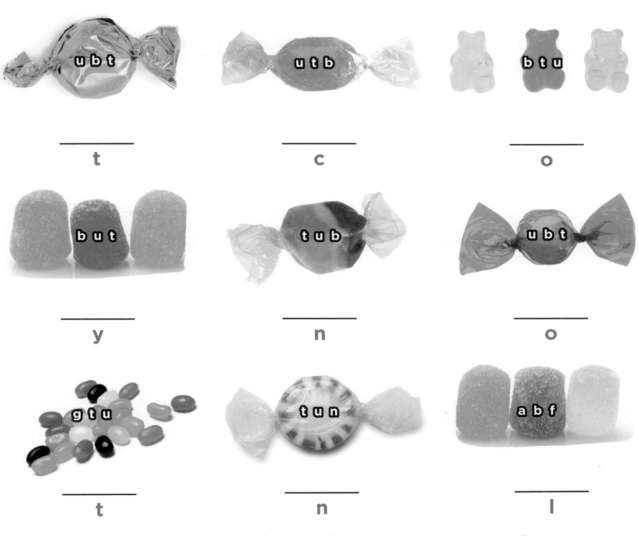

t

c

o

y

n

o

t

n

l

What kind of candy can you wear?

a

d

look

Trace the word look and say it aloud.

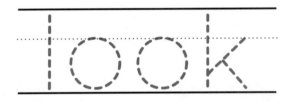

Practice writing the word look.

_____   _____

_____   _____

_____   _____

_____   _____

I _____ at the book.

Boxcar Race

Draw a box around the word look when you see it hiding inside another word. The car with more boxes wins the race.

outlook   unlock

looks   dislike

likes   lucky

overlook   lookup   looking

---

locker   sleek

leaky   looked

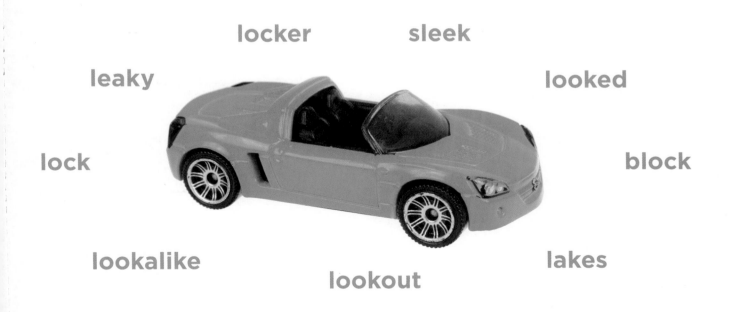

lock   block

lookalike   lakes

lookout

 **Trace the word on and say it aloud.**

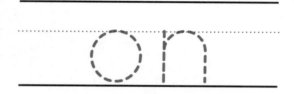

Practice writing the word on.

I sit _____ the bed.

Lucky Card

Color all the shapes that have the word on inside.

Circle the card suit that has all the shapes colored.

yes

Trace the word **yes** and say it aloud.

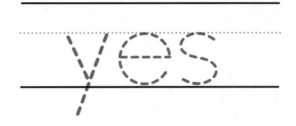

Practice writing the word **yes**.

Are you home? _____ , I am.

Around the Clock

Draw a line from the middle of the clock to the word **yes**. Follow each line to fill in the correct letter below.

his

west   yes

yes   yes

yes   vest

ye   yes

yes   best

yet

Why did the burglar get caught in the clock store?

___ ___   ___ ___ ___ k   ___ ___ s   ___ ___ ___ ___
7   4   1   10 10   7   9   1   9   2   4

 **three**

Trace the word three and say it aloud.

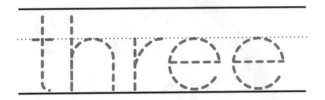

Practice writing the word three.

_____   _____

_____   _____

_____   _____

_____   _____

_____   _____

I eat _____ meals a day.

Fishing for Rhymes

Draw a line from each fishing pole to the words that rhyme with three.

throw

free

the

tree

bee

keep

need

he

see

fee

their

knee

tee

Which side caught more fish? _____

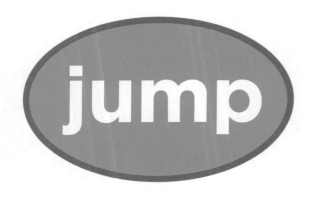

Trace the word **jump** and say it aloud.

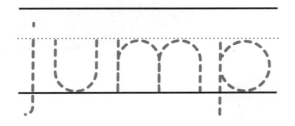

Practice writing the word jump.

_____ _____

_____ _____

_____ _____

_____ _____

_____ _____

We _____ up high.

Fun Fact

Ask an adult to read you the paragraph below. Then shade one box from the bottom up every time you see the word **jump**.

35	jump
30	jump
25	jump
20	jump
15	jump
10	jump
5	jump

Many kinds of frogs can leap and jump. When they are in danger, they can just jump away. Often times, they land in the water to hide. Their back legs are long and strong. Their webbed feet push off the ground. Frogs close their eyes when they jump! This protects their eyes. Not all frogs can jump. Some walk or hop instead.

Use the number at the top of your bar to complete this fun fact:

Some frogs can jump _____ times their body length.

 **funny** Trace the word **funny** and say it aloud.

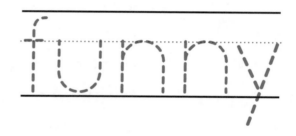

Practice writing the word funny.

The joke is _____.

Beautiful Bubbles

Cross out any bubble that does not have the word funny.

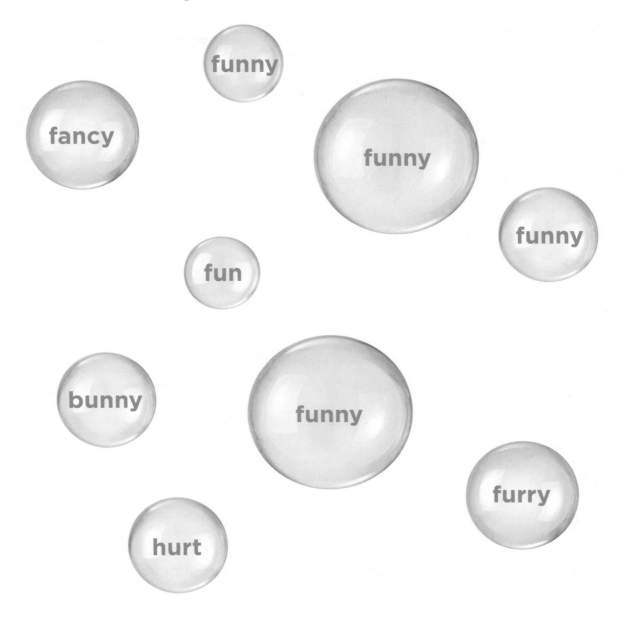

funny

fancy

funny

funny

fun

bunny

funny

furry

hurt

How many bubbles remain? _____

REVIEW: The Bottom Line

Use the codes to help fill in the missing words to the story.

three	make	in	on	funny
——	·····	~~~	═══	- - -

I like to draw _____ pictures _____ my notebooks. _____ the
         - - -   ~~~   ═══

front of my notebook I put my name _____ big letters. First,
                                      ~~~

I _____ the outline _____ pencil. Then I color them _____ with
  ·····   ~~~   ~~~

markers or crayons. I like to sit _____ my bed to _____ these
                                    ═══   ·····

_____ pictures. Once, I drew a monster with _____ heads! I have
- - -   ——

filled _____ notebooks already. Soon I will start _____ my fourth
        ——   ═══

notebook and _____ more _____ pictures.
             ·····   - - -

How many times does each word appear in the story?

three _____   on _____

make _____   funny _____

in _____

REVIEW: Matching Caps

Draw a line to connect the matching sight words. Fill in the letter in the blue circle next to each cap to name the sport below.

1. little

2. yes

3. can

4. jump

5. look

6. but

 jump — i

can — i

but — g

look — n

little — s

yes — k

This sport can be done on the water or on the snow.

$\underline{\hphantom{xx}}$ $\underline{\hphantom{xx}}$ $\underline{\hphantom{xx}}$ $\underline{\hphantom{xx}}$ $\underline{\hphantom{xx}}$ $\underline{\hphantom{xx}}$
  1   2   3   4   5   6

REVIEW: Word Search

Find the review words in the word search.

help   find   look   two   red

where   on   in   away   but   blue

```
K K H K B T W F J Z
L H Q A N W R I J C
O C B B U M O N J V
O R F L Y A S D N H
K E V U E V V F I E
V D W E H E T O Z L
N Y H Q H T W O M P
Y R E Q U L L G Y S
M B R A W A Y S F B
E I E J I F B U T B
```

REVIEW: The Lost Word

Look for each review word from page 106 and circle it below. There is one word from the list that is missing below.

Please help me find my red hat!

It blew away in the wind, and I

don't know where it ended up.

It has two blue flowers on it.

Please look in your neighborhood

for my red hat!

Which review word is missing? _____

Crossword Clues

Complete each sentence with a review word from the box. Use the words to fill in the puzzle on the next page.

down   yellow   come   one   make

little   so   yes   three   jump   funny

Across

1. I can _____ over the rocks.

4. Count to _____ .

6. The lemon is _____ .

7. The joke is _____ .

9. It is _____ cold today.

11. Please _____ with me.

Down

2. I _____ my lunch each day.

3. The baby is _____ .

5. We go _____ the slide.

8. Please say _____ .

10. There is only _____ left.

REVIEW: Crossword Puzzle

Use the clues on page 108 to fill in the puzzle.

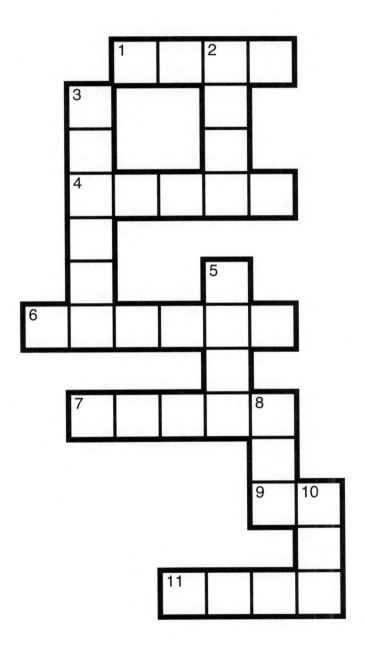

REVIEW: Sentence Sequence

Follow the code in the box to make sentences with sight words.

I	we	it	is	can	go	and	here
!	@	#	$	%	^	&	*

	look	up	you	see	run	in
	+	=	<	>	?	~

1. _____ _____ _____ _____ .
   @   %   >   #

2. _____ _____ _____ .
   !   ^   ~

3. _____ _____ _____ .
   # $ *

4. _____ _____ _____ .
   @   +   =

5. _____ _____ _____ .
   <   %   ?

6. _____ _____ _____ _____ _____ .
   !   ?   &   >   #

REVIEW: Wacky Word Boxes

Some letters are short and some letters are tall.
Find the boxes that fit each word.

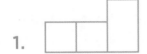

yellow   come   blue   to   yes   a   little
so   not   three   my   where   help   big

1.

2.

3.

4.

5.

6.

7.

8.

9.

10.

11.

12.

13.

14.

REVIEW: Four Squares

Find four sight words in each square.
Draw a box around each correctly spelled word.

the	away
ott	find
down	said
jump	nelp
on	make
me	amd
for	one
two	play
red	funny
kan	but

REVIEW: Framed!

Cross out any words that are not spelled correctly. You should have 22 correct sight words left. Color the frame that has only correct words inside.

the	me	upp
we	iss	I
in	can	sayd

a
three
help
one
away
where
make
so
up

it	my
is	go
soo	mak
to	on
big	

REVIEW: In the End

Draw a line to the correct ending for each sight word. Then write the word on the line.

fi   wn _____   sa   ue _____   s   ee _____

do   nd _____   ju   mp _____   r   es _____

co   me _____   bl   id _____   y   un _____

pl   ay _____   r   ou _____

lo   re _____   n   ed _____

he   ok _____   y   or _____

                                 f   ot _____

a   ut _____   fun   ow   _____

t   nd _____   lit   ny   _____

b   wo _____   yell   tle _____

Section 2

The sight words included in this section are:

all	eat	now	this
am	four	our	too
are	get	out	want
at	good	ran	was
ate	have	saw	well
be	he	say	went
black	into	she	what
brown	like	soon	white
came	must	that	who
did	new	there	will
do	no	they	with

Trace the word do and say it aloud.

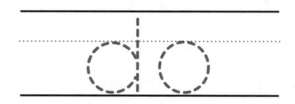

Practice writing the word do.

_____   _____

_____   _____

_____   _____

_____   _____

I can _____ it!

Balloon Buddies

Draw a circle around the word do to make a balloon.
Put an X through the other words.

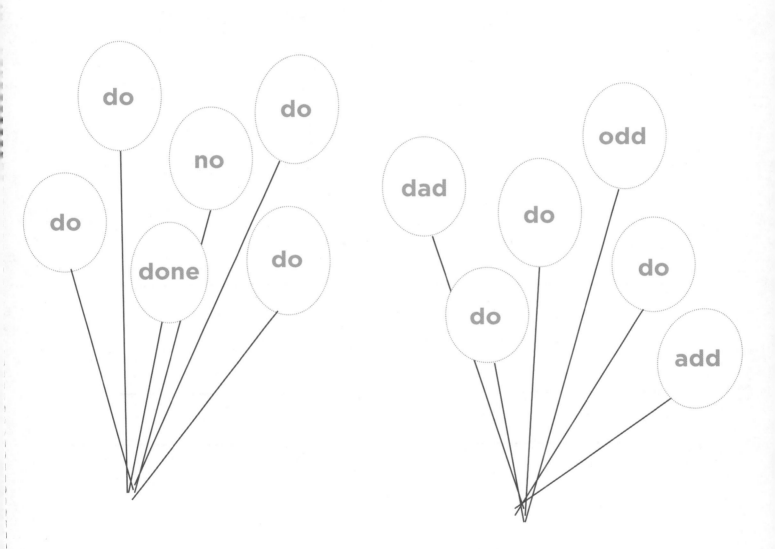

Count the balloons in each bunch.
Circle the bunch that has more balloons.

How many balloons are there altogether? _____

like

Trace the word like and say it aloud.

like

Practice writing the word like.

_____   _____

_____   _____

_____   _____

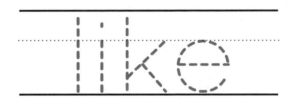

I _____ to play.

Made in the Shade

Shade each box that has the word **like**.
Then match each number to the corresponding letter to fill in the blanks below.

5	like	lick	life	lake	lie
4	lake	lock	like	lime	life
3	lie	bike	luck	lit	like
2	line	like	lie	lack	lick
1	lick	life	line	like	live

p   u   i   t   l

What flower grows best between your nose and chin?

_____ _____ _____ _____ _____
 1   2   3   4   5

Trace the word what and say it aloud.

Practice writing the word what.

_____   _____

....

_____   _____

....

_____   _____

I know _____ to do.

Word Tunnels

Connect the letters of the word what to make a tunnel. Use the number at the tunnel exit to complete the fun fact.

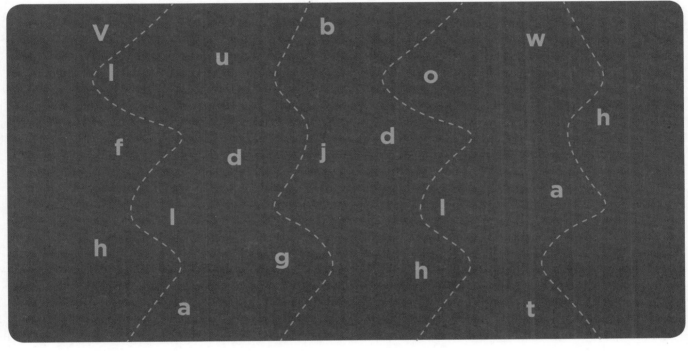

20   200   2,000   20,000

A bullfrog can lay up to _____ eggs!

Circle the rocks that show the word what.

went   want   what   hat   what

say

Trace the word say and say it aloud.

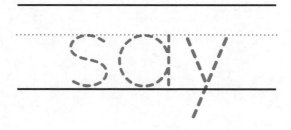

Practice writing the word say.

We _____ it out loud.

Sight Word Slices

Draw a line from the word say in the middle of each pizza to the matching words on the edge of each pizza. See how many slices you make.

Pizza A

said

sat

say

sap

say

save

say

say

zap

Pizza B

soy

say

say

say

yes

sad

say

say   say

Which pizza has more slices?

_____

How many slices in all? _____

with

Trace the word **with** and say it aloud.

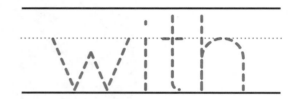

Practice writing the word with.

Please come _____ **me.**

Postcard Puzzler

Circle the word **with** each time it appears on the postcard. Write the number in the stamp in the corner. Find the matching number below to see where the postcard is from.

Dear Luke,

I went with my cousins to the most amazing place! There are beautiful layers of rocks all around. We hiked with a guide down into the deep canyon. I brought lots of water with me. But I forgot to bring my camera with me. I hope you can come back here with me some day.

Love,

Dan

Luke Dobbs

286 Blackwell Ave

San Diego, CA 91945

1. **Mount Everest**
2. **Mississippi River**
3. **Mount Rushmore**
4. **Teton Forest**
5. **Grand Canyon**
6. **Mojave Desert**

into

Trace the word **into** and say it aloud.

into

Practice writing the word into.

_____   _____

_____   _____

_____   _____

_____   _____

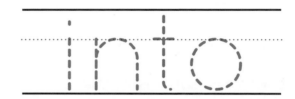

She got _____ bed.

Riddle Row

Circle all rows and columns that have the word into five times. Match the symbols with the letters outside the grid to solve the riddle.

	<	+	#	<	#	
#	into	into	in	to	into	r
+	inn	into	isn't	hint	too	a
#	into	into	into	into	into	n
<	its	into	into	not	info	s
+	into	into	out	into	it'll	d
	v	o	k	e	b	

What do you call a man with a nose but no body?

___ ___ b ___ d y   ___ ___ s e
 #   +   +   #   +

be

Trace the word be and say it aloud.

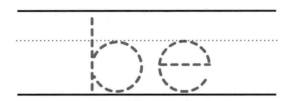

Practice writing the word be.

_____   _____

_____   _____

_____   _____

Let's _____ friends.

Ladder Line Up

Underline **be** if it appears within the longer word. Circle the ladder that has an underlined word on the most steps.

Ladder 1:
- **before**
- **begin**
- **maybe**
- **being**

Ladder 2:
- **below**
- **born**
- **behave**
- **webbing**

Ladder 3:
- **bone**
- **beside**
- **become**
- **deep**

at

Trace the word
at and say
it aloud.

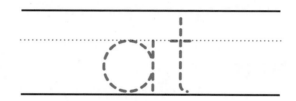

Practice writing the word **at**.

_____   _____

_____   _____

_____   _____

_____   _____

_____   _____

I am_____ home.

Follow the Chain

Draw a circle every time you see the word **at**.
If your circles make a chain, write the number
of times the word **at** appears.

a t a t a t   t a t a t   _____

a t a t a t a t a t   _____

a t a t a t a t a t a t   _____

a t a t a t a t a t   _____

a t a t a t a t   _____

all

Trace the word all and say it aloud.

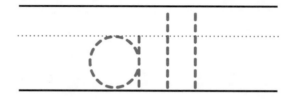

Practice writing the word all.

I ate _____ my dinner.

Rhyme Score

Circle the word all each time it appears on the field. Underline any words that rhyme with all. Count the total for each and fill in the score board.

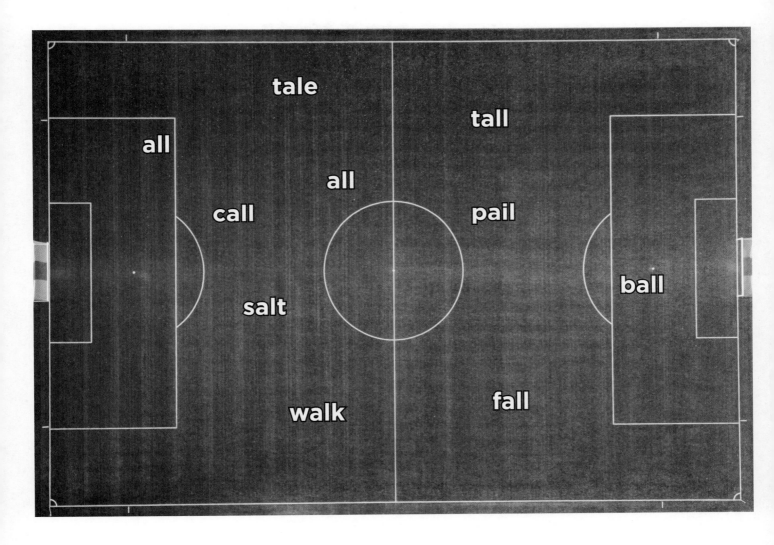

tale

tall

all

all

pail

call

ball

salt

walk

fall

ALL   RHYMES WITH ALL

_____   _____

 **too**

Trace the word too and say it aloud.

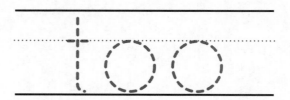

Practice writing the word too.

_____   _____

_____   _____

_____   _____

_____   _____

Can I come _____ ?

Three Ring Circus

Find the word too three times inside
each ring and circle it.

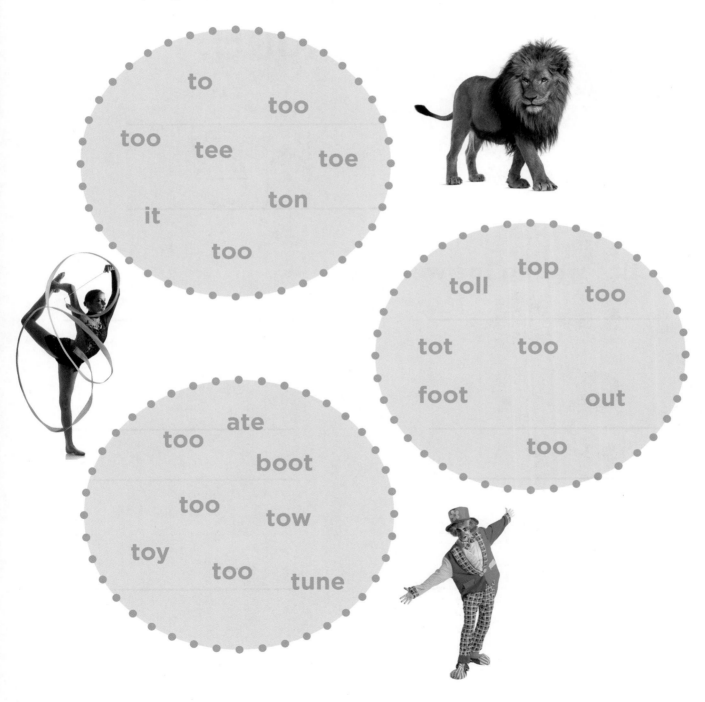

to

too

too

tee

toe

ton

it

too

top

toll

too

tot

too

foot

out

too

ate

too

boot

too

tow

toy

too

tune

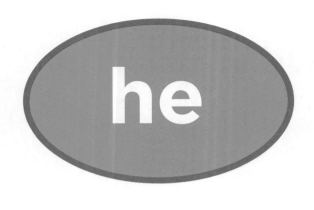

Trace the word **he** and say it aloud.

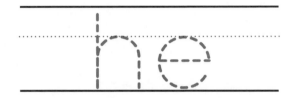

Practice writing the word he.

_____   _____

_____   _____

_____   _____

I hope _____ can play.

Play Along

Draw a circle around the word **he** to make a music note. Follow the code for the circled notes to answer the joke.

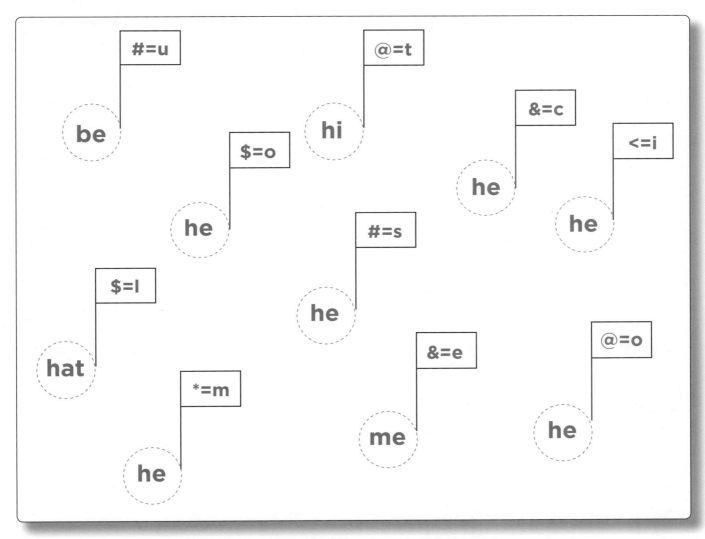

What do cows like to sing along to?

___ ___ ___ ___ ___ ___

   *   \$ @   #   <   &

REVIEW: The Bottom Line

Use the codes to help fill in the missing words to the story.

he	into	all	at	with
——	·····	～～	══	---

Today I went swimming _____ my brother _____ the pool.
                                                    ---   ══

I jumped _____ the water first. _____ waited _____ the side for
  ·····   ——   ══

a while. Then _____ jumped _____ the pool _____ a big noodle.
                 ——   ·····   ---

I swam _____ the way across the pool. _____ waited _____ the
    ～～   ——   ══

shallow end. We swam _____ day. Then we changed _____ dry
                      ～～   ·····

clothes and walked _____ the way home.
                 ～～

How many times does each word appear in the story?

he _____   at _____

into _____   with _____

all _____

REVIEW: Matching Caps

Draw a line to connect the matching sight words.
Fill in the letter in the blue circle next to each cap to
name the sport below.

1. do

2. like

3. what

4. say

5. be

6. too

what — c

do — h

like — o

say — k

too — y

be — e

This sport can be played on ice, a field, or a roller rink.

___ ___ ___ ___ ___ ___
 1   2   3   4   5   6

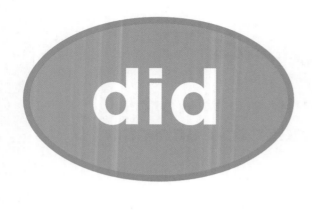

did

Trace the word did and say it aloud.

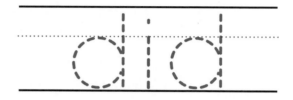

Practice writing the word did.

_____   _____

_____   _____

_____   _____

_____   _____

I _____ all my work.

Button Up

Draw a circle around the word did to make buttons on the sweaters. Circle the sweater with more buttons.

did
bid
did
lid
did
did

did
did
dig
did
did
did

Trace the word **want** and say it aloud.

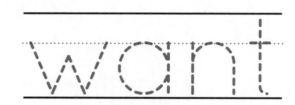

Practice writing the word want.

_____   _____
. . . .
_____   _____
_____   _____
. . . .
_____   _____

I _____ that one, please.

Funny Food

Circle the word **want** each time you see it. Write the total under each can, and use the code to answer the joke.

want	water	ant
want	want	want
wet	wait	what
want	won't	want
with	went	want
went	watt	want

_____ = u   _____ = n   _____ = o

want	want	wand
want	want	want
van	want	wallet
want	want	wart
want	want	town
want	want	want

_____ = a   _____ = t   _____ = d

What kind of nut has a hole?

____   ____ ____ ____ ____ ____
5   2   4   1   3   6

 **Trace the word good and say it aloud.**

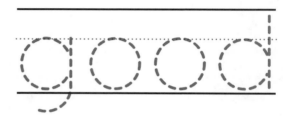

Practice writing the word good.

_____   _____

_____   _____

_____   _____

_____   _____

You did a _____ job.

Check It Out

Put a check mark by the word good in the book titles. If the title does not have the word good, leave it blank.

Good Recipes

The Good Dog

Finding Gold

Making Good Choices

All the Good Stuff

Hotel Guide

Good Ideas for Rainy Days

Feeling Good

How many book titles have the word good?

_____

 **was**

Trace the word was and say it aloud.

Practice writing the word was.

_____   _____

_____   _____

_____   _____

He _____ sick yesterday.

Prize Tickets

Underline the word was each time you see it on the ticket. Write the number on the line.

w a s a w a s w ____

W A W A S A W A ____

s a w a s w a s ____

w a a w a s a w ____

W A S W A S W A ____

s w a w a a s w ____

Add up the numbers on all the tickets. _____

10　　　**2**　　　**5**　　　**2**　　　**1**

Circle the prize or prizes that equals the number of underlined words.

Trace the word **went** and say it aloud.

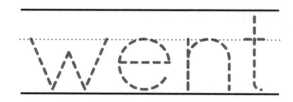

Practice writing the word went.

_____   _____

_____   _____

_____   _____

_____   _____

We _____ away for the summer.

Candy Code

Look at the letters inside each candy. If you can unscramble the letters to make the word **went**, then write went on the line and follow the code. If not, leave it blank.

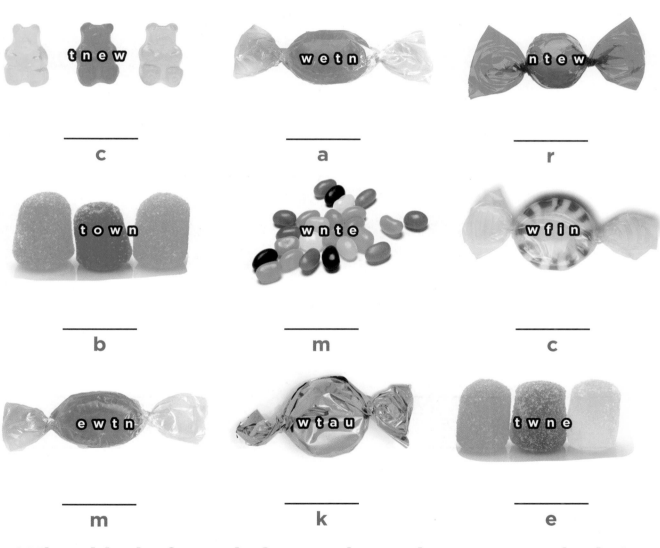

t n e w	w e t n	n t e w
_____	_____	_____
c	a	r

t o w n	w n t e	w f i n
_____	_____	_____
b	m	c

e w t n	w t a u	t w n e
_____	_____	_____
m	k	e

What kind of candy is good to take on a road trip?

_____ _____ _____ _____ _____ _____ l

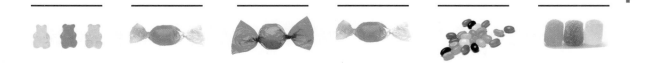

Trace the word ran and say it aloud.

Practice writing the word ran.

The dog _____ **to the ball.**

Boxcar Race

Draw a box around the word ran when you see it hiding inside another word. The car with more boxes wins the race.

rank

friend

runs

grand

bran

trap

ranch

ramp

rain

---

grape

brain

wrong

strand

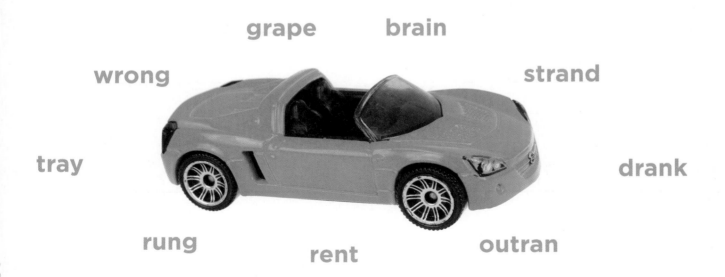

tray

drank

rung

rent

outran

Trace the word am and say it aloud.

Practice writing the word am.

I _____ happy.

Lucky Card

Color all the shapes that have the word **am** inside.

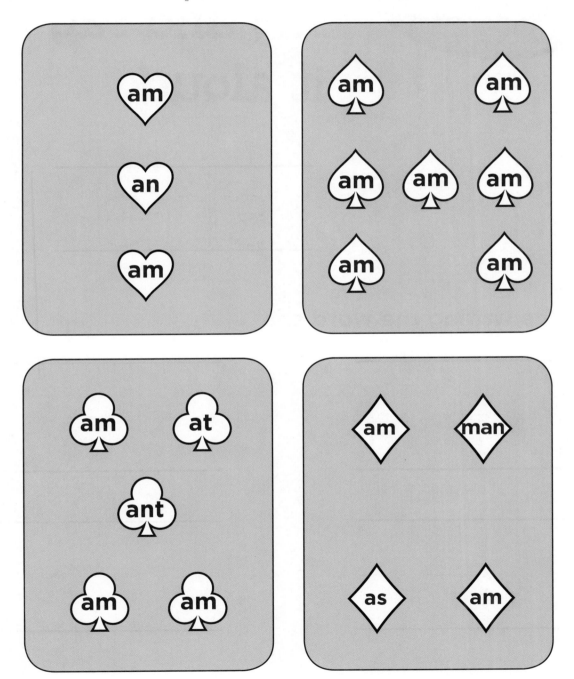

**she**

Trace the word she and say it aloud.

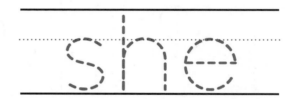

Practice writing the word she.

_____   _____

_____   _____

_____   _____

Can _____ come to my party?

Around the Clock

Draw a line from the middle of the clock to the word she each time it appears. Follow each line to fill in the correct letter below.

Why did the boy throw the clock in the trash?

__ __	__ __ __ __ __	__ __ __ __
8 3	11 1 2 8 5	8 7 10 5

**came**

Trace the word came and say it aloud.

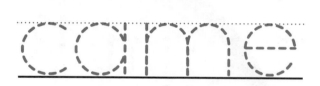

Practice writing the word came.

_____ _____

....

_____ _____

_____ _____

....

_____ _____

We _____ here last week.

Fishing for Rhymes

Draw a line from each fishing pole to the words that rhyme with came.

blame

fame

clam

game

camp

lamp

flame

name

lamb

same

tame

frame

Which side caught more fish? _____

brown

Trace the word brown and say it aloud.

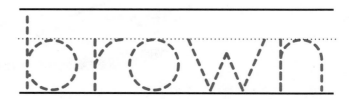

Practice writing the word brown.

My hair is _____ .

Fun Fact

Ask an adult to read you the paragraph below. Then, shade one box from the bottum up every time you see the word **brown**.

6	brown
5	brown
4	brown
3	brown
2	brown
1	brown

Owls have feathers that help them blend in. Their feathers might be brown, gray, or white. They make nests in the brown tree trunks and branches. Barns also make good homes for owls. Owls can hide in logs, grass, or bushes. They have good eye-sight. Owls with brown or black eyes like to hunt at night.

Use the number at the top of your bar to complete this fun fact:

Owls have _____ eyelids.

**four**

Trace the word four and say it aloud.

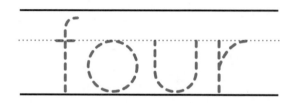

Practice writing the word four.

_____   _____

_____   _____

_____   _____

I ate _____ cookies.

Beautiful Bubbles

Cross out any bubble that does not have the word **four**.

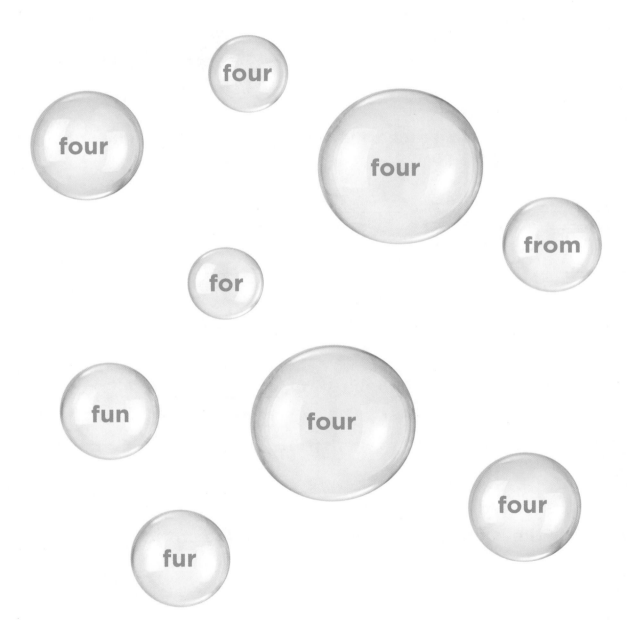

How many bubbles remain? _____

REVIEW: The Bottom Line

Use the codes to help fill in the missing words to the story.

went	ran	she	was	came
▬▬▬	• • • • •	∼∼∼	═══	▬ ▬ ▬

My sister _____ in a race today. I _____ to watch her run.
          • • • • •   ═══

It _____ a relay race. _____ _____ first. _____
   ═══   ∼∼∼   ═══   ∼∼∼

_____ around the track once. When _____ _____ back to
• • • • •   ∼∼∼   ▬ ▬ ▬

the starting line, another runner _____ waiting. Each person
                                   ═══

on the team _____ when her turn _____. They all _____
            • • • • •   ▬ ▬ ▬   • • • • •

so fast! Their team _____ in first. It _____ a great race!
                    ▬ ▬ ▬   ═══

How many times does each word appear in the story?

went _____   was _____

ran _____   came _____

she _____

REVIEW: Matching Caps

Draw a line to connect the matching sight words. Fill in the letter in the blue circle next to each cap to name the sport below.

1. did

2. want

3. good

4. am

5. brown

6. four

 brown — o

 did — p

 am — g

 good — n

 want — i

 four — n

This sport is also called "table tennis."

___ ___ ___ ___ ___ ___ ___
1   2   3   4   1   5   6   4

REVIEW: Word Search

Find the review words in the word search.

do	with	into	at	he	want
good	am	brown	four	ran	

```
A  E  R  D  W  T  M  C  Y  S
Y  E  F  O  U  R  I  H  U  N
J  V  C  B  H  G  C  I  Q  U
L  W  H  R  I  N  V  N  W  J
W  B  M  O  R  A  N  T  I  R
G  H  R  W  D  M  F  O  T  G
N  O  S  N  J  H  I  R  H  O
G  D  O  O  Z  E  R  E  K  O
C  X  N  D  X  S  Z  A  L  E
W  A  N  T  U  P  D  J  T  B
```

REVIEW: The Lost Word

Look for each review word from page 164 and circle it below. There is one word from the list that is missing.

> My dog ran into the woods four
> days ago! He has brown fur with
> white spots. I am so worried, and I
> want to find him. He is a good dog.
> If you see him, call me at 555-7456.
> Thank you!

Which review word is missing? _____

Crossword Clues

Complete each sentence with a review word from the box. Use the words to fill in the puzzle on the next page.

like   what   say   be   all   too

did   was   went   she   came

Across

2. She _____ there early.

4. I _____ pizza.

6. _____ is your name?

9. My mom _____ to get me.

Down

1. We _____ our homework.

2. I _____ to the game.

3. Can you _____ it?

5. I think _____ is funny!

7. It is _____ cold outside.

8. I want to _____ an artist.

10. I was _____ alone.

Use the clues on page 166 to fill in the puzzle.

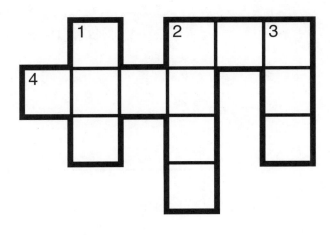

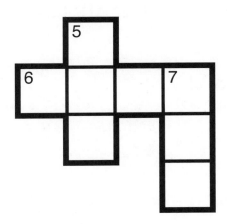

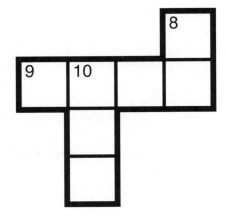

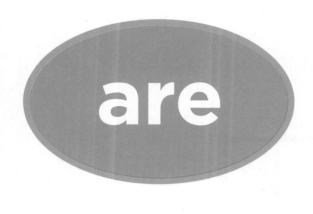

are

Trace the word are and say it aloud.

Practice writing the word are.

You _____ my friend.

Balloon Buddies

Draw a circle around the word are to make a balloon.
Put an X through the other words.

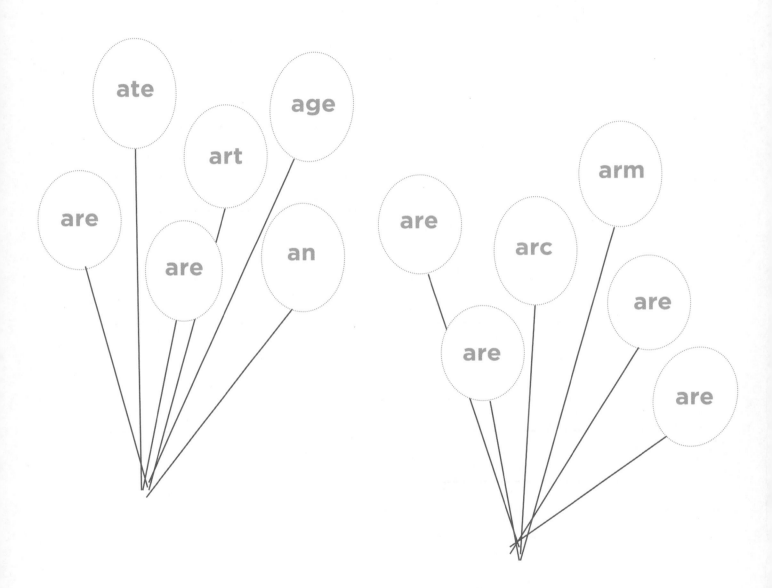

Count the balloons in each bunch.
Circle the bunch that has more balloons.

How many balloons are there altogether? _____

Trace the word that and say it aloud.

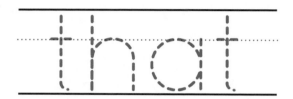

Practice writing the word that.

_____   _____

....

_____   _____

_____   _____

....

_____   _____

Let's go _____ way.

Made in the Shade

Shade each box that has the word that. Then match each number to the corresponding letter to fill in the blanks below.

5	hat	that	tot	than	path
4	that	thank	math	thaw	hat
3	than	hot	fat	ham	that
2	hit	them	their	that	half
1	then	hat	that	ten	this
	s	w	s	e	a

How do you cut the sea in half?

With a ___ ___ ___ ___ ___ ___
       1   2   3   4   3   5

 **black** Trace the word black and say it aloud.

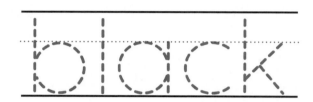

Practice writing the word **black.**

_____   _____

_____   _____

_____   _____

_____   _____

The car is _____ .

Word Tunnels

Connect the letters of the word **black** to make a tunnel. Use the number at the tunnel exit to complete the fun fact.

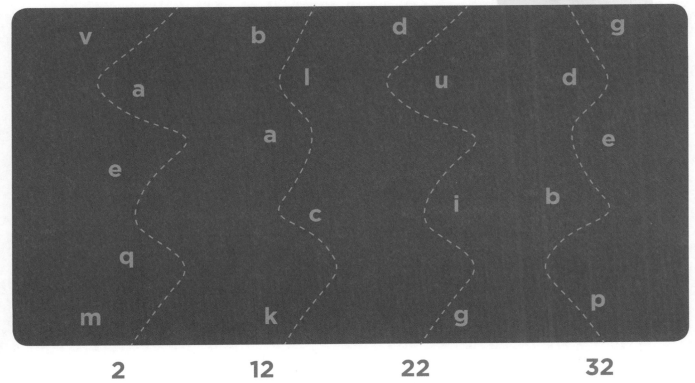

2   12   22   32

The goliath frog can be over _____ inches long!

Circle the rocks that show the word black.

 block
 black
 blink
 black
 back

now

Trace the word now and say it aloud.

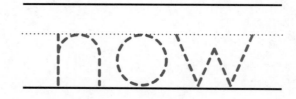

now

Practice writing the word now.

_____   _____

_____   _____

_____   _____

Please come here _____.

Sight Word Slices

Draw a line from the word now in the middle of each pie to matching words on the edge of each pie. See how many slices you make.

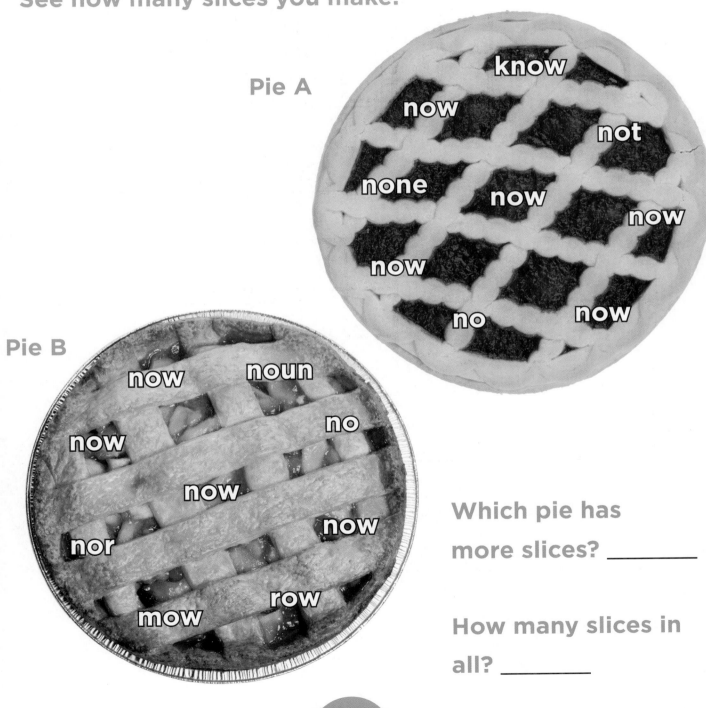

Pie A

know

now

not

now

now

now

no

now

Pie B

now

noun

now

no

now

nor

now

row

mow

Which pie has more slices? _____

How many slices in all? _____

saw

Trace the word saw and say it aloud.

Practice writing the word saw.

_____   _____

························   ····························

_____   _____

_____   _____

························   ····························

_____   _____

We _____ a bird.

Postcard Puzzler

Circle the word **saw** each time it appears on the postcard. Write the number in the stamp in the corner. Find the matching number below to see where the postcard is from.

Dear Laura,

This city is amazing! Today, I saw famous paintings at a museum. I also saw some very old churches and the Eiffel Tower. Last night, we saw an opera! The food here is wonderful. Some people say this is "The City of Lights." I'll see you soon when I get home.

Greg Millard

42 Kelton Street

Boston, MA 02101

1. Tokyo

2. Calgary

3. Paris

4. Rio de Janeiro

5. Los Angeles

6. London

 **they** Trace the word they and say it aloud.

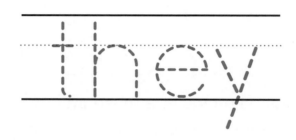

Practice writing the word they.

_____   _____
....
_____   _____
_____   _____
....
_____   _____

_____ **are my friends.**

Riddle Row

Circle all rows and columns that have the word they five times. Match the symbols with the letters outside the grid to solve the riddle.

	+	*	+	*	+	
*	hey	they	the	they	they	a
+	them	their	thee	here	they	w
*	the	they	hey	them	they	v
+	they	they	ten	they	they	l
*	they	they	they	they	they	s

t p h b e

What kind of shoes do spies wear?

___ n ___ a k ___ r ___

* + + *

179

Trace the word eat and say it aloud.

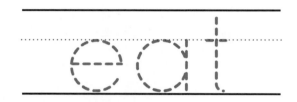

Practice writing the word eat.

_____   _____

_____   _____

_____   _____

_____   _____

Let's _____ lunch.

Ladder Line Up

Underline eat if it appears within the longer word. Circle the ladder that has an underlined word on the most steps.

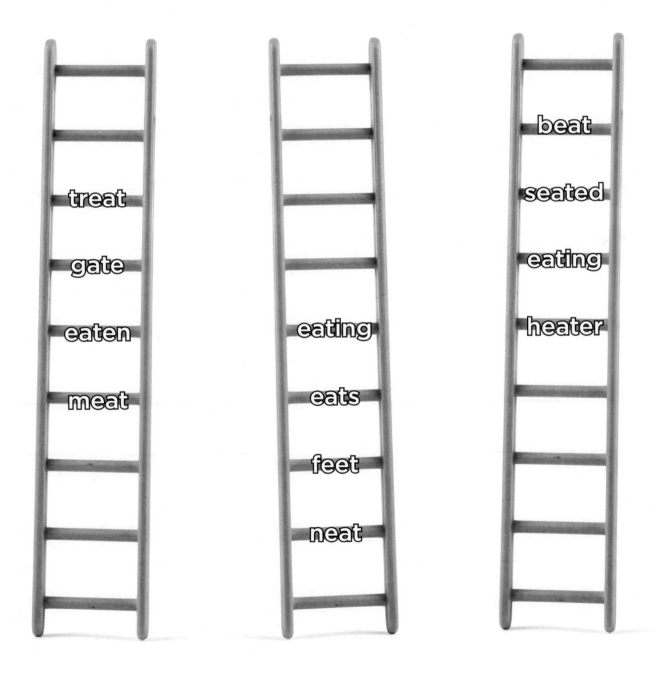

treat

gate

eaten

meat

eating

eats

feet

neat

beat

seated

eating

heater

Trace the word will and say it aloud.

will

Practice writing the word will.

_____   _____

_____   _____

_____   _____

I _____ be there soon.

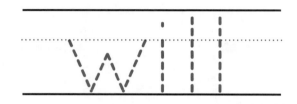

Follow the Chain

Draw a circle every time you see the word will.
If your circles make a chain, write the number of
times the word will appears.

will will will _____

will will will wll _____

will will will _____

will wil will will _____

will will _____

well

Trace the word well and say it aloud.

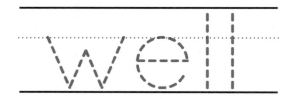

Practice writing the word well.

_____   _____

_____   _____

_____   _____

I did _____ on the test.

Rhyme Score

Circle the word **well** each time it appears on the field. Underline any words that rhyme with **well**. Count the total for each and fill in the score board.

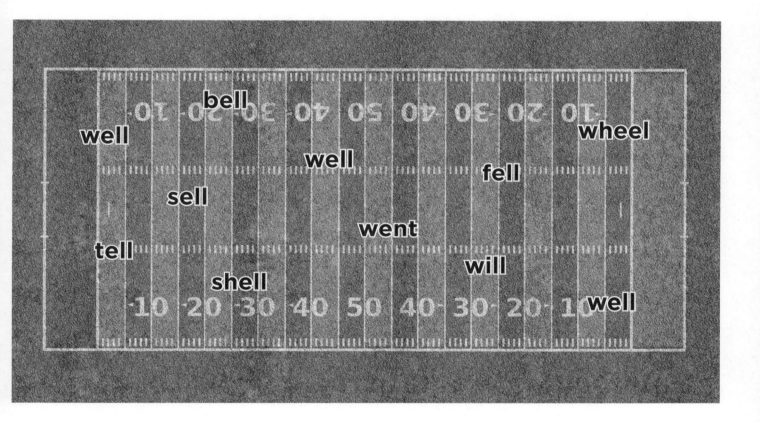

WELL   RHYMES WITH WELL

_____   _____

**have**

Trace the word have and say it aloud.

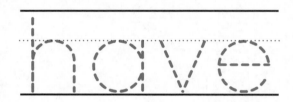

Practice writing the word have.

_____   _____

_____   _____

_____   _____

I _____ a new book.

Three Ring Circus

Find the word have three times inside each ring and circle it.

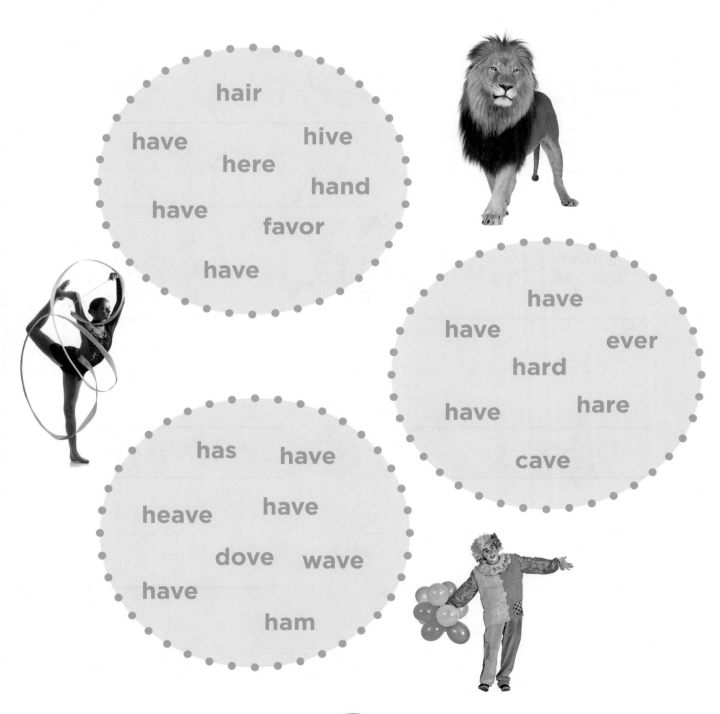

hair

have   hive

here

    hand

have

   favor

have

have

have   ever

   hard

have   hare

   cave

has   have

heave   have

dove   wave

have

ham

who

Trace the word who and say it aloud.

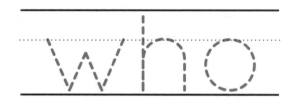

who

Practice writing the word who.

_____   _____

....

_____   _____

_____   _____

....

_____   _____

_____ **is at the door?**

Play Along

Draw a circle around the word **who** to make a music note. Follow the code for the circled notes to answer the joke.

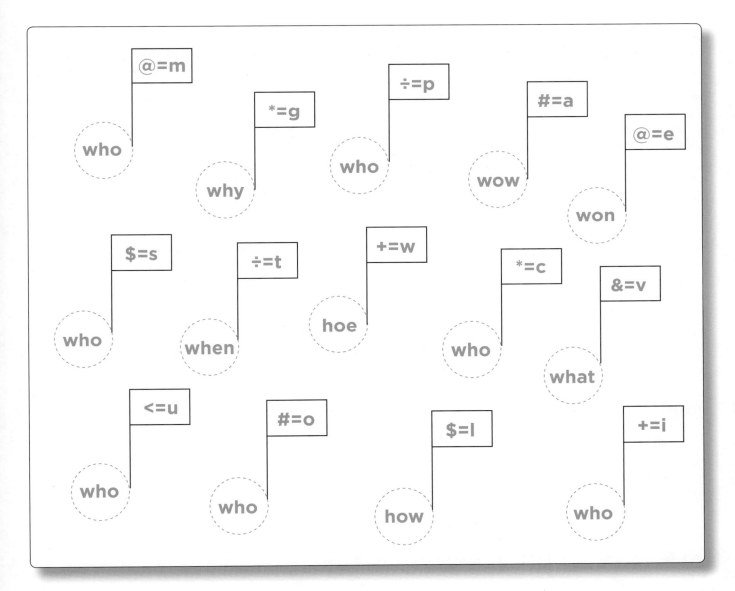

What kind of music are balloons afraid of?

___ ___ ___   ___ ___ ___ ___ ___

÷ # ÷   @ < $ + *

REVIEW: The Bottom Line

Use the codes to help fill in the missing words to the story.

eat	well	they	are	black
▬▬▬	• • • • •	∼∼∼	═══	▬ ▬ ▬

_____ bears _____ not always _____ ! They can
▬ ▬ ▬   ═══   ▬ ▬ ▬

have _____ , brown, or even white fur. _____ bears live in
▬ ▬ ▬   ▬ ▬ ▬

forests, and _____ like to be near trees and rivers. Their
∼∼∼

claws _____ sharp. This helps them climb trees _____ and
═══   • • • • •

catch fish to _____ . _____ bears also _____ berries, plants,
▬▬▬   ▬ ▬ ▬   ▬▬▬

and grass. _____ _____ amazing animals!
∼∼∼   ═══

How many times does each word appear in the story?

eat _____   are _____

well _____   black _____

they _____

REVIEW: Matching Caps

Draw a line to connect the matching sight words.
Fill in the letter in the pink circle next to each cap
to name the sport below.

1. saw

2. that

3. now

4. will

5. here

6. who

 that — o

 will — b

 saw — f

 now — t

 who — l

 here — a

In this sport, players try to get the ball to the "end zone."

__ __ __ __ __ __ __
1   2   2   3   4   5   6   6

Trace the word get and say it aloud.

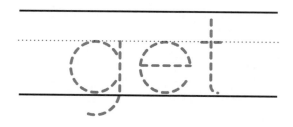

Practice writing the word get.

_____   _____

....

_____   _____

_____   _____

....

_____   _____

Let's _____ ice cream.

Button Up

Draw a circle around the word get to make buttons on the shirts. Circle the shirt with more buttons.

get
tag
get
ten
pet
gem

get
got
get
gel
get
goat

**must**

Trace the word must and say it aloud.

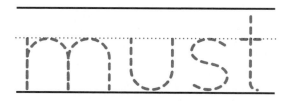

Practice writing the word must.

_____   _____

....

_____   _____

_____   _____

....

_____   _____

We _____ clean up.

Funny Food

Circle the word must each time you see it. Write the total under each can, and use the code to answer the joke.

must
mist
money
mast
must
miss

_____ = o

must
must
nest
must
just
must

_____ = b

mist
muse
most
mutt
must
meet

_____ = r

must
moss
mat
must
sum
must

_____ = t

must
must
must
must
must
must

_____ = r

must
mess
must
must
must
must

_____ = e

What do trees like to drink?

___ ___ ___ ___   ___ ___ ___ ___
 1   2   2   3   4   5   5   6

 **white**

Trace the word **white** and say it aloud.

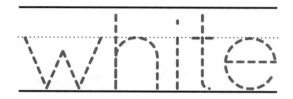

Practice writing the word white.

_____   _____

. . . .

_____   _____

_____   _____

. . . .

_____   _____

The paper is _____.

Check It Out

Put a check mark by the word **white** in the book titles. If the title does not have the word **white**, leave it blank.

While You Were Away

Black and White Photography

Whispers in the Wind

The White House

What Do You Want to Be?

Wait for the Winter

How to Make White Lace

Rafting on White Water

How many book titles have the word **white**?

_____

 **new**

Trace the word new and say it aloud.

Practice writing the word new.

I got _____ shoes.

Prize Tickets

Underline the word new each time you see it on the ticket. Write the number on the line.

n e n w e w n e ___

N E W E N E W N ___

n e w e n e w n ___

n w e w e n e w ___

E W N E W N E E ___

n e w n e w n e w ___

Add up the numbers on all the tickets. _____

9   2   5   2   1

Circle the prize that equals the number of underlined words.

this

Trace the word this and say it aloud.

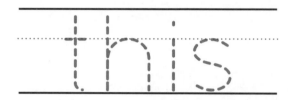

Practice writing the word this.

I like _____ book.

Candy Code

Look at the letters inside each candy. If you can unscramble the letters to make the word this, then write this on the line and follow the code. If not, leave it blank.

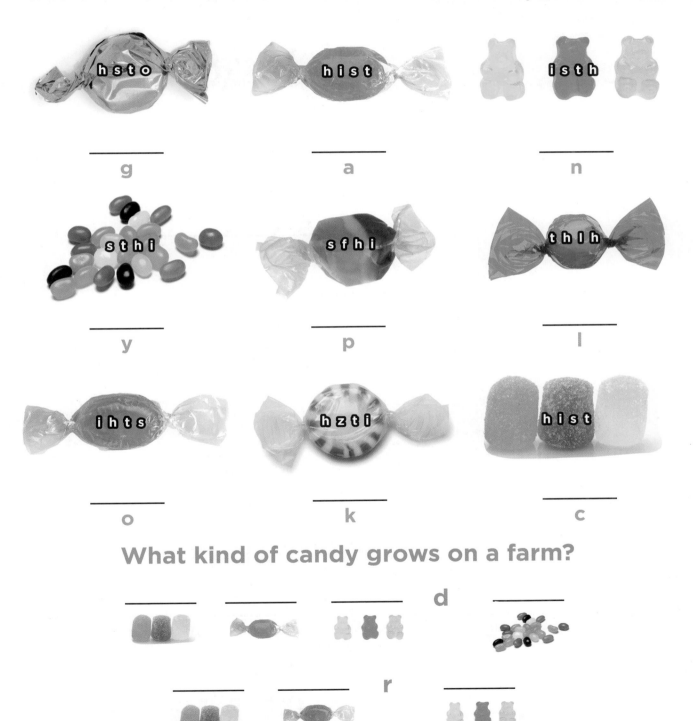

hsto	hist	isth
___	___	___
g	a	n

sthi	sfhi	thlh
___	___	___
y	p	l

ihts	hzti	hist
___	___	___
o	k	c

What kind of candy grows on a farm?

___ ___ ___ ___ d ___

___ ___ r ___

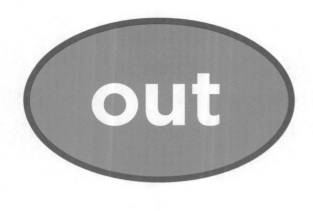

out

Trace the word **out** and say it aloud.

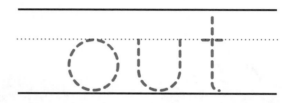

out

Practice writing the word out.

_____   _____

_____   _____

_____   _____

I got _____ of the car.

Boxcar Race

Draw a box around the word **out** when you see it hiding inside another word. The car with more boxes wins the race.

tote   butter

outer   hour

loud   once

touch   spout

outside

---

shout   scout

mount   tryout

fort   ouch

pout   about

lookout

Trace the word no and say it aloud.

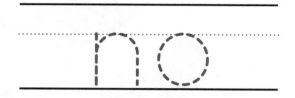

Practice writing the word no.

I have _____ shoes on.

Lucky Card

Color all the shapes that have the word **no** inside.

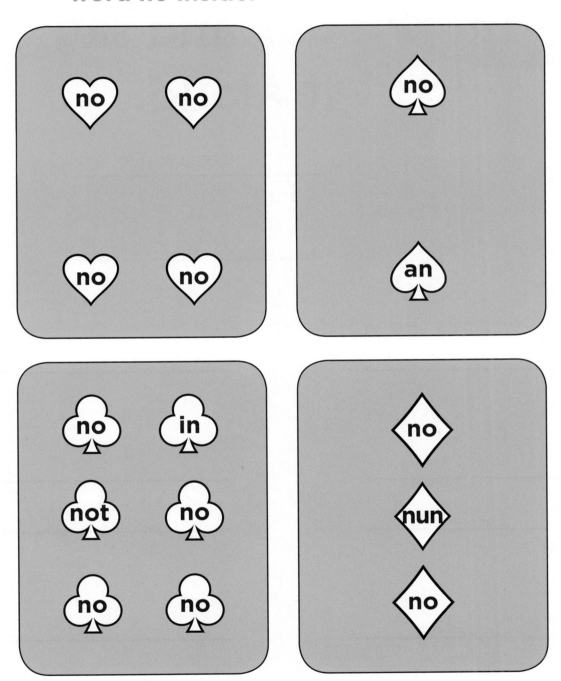

Circle the card suit that has all the shapes colored.

**our**

Trace the word our and say it aloud.

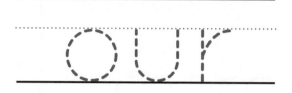

Practice writing the word our.

_____   _____

_____   _____

_____   _____

We like _____ teacher.

Around the Clock

Draw a line from the middle of the clock to the word our every time it appears. Follow each line to fill in the correct letter below.

What did the clock hands say when they passed each other?

__ __ __ __ __   __ __ __

5 1 6 11 7   9 3 6

Trace the word ate and say it aloud.

Practice writing the word ate.

I _____ too much!

Fishing for Rhymes

Draw a line from each fishing pole to the words that rhyme with **ate**.

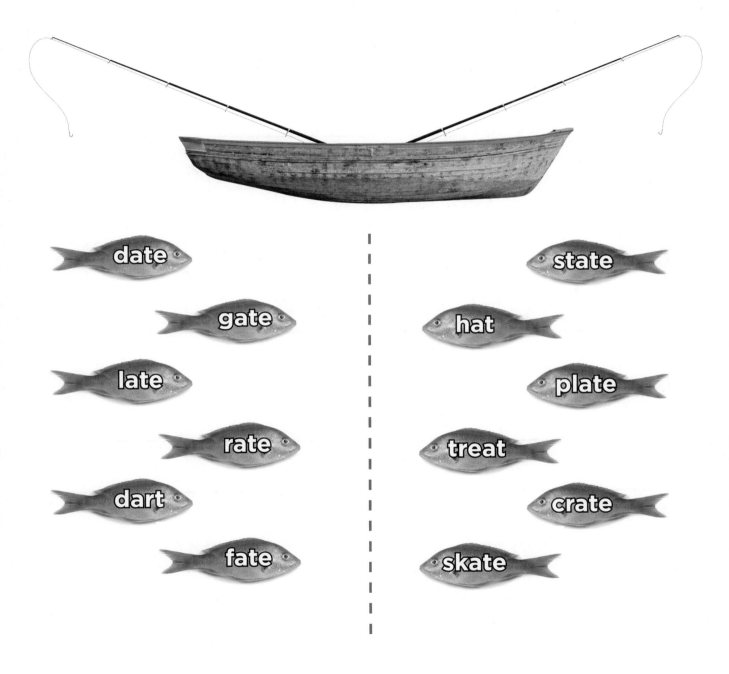

date

gate

late

rate

dart

fate

state

hat

plate

treat

crate

skate

Which side caught more fish? _____

 **there**

Trace the word there and say it aloud.

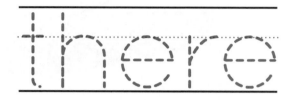

Practice writing the word there.

_____ _____

....

_____ _____

_____ _____

....

_____ _____

Please sit over _____.

Fun Fact

Ask an adult to read you the paragraph below. Then shade one box from the bottom up on the graph every time you see the word there.

70	there
60	there
50	there
40	there
30	there
20	there
10	there

There are not many giant pandas left in the wild. Pandas live in the mountains of China. They like the bamboo trees there. But bamboo forests can get cut down. Pandas lose their homes and their food. There are many people trying to help save pandas. These people protect the bamboo forests. Is there something you can do to help too?

Use the number at the top of your bar to complete this fun fact:

Giant pandas eat 20 to _____ pounds of bamboo a day.

Trace the word soon and say it aloud.

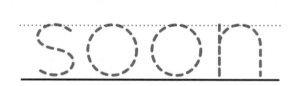

Practice writing the word soon.

We will be home _____.

Beautiful Bubbles

Cross out any bubble that does not have the word **soon**.

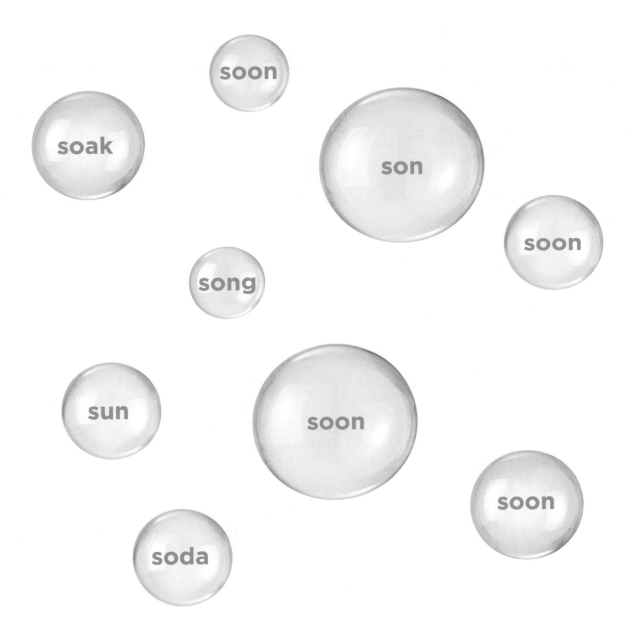

soon

soak

son

soon

song

sun

soon

soon

soda

How many bubbles remain? _____

REVIEW: The Bottom Line

Use the codes to help fill in the missing words to the story.

new	this	our	there	soon
▬▬	• • • • •	∼∼	═══	▬ ▬ ▬

I went to a _____ camp _____ summer. As _____ as I got
_____ (new) _____ (this) _____ (soon)

_____ , I went to my cabin. I made a lot of _____ friends
_____ (there) _____ (new)

_____ . _____ cabin was _____ and very clean. _____ was
_____ (there) _____ (our) _____ (new) _____ (there)

a lake with canoes near _____ cabin. _____ was _____
_____ (our) _____ (this) _____ (our)

favorite part of camp! I hope I can see my friends again _____ . I
_____ (soon)

want to go to _____ summer camp again next year.
_____ (this)

How many times does each word appear in the story?

new _____   there _____

this _____   soon _____

our _____

REVIEW: Matching Caps

Draw a line to connect the matching sight words. Fill in the letter in the blue circle next to each cap to name the sport below.

1. get

2. must

3. are

4. no

5. out

6. white

 g

 k

 a

 i

 y

 n

This name of this sport means "hunter's boat."

___ ___ ___ ___ ___ ___ ___ ___
 4   2   1   2   4   6   5   3

REVIEW: Word Search

Find the review words in the word search.

black   saw   will   who   get   must

white   new   out   there   soon

G A L M A W H I

W S B U T S A W

I O L S H N E H

L O A T E R E I

L U C K R G E T

N T K B E L L E

W H O L S O O N

E T L E N E W I

REVIEW: The Lost Word

Look for each review word from page 216 and circle it below. There is one word from the list that is missing.

Who can help me find my black backpack? It is a new backpack with white stripes. I left it out on the grass after school. Now, it's not there. I must find it soon!

If you find it, you will get a reward!

Which review word is missing? _____

Crossword Clues

Complete each sentence with a review word from the box. Use the words to fill in the puzzle on the next page.

are	that	now	eat	well
have	they	this	no	our	ate

Across

2. I like _____ one here.

4. We _____ it all up!

5. We washed _____ car.

6. It's time for dinner _____.

8. Let's _____ lunch outside.

Down

1. Where is _____ book I was reading?

3. We _____ a pet dog.

4. They _____ sisters.

6. There is _____ food inside.

7. She does not feel _____.

9. I hope _____ get home soon.

Use the clues on **page 218** to fill in the puzzle.

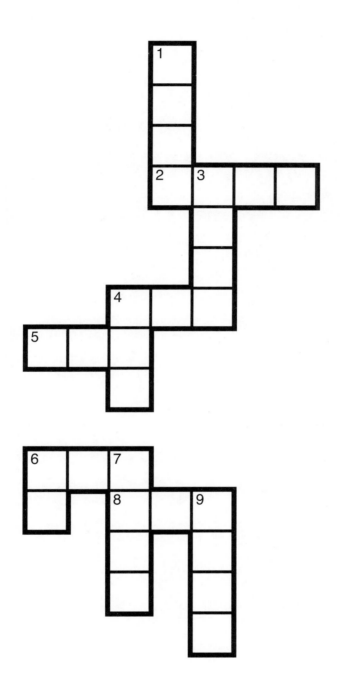

REVIEW: Sentence Sequence

Follow the code in the box to make sentences with sight words.

what	he	she	did	they	want	eat	out
!	@	#	$	%	^	&	*

there	was	good	that	will	have
+	=	<	>	?	~

1. _____ _____ _____ _____ .
   \#   ?   ~   >

2. _____ _____ _____ _____ ?
   ! $ %   &

3. _____ _____ _____ _____ .
   @   =   *   +

4. _____ _____ _____ .
   %   ^   >

5. _____ _____ _____ .
   >   =   <

6. _____ _____ _____ _____ .
   @   ?   &   >

REVIEW: Wacky Word Boxes

Some letters are short and some letters are tall.
Find the boxes that fit each word.

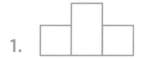

ate	say	black	must	came	with	do
all	get	no	who	this	white	four

1.

2.

3.

4.

5.

6.

7.

8.

9.

10.

11.

12.

13.

14.

REVIEW: Four Squares

Find four sight words in each square. Draw a box around each correctly spelled word.

whot	be
at	went
too	eet
new	are
soon	our
ran	like
now	wint
blak	am
well	brown
are	into

REVIEW: Framed!

Cross out any words that are not spelled correctly. You should have 22 correct sight words left. Color the frame that has only correct words inside.

like
want
will
must
new
soon
no
white

am   ran
he   good
ar   went
saw   she
too   thew

are   our   they
lik   att   have
say   what   wuz

REVIEW: In the End

Draw a line to the correct ending for each sight word. Then write the word on the line.

d   e   _____   o   id   _____   th   ur   _____

b   o   _____   w   as   _____   fo   is   _____

a   t   _____   d   ut   _____   we   ll   _____

a   ow   _____   ca   at   _____

n   ll   _____   in   th   _____

e   at   _____   th   me   _____

                               wi   to   _____

a   et   _____   br   ack   _____

w   ho   _____   bl   ere   _____

g   te   _____   th   own   _____

Section 3

The sight words included in this section are:

after	give	live	some
again	going	may	stop
an	had	of	take
any	has	old	thank
as	her	once	them
ask	him	open	then
by	his	over	think
could	how	please	under
every	just	pretty	walk
fly	know	put	were
from	let	ride	when

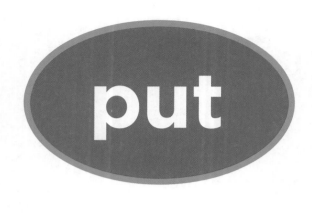

Trace the word put and say it aloud.

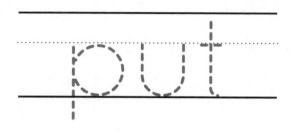

Practice writing the word put.

Please _____ your shoes on.

Balloon Buddies

Draw a circle around the word **put** to make
a balloon. Put an X through the other words.

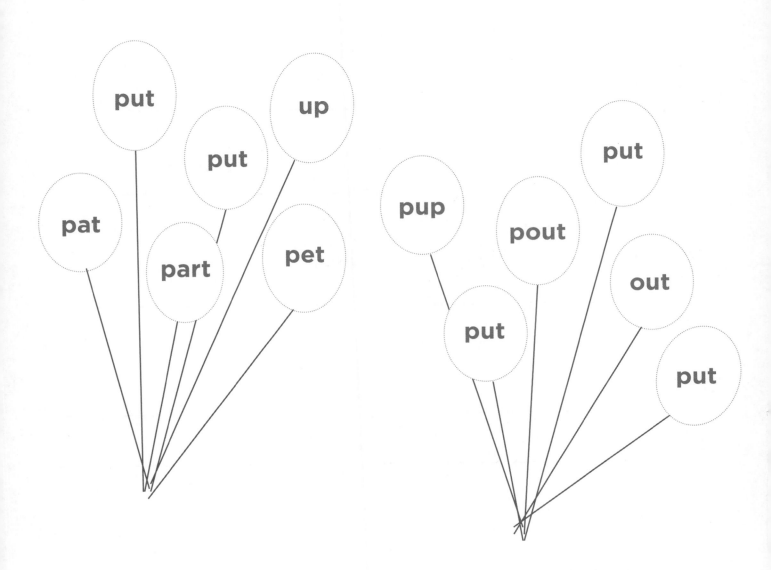

Count the balloons in each bunch.
Circle the bunch that has more balloons.

How many balloons are there altogether? _____

**under**

Trace the word under and say it aloud.

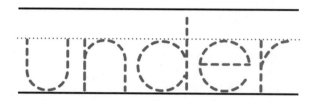

Practice writing the word under.

_____   _____
....

_____   _____

_____   _____
....

_____   _____

I hide _____ the table.

Made in the Shade

Shade each box that has the word under. Then match each number to the corresponding letter to fill in the blanks below.

5	up	ugly	uncle	under	until
4	under	until	up	end	onto
3	fun	undo	untie	upper	under
2	upset	under	and	bun	wander
1	until	undone	under	dunk	ending

l   c   a   d   o

What can you catch but never throw?

_____   _____   _____   _____   _____
   1   2   3   4   5

**please**

Trace the word please and say it aloud.

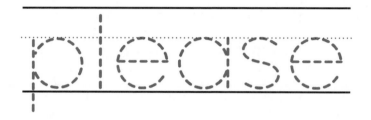

Practice writing the word please.

_____   _____

_____   _____

_____   _____

I always say _____.

Word Tunnels

Connect the letters of the word **please** to make a tunnel. Use the number at the tunnel exit to complete the fun fact.

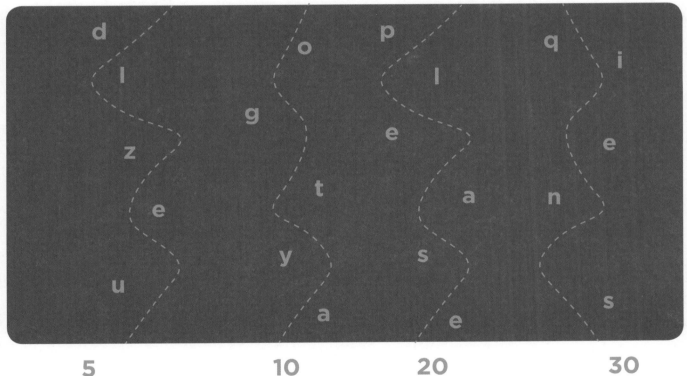

5	10	20	30

Squirrels can run up to _____ miles an hour!

Circle the berries that show the word **please**.

please   leaps   place   please   sleeps

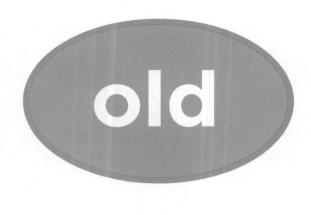

Trace the word old and say it aloud.

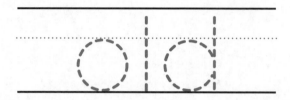

Practice writing the word old.

_____   _____

_____   _____

_____   _____

How _____ are you?

Sight Word Slices

Draw a line from the word old in the middle of each pizza to the matching words on the edge of each pizza. See how many slices you make.

Pizza A

old   all

goal

old

old

old   old

bowl   old

Pizza B

old

doll   and

odd   add

old

loud   old

old

Which pizza has more slices?

_____

How many slices in all? _____

233

pretty

Trace the word pretty and say it aloud.

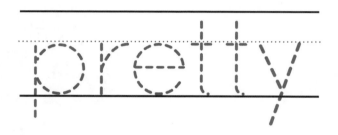

Practice writing the word pretty.

She is very _____.

Postcard Puzzler

Circle the word **pretty** each time it appears on the postcard. Write the number in the stamp in the corner. Find the matching number below to see where the postcard is from.

Dear Lauren,

I love camping! This place is so pretty. We go hiking in the mountains every day. Then I watch the sunset. I can see all the pretty stars at night. We went to see a geyser today. Hot water shoots out of the ground. It's pretty amazing. It's called "Old Faithful." I'll be home soon!

Love,
Rita

Lauren Harris

212 Parker Drive

Phoenix, AZ 85001

1. Niagara Falls

2. The Pacific Ocean

3. Yellowstone

4. Rocky Mountains

5. Crater Lake

6. Sequoia

Trace the word once and say it aloud.

Practice writing the word once.

My birthday is _____ a year.

Riddle Row

Circle all rows and columns that have the word **once** five times. Match the symbols with the letters outside the grid to solve the riddle.

	+	<	*	+	<	
*	once	one	once	once	no	h
<	once	once	once	once	once	a
*	once	once	once	once	once	e
+	nice	once	since	once	once	p
<	one	on	one	once	sons	t
	s	r	i	b	j	

Who can shave all day and still have a beard?

___   ___ ___ r ___ ___ r

   <   +   <   +   *

some

Trace the word some and say it aloud.

Practice writing the word some.

I want _____ candy, please.

Ladder Line Up

Underline some if it appears within the longer word. Circle the ladder that has an underlined word on the most steps.

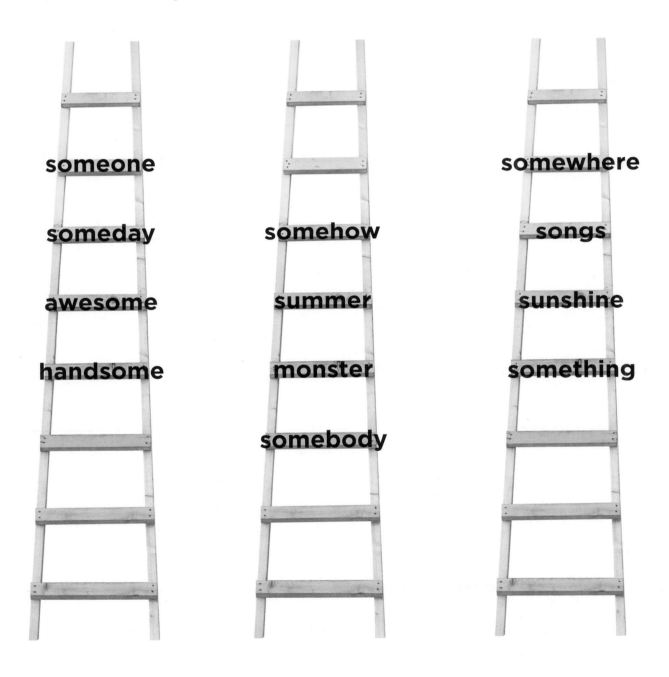

someone		somewhere
someday	somehow	songs
awesome	summer	sunshine
handsome	monster	something
	somebody	

 **had**

Trace the word had and say it aloud.

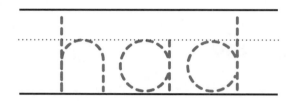

Practice writing the word had.

_____   _____

_____   _____

_____   _____

_____   _____

We _____ a great day!

Follow the Chain

Draw a circle every time you see the word had.
If your circles make a chain, write the number of
times the word had appears.

h a d h a d h o d h a d   _____

h a d h a d h a d h a d   _____

h a d h a d h a d   _____

h a d h a d h a d   _____

h a d h a d h a d h a d   _____

 **ride**

Trace the word ride and say it aloud.

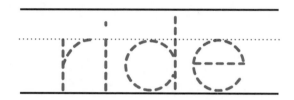

Practice writing the word ride.

_____

_____

_____

_____

_____

_____

I _____ the bus.

Rhyme Score

Circle the word ride each time it appears on the field. Underline any words that rhyme with ride. Count the total for each and fill in the score board.

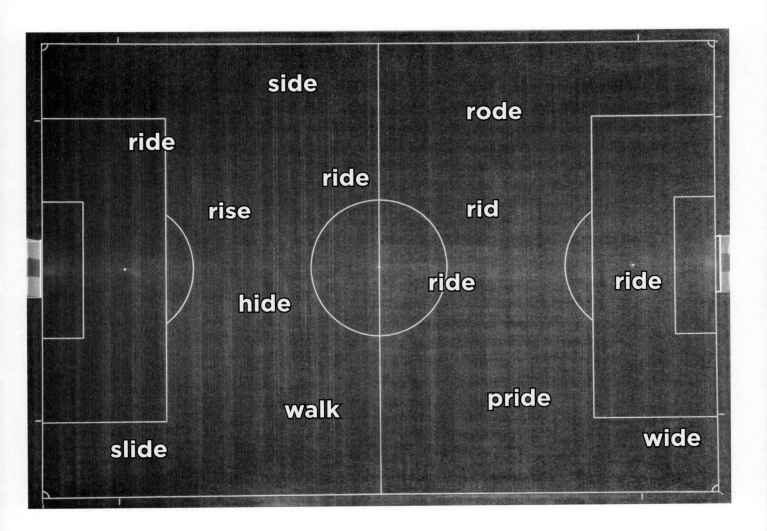

side

rode

ride

rise

ride

rid

hide

ride

ride

walk

pride

slide

wide

RIDE

RHYMES WITH RIDE

_____

_____

 **after**

Trace the word after and say it aloud.

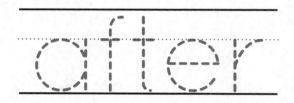

Practice writing the word after.

_____   _____

_____   _____

_____   _____

_____   _____

We walk home _____ school.

Three Ring Circus

Find the word **after** three times inside each ring and circle it.

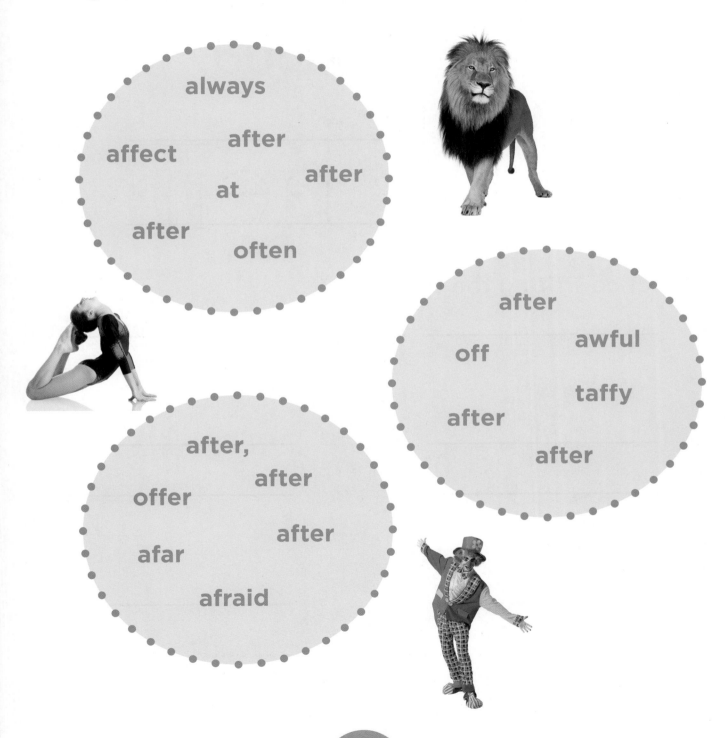

always

after

affect

after

at

after

often

after

awful

off

taffy

after

after

after,

after

offer

after

afar

afraid

her

Trace the word her and say it aloud.

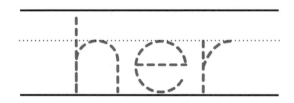

Practice writing the word her.

_____   _____

-        -

_____   _____

_____   _____

-        -

_____   _____

This is _____ book.

Play Along

Draw a circle around the word her to make a music note. Follow the code for the circled notes to answer the joke.

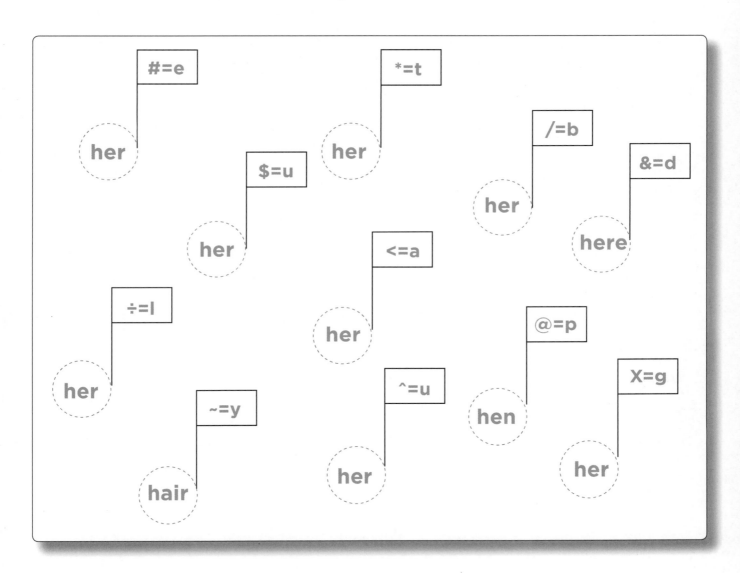

How do you fix a tuba?

With ___   ___ ___ ___ ___   ___ ___ ___ ___
       <   * $ /   <   X   ÷   ^   #

REVIEW: The Bottom Line

Use the codes to help fill in the missing words to the story.

once	old	had	some	under
▬▬	·····	〰	══	▬ ▬ ▬

_____ I found a nest _____ an _____ bridge. The nest _____ a

bird in it. I wondered if the bird _____ _____ babies in the nest, too.

I _____ to wait quietly for a long time. _____ the bird flew away,

I saw _____ small baby birds in the nest! They were probably a few

weeks _____. The mother bird came back with _____ food for the

babies. I _____ so much fun watching these birds _____ the bridge!

How many times does each word appear in the story?

once	_____	some	_____
old	_____	under	_____
had	_____		

REVIEW: Matching Caps

Draw a line to connect the matching sight words. Fill in the letter in the blue circle next to each cap to name the sport below.

1. put

2. please

3. pretty

4. ride

5. after

6. her

 after   n

 pretty   x

 ride   i

please   o

her   g

put   b

This sport is played in a ring and has "rounds."

___ ___ ___ ___ ___ ___
1   2   3   4   5   6

fly

Trace the word fly and say it aloud.

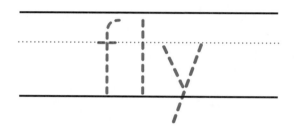

Practice writing the word fly.

See the bird _____.

Button Up

Draw a circle around the word fly to make buttons on the sweaters. Circle the sweater with more buttons.

fly

try

fly

lay

sly

fly

flight

fly

fly

fly

ry

fly

Trace the word open and say it aloud.

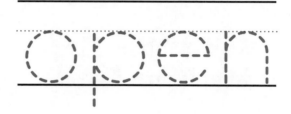

Practice writing the word open.

We _____ the box.

Funny Food

Circle the word open each time you see it. Write the total under each bag, and use the code to answer the joke.

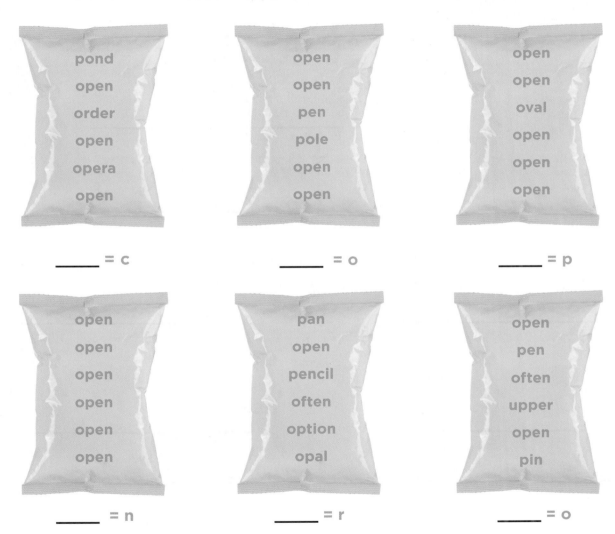

pond
open
order
open
opera
open

_____ = c

open
open
pen
pole
open
open

_____ = o

open
open
oval
open
open
open

_____ = p

open
open
open
open
open
open

_____ = n

pan
open
pencil
often
option
opal

_____ = r

open
pen
often
upper
open
pin

_____ = o

What did the baby corn call its dad?

___ ___ ___ ___ ___ ___ ___
5   2   5   3   4   1   6

**from**

Trace the word from and say it aloud.

Practice writing the word from.

I went home _____ school.

Check It Out

Put a check mark by the word **from** in the book titles. If the title does not have the word **from**, leave it blank.

From East to West

On the Front Lines

Recipes from Around the World

Stories for Bedtime

The Little Frog

Far Away Places

From Me to You

Letters from Kings

How many book titles have the word **from**?

_____

how

Trace the word how and say it aloud.

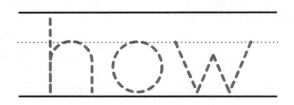

Practice writing the word how.

_____   _____

_____   _____

_____   _____

_____   _____

I know _____ to do it.

Prize Tickets

Underline the word how each time you see it on the ticket. Write the number on the line.

howhowow ___

HOWHOHOWH ___

wowhowhow ___

howhowhow ___

HOHOWOWH ___

hovowhow ___

Add up the numbers on all the tickets. _____

11   **2**   **5**   **2**   **1**

Circle the prize that equals the number of underlined words.

 **give**

Trace the word give and say it aloud.

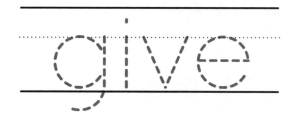

Practice writing the word give.

_____   _____

_____   _____

_____   _____

_____   _____

Let's _____ her a treat.

Candy Code

Look at the letters inside each candy. If you can unscramble the letters to make the word **give**, then write **give** on the line and follow the code. If not, leave it blank.

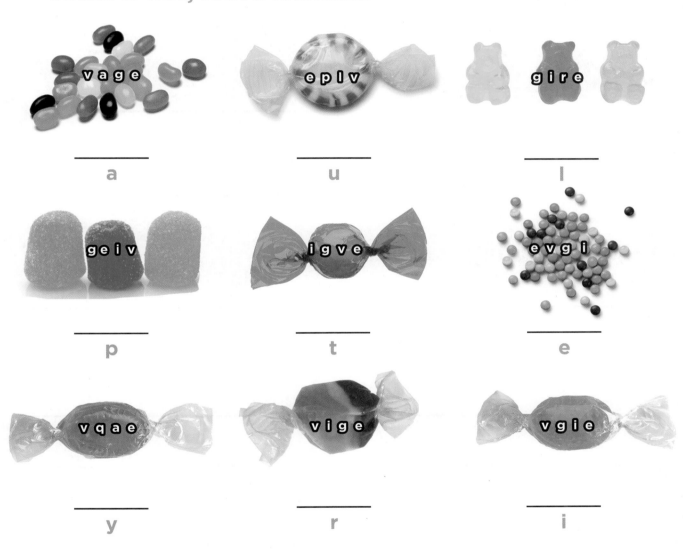

v a g e

_____
a

e p l v

_____
u

g i r e

_____
l

g e i v

_____
p

i g v e

_____
t

e v g i

_____
e

v q a e

_____
y

v i g e

_____
r

v g i e

_____
i

What kind of candy might make you sneeze?

_____ _____ _____ _____ _____ _____ m _____ n _____

Trace the word ask and say it aloud.

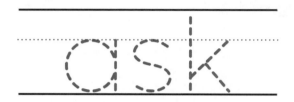

Practice writing the word ask.

I _____ a question.

Boxcar Race

Draw a box around the word **ask** when you see it hiding inside another word. The car with more boxes wins the race.

task

mask

last

taps

asks

skip

basket

sack

skate

---

asking

past

bask

masks

Alaska

asked

as

stack

packs

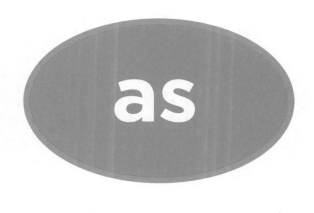

Trace the word as and say it aloud.

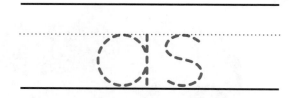

Practice writing the word as.

_____   _____

....

_____   _____

_____   _____

....

_____   _____

We talk _____ **we walk to school.**

Lucky Card

Color all the shapes that have the word as inside.

Circle the card suit that has all the shapes colored.

Trace the word him and say it aloud.

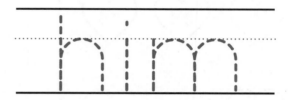

Practice writing the word him.

_____   _____
....

_____   _____

_____   _____
....

_____   _____

I talk to _____.

Around the Clock

Draw a line from the middle of the clock to the word him every time it appears. Follow each line to fill in the correct letter below.

When do clocks speed up?

___ ___ ___ ___ ___ ___   ___ ___ ___ ___
8   3   12   2   7   9   12   3   6   1

___ ___ ___ ___
1   11   3   12

Trace the word stop and say it aloud.

stop

Practice writing the word stop.

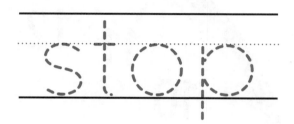

I _____ to help my dad.

Fishing for Rhymes

Draw a line from each fishing pole to the words that rhyme with **stop**.

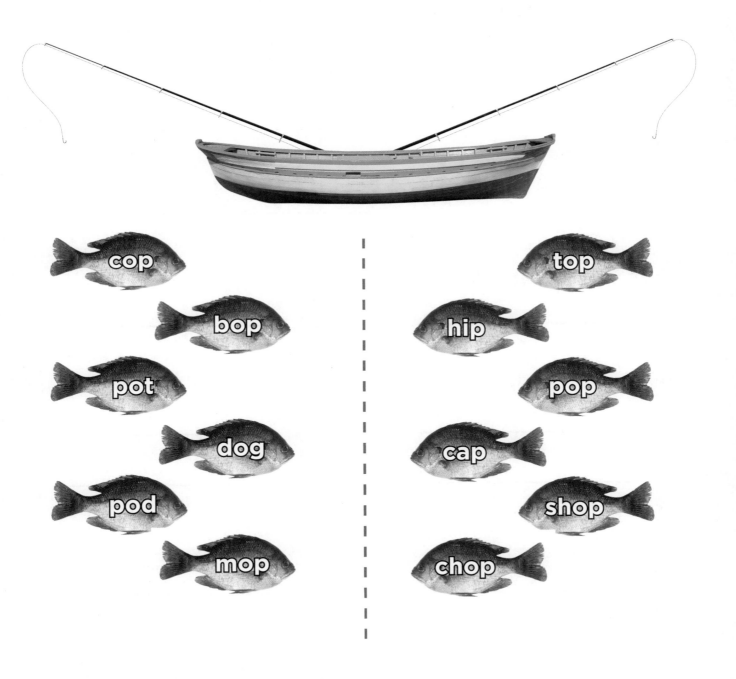

cop

bop

pot

dog

pod

mop

top

hip

pop

cap

shop

chop

Which side caught more fish? _____

 **has**

Trace the word has and say it aloud.

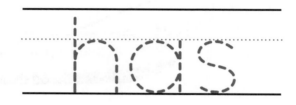

Practice writing the word has.

He _____ a new book.

Fun Fact

Ask an adult to read you the paragraph below. Then shade one box from the bottom up every time you see the word has.

24	has
21	has
18	has
15	has
12	has
9	has
6	has

Koala bears live in eucalyptus trees. A koala has sharp claws to grip the branches. Eucalyptus leaves are the main food for a koala. This leaf has a strong smell, like a cough drop. A koala bear has the same smell because it eats so many leaves! The number of trees has gone down over the years. So, it's harder for a koala to find a home and food. Everyone has to work together to protect the trees and the koalas.

Use the number at the top of your bar to complete this fun fact:

A koala can sleep up to _____ hours a day.

 **going** Trace the word going and say it aloud.

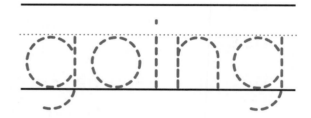

Practice writing the word going.

_____   _____

....

_____   _____

_____   _____

....

_____   _____

We are _____ **now.**

Beautiful Bubbles

Cross out any bubble that does not have the word going.

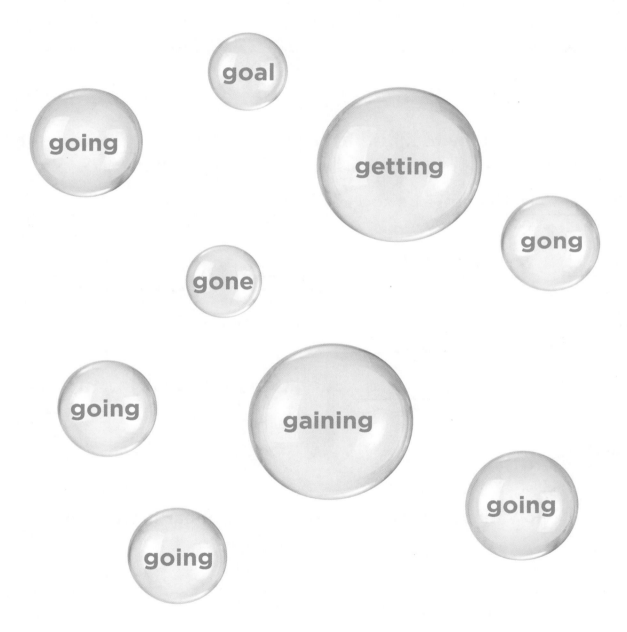

How many bubbles remain? _____

REVIEW: The Bottom Line

Use the codes to help fill in the missing words to the story.

give	from	open	him	going
———	•••••	~~~	═══	– – –

I am _____ (going) to my friend's birthday party. I'm _____ (going) to get a

gift _____ (from) the store as soon as it is _____ (open) . I want to _____ (give)

_____ (him) a baseball. My friend is _____ (going) to _____ (give) _____ (him) a glove.

We are _____ (going) to _____ (open) them together. It will be _____ (from) both

of us. We hope he will _____ (open) our gift first! We really want _____ (him)

to like it.

How many times does each word appear in the story?

give _____   him _____

from _____   going _____

open _____

REVIEW: Matching Caps

Draw a line to connect the matching sight words. Fill in the letter in the blue circle next to each cap to name the activity below.

1. fly

2. how

3. ask

4. as

5. stop

6. has

 as — i

 fly — r

 has — g

 ask — n

 stop — n

how — u

In a marathon, people do this for over 26 miles.

___ ___ ___ ___ ___ ___
1   2   3   3   4   5   6

REVIEW: Word Search

Find the review words in the word search.

put	under	please	old	some	after
from	give	ask	has	going	

```
T  G  I  V  E  P  U  T
P  O  K  M  A  F  N  U
L  I  P  U  E  R  D  N
E  N  L  S  T  O  L  D
A  G  U  B  R  M  R  E
S  O  M  E  T  I  V  R
E  H  A  S  F  A  S  K
S  A  F  T  E  R  O  M
```

REVIEW: The Lost Word

Look for each review word from page 274 and circle it below. There is one word from the list that is missing.

Please help me find my old baseball mitt! I put it under the bench after the game. This mitt was a gift from my dad. I am going to give it to my brother. Please ask around and see if anyone on that team has seen it!

Which review word is missing? _____

Crossword Clues

Complete each sentence with a review word from the box. Use the words to fill in the puzzle on the next page.

pretty	once	ride	her	fly	open
how	as	him	stop	had	

Across

1. _____ can I help you?

3. Clap your hands only _____.

4. Please _____ that now.

6. That dress is so _____.

8. I _____ a cold last week.

Down

1. I like _____ picture!

2. He is _____ tall as you.

3. Please _____ the window.

5. We will _____ on a plane.

7. I _____ the train every day.

8. Let's sing a song to _____.

Use the clues on page 276 to fill in the puzzle.

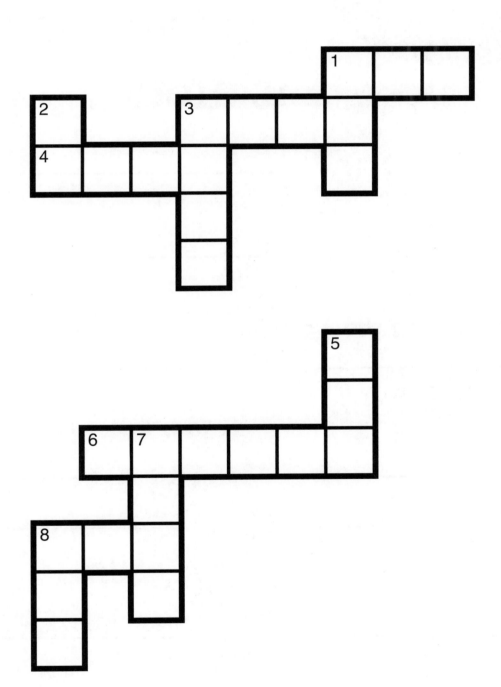

just

Trace the word just and say it aloud.

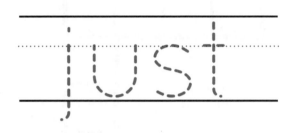

Practice writing the word just.

_____   _____

_____   _____

_____   _____

_____   _____

We _____ got here.

Balloon Buddies

Draw a circle around the word just to make a balloon.
Put an X through the other words.

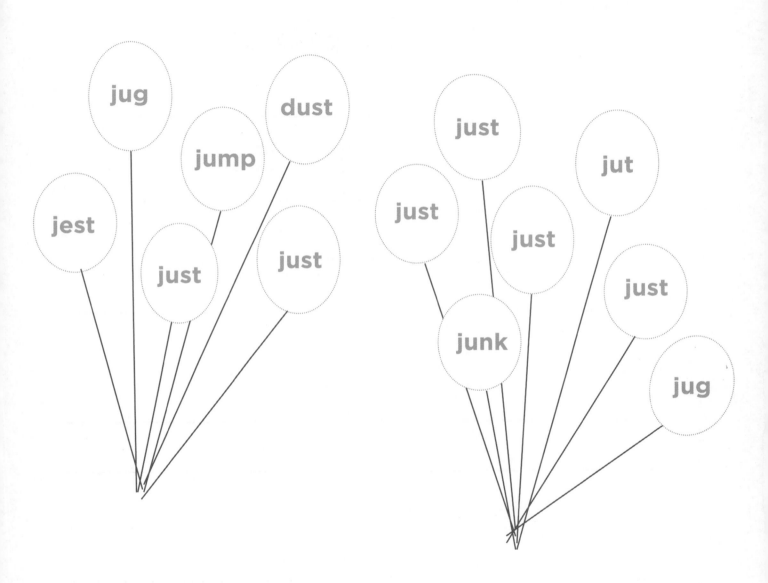

Count the balloons in each bunch.
Circle the bunch that has more balloons.

How many balloons are there altogether? _____

 **them**

Trace the word **them** and say it aloud.

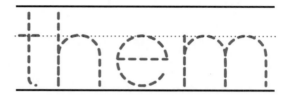

Practice writing the word **them**.

_____   _____

_____   _____

_____   _____

_____   _____

Put _____ in the bag.

Made in the Shade

Shade each box that has the word **them**. Then match each number to the corresponding letter to fill in the blanks below.

5	then	them	their	hen	ten
4	the	they	them	these	met
3	them	ten	the	mesh	than
2	there	these	they	them	hem
1	hem	then	tent	there	them

o   d   u   l   c

What do you call a sheep with no head and no legs?

a _____ _____ _____ _____ _____

    1   2   3   4   5

thank

Trace the word thank and say it aloud.

Practice writing the word thank.

Don't forget to _____ her.

Word Tunnels

Connect the letters of the word thank to make a tunnel. Use the number at the tunnel exit to complete the fun fact.

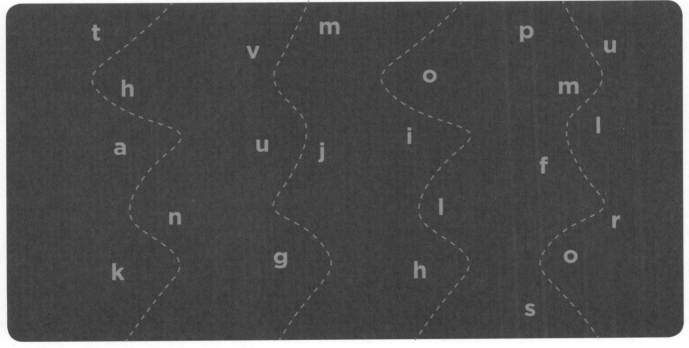

t		m		p	
	v				u
h			o		m
			i		l
a	u	j			f
				l	
n					r
k	g		h		o
					s

5   10   15   20

Squirrels can jump about _____ feet up!

Circle the berries that show the word thank.

think   thank   tank   thick   thank

Trace the word by and say it aloud.

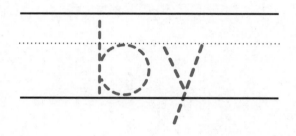

Practice writing the word by.

I wait _____ the door.

Sight Word Slices

Draw a line from the word by in the middle of each pie to the matching words on the edge of each pie. See how many slices you make.

Pie A

Pie B

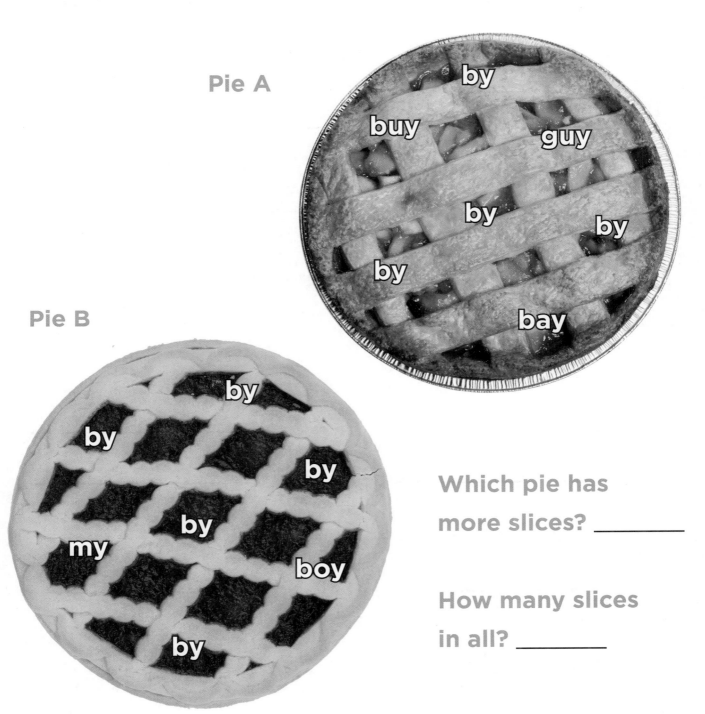

by
buy   guy
by   by
by
bay

by
by   by
by
my   boy
by

Which pie has
more slices? _____

How many slices
in all? _____

 **were**

Trace the word were and say it aloud.

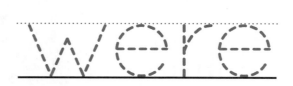

Practice writing the word were.

_____   _____

_____   _____

_____   _____

We _____ out all day.

Postcard Puzzler

Circle the word **were** each time it appears on the postcard. Write the number in the stamp in the corner. Find the matching number below to see where the postcard is from.

Dear Tom,

I wish you were here! My parents were right about going on a cruise. It's amazing. Yesterday we saw big, icy glaciers. Big chunks of ice were breaking off and splashing into the water. Today our ship stopped in Skagway. We were going to ride a train into the mountains. But instead, we went on a wildlife tour. We saw bears! There were also tons of bald eagles. I'm so glad I came!

Love,
Rudy

Tom Moore

44 Pine Street

Portland, Oregon 97035

1. Bahamas

2. Mexico

3. Canada

4. Florida

5. Alaska

6. California

**when**

Trace the word when and say it aloud.

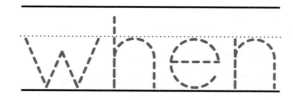

Practice writing the word when.

Tell me _____ to go.

Riddle Row

Circle all rows and columns that have the word when five times. Match the symbols with the letters outside the grid to solve the riddle.

	*	@	#	*	#	
#	when	when	west	went	want	l
*	when	when	what	when	new	y
@	we	when	when	hen	wheat	m
#	when	when	when	when	when	t
@	where	when	wheel	when	where	o
	p	i	r	a	w	

What's the best way to get on TV?

s __ __ on __ __
  @ #   @ #

289

 **over**

Trace the word over and say it aloud.

Practice writing the word over.

I go _____ the bridge.

Ladder Line Up

Underline **over** if it appears within the longer word. Circle the ladder that has an underlined word on the most steps.

clover

oven

oversee

voted

rover

overdo

overmix

flyover

overdone

lovely

overlap

playoff

Trace the word his and say it aloud.

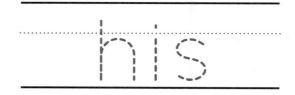

Practice writing the word his.

_____   _____

_____   _____

_____   _____

_____   _____

This is _____ pen.

Follow the Chain

Draw a circle every time you see the word **his**.
If your circles make a chain, write the number
of times the word **his** appears.

h i s h i s h i s   _____

h i s s h i s i s h i s   _____

h i s h i s h i s   _____

h i s h i s h i s h i s   _____

h i s h i s h s i   _____

take

Trace the word take and say it aloud.

Practice writing the word take.

_____   _____

_____   _____

_____   _____

_____   _____

I _____ my bag with me.

Rhyme Score

Circle the word take each time it appears on the field. Underline any words that rhyme with take. Count the total for each and fill in the score board.

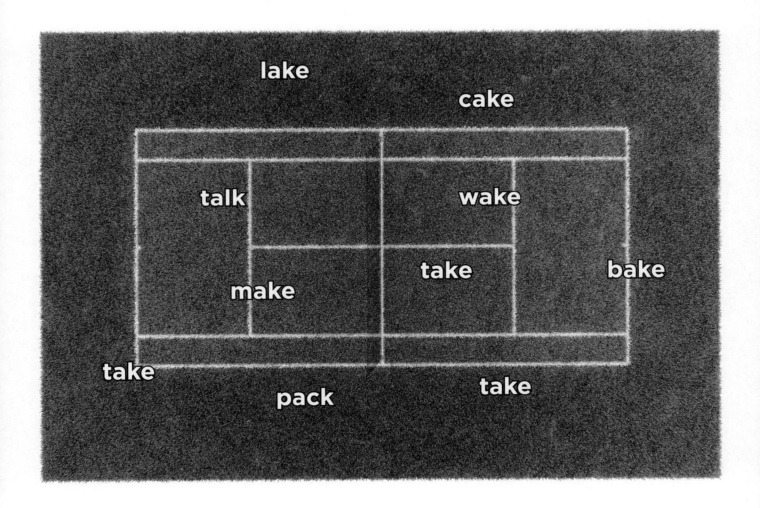

TAKE

RHYMES WITH TAKE

_____   _____

Trace the word again and say it aloud.

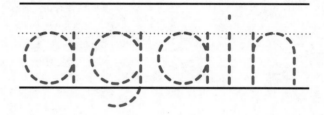

Practice writing the word again.

Let's sing it _____ !

Three Ring Circus

Find the word again three times inside
each ring and circle it.

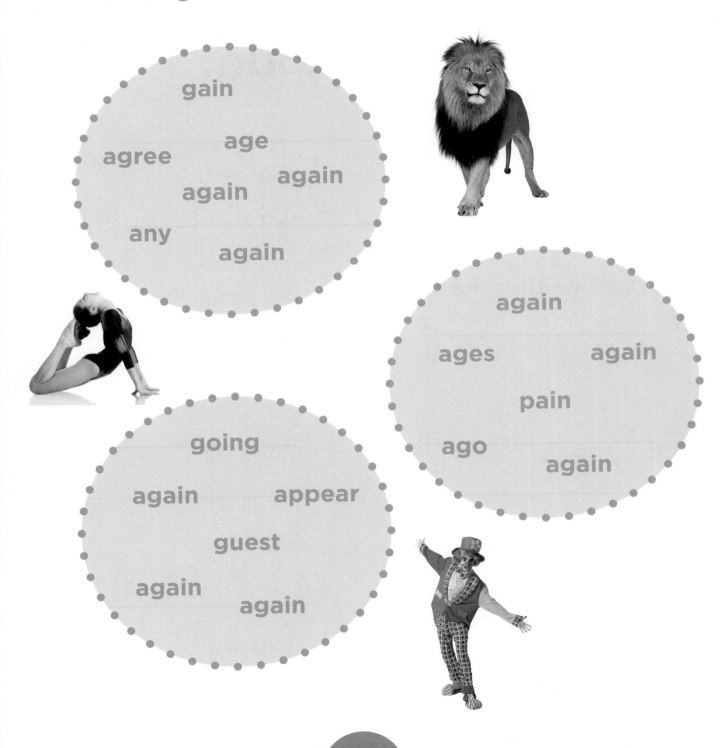

gain

age

agree

again

again

any

again

again

ages

again

pain

ago

again

going

again

appear

guest

again

again

Trace the word an and say it aloud.

Practice writing the word an.

I have _____ apple.

Play Along

Draw a circle around the word **an** to make a music note. Follow the code for the circled notes to answer the joke.

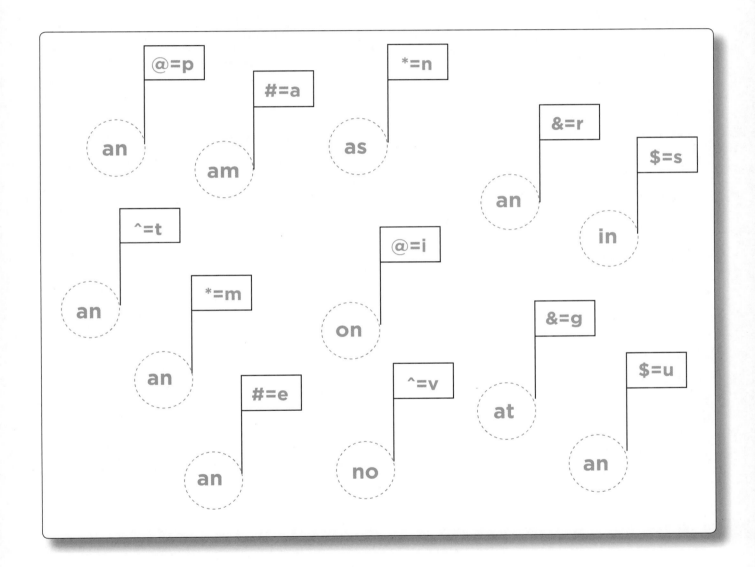

What pet makes loud music?

___ ___ ___ ___ ___ ___ ___
^   & $ *   @   #   ^

REVIEW: The Bottom Line

Use the codes to help fill in the missing words to the story.

over	take	again	were	them
——	·····	~~~	══	▬ ▬ ▬

Our neighbors _____ moving away. I decided to _____ some
         ══   ·····

boxes _____ to _____. Pretty soon, all those boxes _____ full.
      ——   ▬ ▬ ▬   ══

So I brought boxes from home _____. We helped _____ _____
                             ~~~   ▬ ▬ ▬ ·····

the boxes to the truck. We _____ sad to say good-bye. I hope we see
                          ══

our neighbors _____. I'd like to _____ a trip to visit _____.
              ~~~   ·····   ▬ ▬ ▬

How many times does each word appear in the story?

over _____   were _____

take _____   them _____

again _____

REVIEW: Matching Caps

Draw a line to connect the matching sight words.
Fill in the letter in the blue circle next to each cap
to name the sport below.

1. just

2. thank

3. by

4. when

5. his

6. an

 thank r

an y

when h

his e

by c

just a

In this sport, people use a bow to shoot arrows at targets.

___ ___ ___ ___ ___ ___ ___
 1   2   3   4   5   2   6

may

Trace the word may and say it aloud.

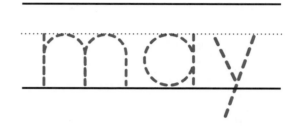

Practice writing the word may.

You _____ have a treat.

Button Up

Draw a circle around the word **may** to make buttons on the sweaters. Circle the sweater with more buttons.

may
my
may
way
may
may

why
made
may
me
may
am

walk

Trace the word **walk** and say it aloud.

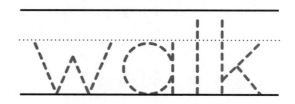

Practice writing the word **walk**.

_____   _____

_____   _____

_____   _____

_____   _____

We _____ home.

Funny Food

Circle the word **walk** each time you see it. Write the total under each can, and use the code to answer the joke.

walk	well	wake
walk	walk	wall
walk	law	wacky
walk	walk	work
walk	was	walk
walk	walk	want
_____ = p	_____ = e	_____ = s

won't	lock	walk
walk	walk	will
wait	walk	walk
what	want	walk
wink	walk	walk
walk	walk	walk
_____ = w	_____ = t	_____ = o

What is the kindest vegetable?

___ ___ ___ ___ ___   ___ ___ ___ a ___ ___
 1   2   3   3   4   6   5   4   4   5

 **live**

Trace the word live and say it aloud.

Practice writing the word live.

_____   _____

_____   _____

_____   _____

_____   _____

Fish _____ in the sea.

Check It Out

Put a check mark by the word live in the book titles. If the title does not have the word live, leave it blank.

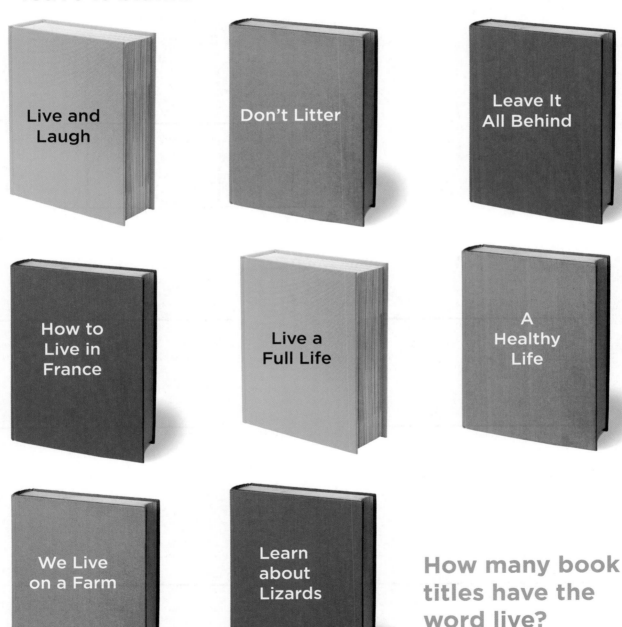

Live and Laugh

Don't Litter

Leave It All Behind

How to Live in France

Live a Full Life

A Healthy Life

We Live on a Farm

Learn about Lizards

How many book titles have the word live?

_____

then

Trace the word then and say it aloud.

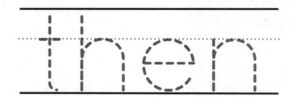

Practice writing the word then.

_____ _____

_____ _____

_____ _____

I woke up, and _____ I ate.

Prize Tickets

Underline the word **then** each time you see it on the ticket. Write the number on the line.

t h e n t h e n ____

T H E T H E N T ____

t h n t h e n t h ____

t h e n t e n h t ____

T H E N T H E N ____

h e n t h e t h e n ____

Add up the numbers on all the tickets. _____

10   2   8   2   1

Circle the prize that equals the number of underlined words.

 **know**

Trace the word **know** and say it aloud.

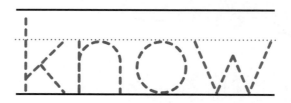

Practice writing the word know.

I _____ how to bake.

Candy Code

Look at the letters inside each candy. If you can unscramble the letters to make the word know, then write know on the line and follow the code. If not, leave it blank.

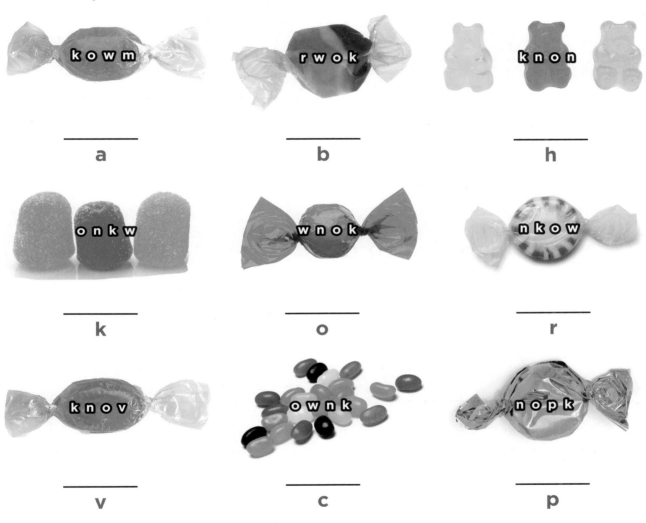

k o w m

_____
a

r w o k

_____
b

k n o n

_____
h

o n k w

_____
k

w n o k

_____
o

n k o w

_____
r

k n o v

_____
v

o w n k

_____
c

n o p k

_____
p

What kind of candy do guitar players like?

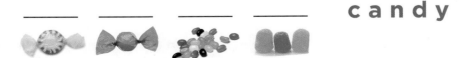

____ ____ ____ ____   c a n d y

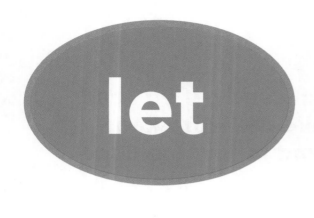

Trace the word let and say it aloud.

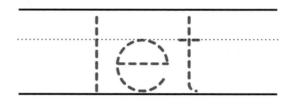

Practice writing the word let.

_____ _____

_____ _____

_____ _____

_____ _____

I _____ the dog out.

Boxcar Race

Draw a box around the word let when you see it hiding inside another word. The car with more boxes wins the race.

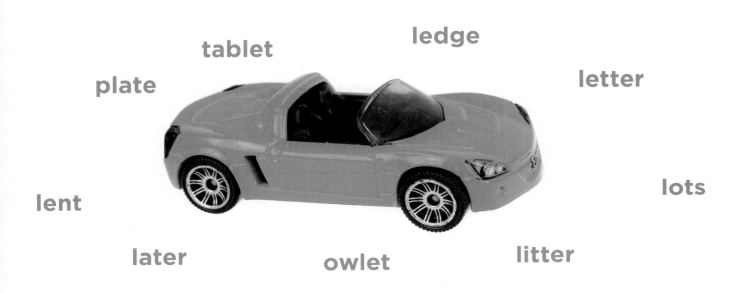

tablet

ledge

plate

letter

lent

lots

later

owlet

litter

leader

let's

lettuce

lantern

wallet

toilet

plant

listen

lend

of

Trace the word of and say it aloud.

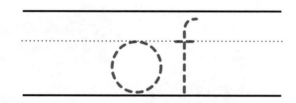

Practice writing the word of.

I am scared _____ bees.

Lucky Card

Color all the shapes that have the word of inside.

Circle the card suit that has all the shapes colored.

 **any**

Trace the word any and say it aloud.

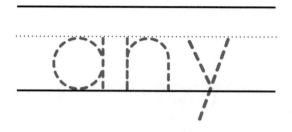

Practice writing the word any.

Do you see _____ stars?

Around the Clock

Draw a line from the middle of the clock to the word **any** every time it appears. Follow each line to fill in the correct letter below.

army

and

ant

Why wasn't the clock working?

___ ___ w ___ ___   ___ ___ ___ ___ ___ g
 4   1   6   2   1   6   8   4 10

___ ___ ___ e   ___ ___ ___.
 1   4 11   12   3   3

 **think**

Trace the word think and say it aloud.

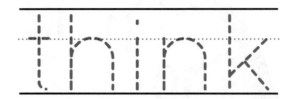

Practice writing the word think.

_____   _____

_____   _____

_____   _____

_____   _____

What do you _____ ?

Fishing for Rhymes

Draw a line from each fishing pole to the words that rhyme with think.

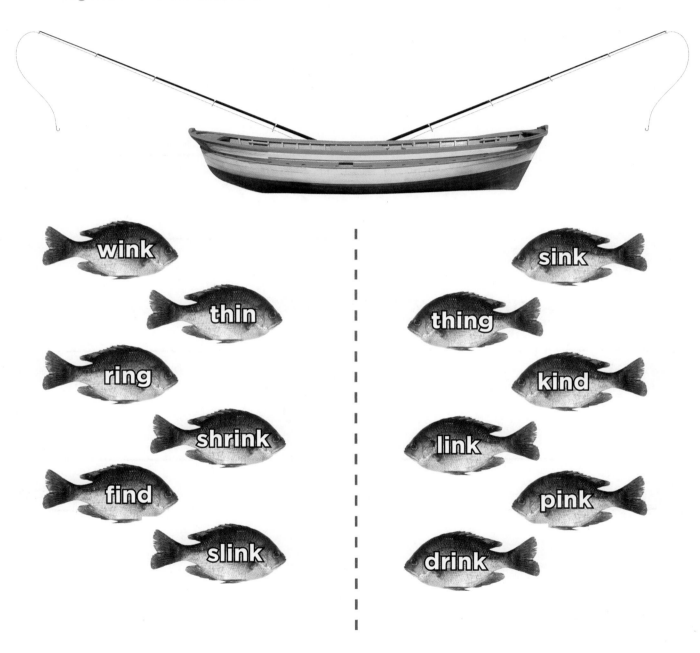

wink

thin

ring

shrink

find

slink

sink

thing

kind

link

pink

drink

Which side caught more fish? _____

 **could**

Trace the word could and say it aloud.

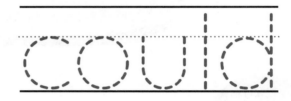

Practice writing the word could.

_____   _____

....

_____   _____

_____   _____

....

_____   _____

We _____ go that way.

Fun Fact

Ask an adult to read you the paragraph below. Then shade one box from the bottom up every time you see the word could.

20,000	could
1,600	could
1,200	could
800	could
400	could

Imagine you are in the dark. Could you still find something to eat? A bat could! Bats send out a sound wave. They listen for an echo to bounce back. The echo helps bats find food in the dark. This is called echolocation. It could even work to help bats find tiny insects!

Use the number at the top of your bar to complete this fun fact:

Bats can eat up to _____ mosquitoes per hour!

 **every**

Trace the word every and say it aloud.

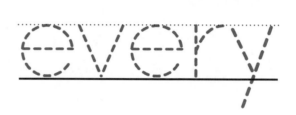

Practice writing the word every.

_____   _____

_____   _____

_____   _____

I like _____ kid in my class.

Beautiful Bubbles

Cross out any bubble that does not have the word **every**.

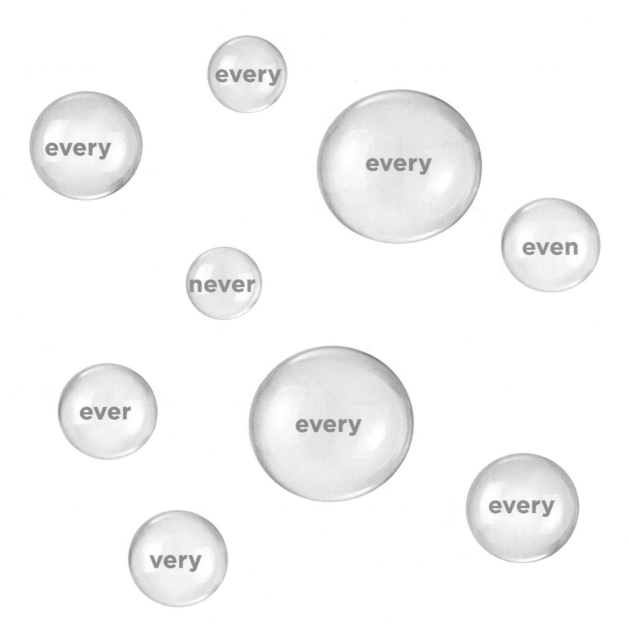

How many bubbles remain? _____

REVIEW: The Bottom Line

Use the codes to help fill in the missing words to the story.

walk	then	think	every	know
——	·····	～～	═══	– – –

I _____ home from school _____ day. I _____ the way.
— — (═══) (– – –)

I always _____ about my day as I _____. When I get home, I
(～～) (——)

_____ I need to do my homework. _____ I have a snack. I _____
(– – –) (·····) (– – –)

how to make _____ snack in our recipe book. _____, I play
(═══) (·····)

outside with my friends. I _____ I _____ _____ kid on my street!
(～～) (– – –) (═══)

How many times does each word appear in the story?

walk _____   every _____

then _____   know _____

think _____

REVIEW: Matching Caps

Draw a line to connect the matching sight words. Fill in the letter in the blue circle next to each cap to name the sport below.

1. may

2. live

3. let

4. of

5. any

6. could

 live   o

 of   l

 may   v

 let   l

 could   y

 any   e

There are six positions in this sport:
setter, server, spotter, spiker, passer, digger.

___ ___ ___ ___ ___ ___ b a l l
1   2   3   4   5   6

REVIEW: Word Search

Find the review words in the word search.

them	by	were	over	an	know
let	of	think	could	then	

```
E  T  L  N  O  W  U  N  V  C
W  E  E  R  B  C  G  X  O  F
L  E  T  K  N  O  W  D  L  M
O  T  H  Y  I  U  V  Z  I  T
T  H  E  N  D  L  O  D  W  H
Y  I  U  C  L  D  T  B  R  E
K  N  F  K  W  O  H  W  L  M
B  K  P  N  K  V  L  A  J  K
Y  N  W  E  R  E  M  Y  A  I
R  I  F  D  Y  R  I  F  N  P
```

REVIEW: The Lost Word

Look for each review word from page 326 and circle it below. There is one word from the list that is missing.

Do you know where the school Lost and Found is? It is over by the lunch area. If you think your things were lost at school, then please tell an aide. The aides let students check the Lost and Found before school. You could also ask them for help after school.

Which review word is missing? _____

Crossword Clues

Complete each sentence with a review word from the box. Use the words to fill in the puzzle on the next page.

> just   thank   when   his   take
>
> again   may   walk   live   any   every

Across

4. We _____ in that house.

5. _____ you so much!

6. I know _____ the show starts.

8. We _____ read or draw.

10. I _____ got home.

Down

1. We _____ across the street.

2. I want to play _____ .

3. Check _____ name on the list.

7. He eats _____ lunch.

9. You may choose _____ book.

11. Let's _____ the ball to the park.

Use the clues on page 328 to fill in the puzzle.

REVIEW: Sentence Sequence

Follow the code in the box to make sentences with sight words.

please	over	him	again	ask	her	put	after
!	@	#	$	%	^	&	*

them	by	take	give	ride	some
+	=	<	>	?	~

1. _____ _____ _____ _____ _____ .
   ! & + = ^

2. _____ _____ _____ .
   % # $

3. _____ _____ _____ _____ .
   ! > ^ ~

4. _____ _____ _____ _____ .
   ! ? * #

5. _____ _____ _____ _____ _____ .
   & ~ @ = +

6. _____ _____ _____ _____ .
   ! < + $

REVIEW: Wacky Word Boxes

Some letters are short and some letters are tall.
Find the boxes that fit each word.

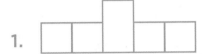

once   stop   may   just   under   walk   of

his   know   open   live   had   think   just

1.

2.

3.

4.

5.

6.

7.

8.

9.

10.

11.

12.

13.

14.

REVIEW: Four Squares

Find four sight words in each square.
Draw a box around each correctly spelled word.

fly	could
thank	pretty
plees	old
when	has
going	wen
evry	were
from	then
any	an
as	wons
how	every

REVIEW: Framed!

Cross out any words that are not spelled correctly. You should have 22 correct sight words left. Color the frame that has only correct words inside.

put
pretty
wer
open
as
again
hiz
live
think

them   by
aftur   his
how   liv
any   from
som

please   him   know
had   has   of
give   an   were

REVIEW: In the End

Draw a line to the correct ending for each word. Write the word on the line.

st   de   _____   tha   nk   _____   a   ly   _____

ri   me   _____   und   ld   _____   m   ay   _____

so   op   _____   cou   er   _____   f   sk   _____

ov   lk   _____   th   ke   _____

wh   er   _____   ta   ce   _____

wa   en   _____   on   en   _____

                            ju   st   _____

o   er   _____

h   ld   _____   af   ery   _____

l   et   _____   go   ter   _____

                           ev   ing   _____

Section 4

The sight words included in this section are:

always	first	pull	upon
around	five	read	us
been	found	right	use
best	gave	round	very
both	goes	sing	wash
buy	green	sit	why
call	its	sleep	wish
cold	made	tell	work
does	many	their	would
don't	off	these	write
fast	or	those	your

 **five**

Trace the word five and say it aloud.

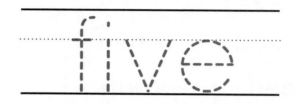

Practice writing the word five.

_____

_____

I have _____ cents.

Balloon Buddies

Draw a circle around the word five to make a balloon.
Put an X through the other words.

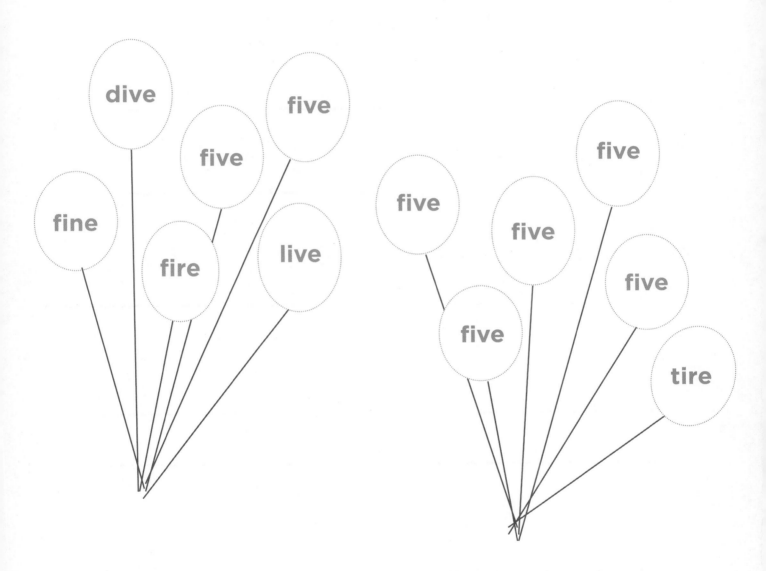

Count the balloons in each bunch.
Circle the bunch that has more balloons.

How many balloons are there altogether? _____

Trace the word cold and say it aloud.

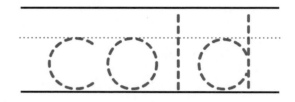

Practice writing the word cold.

_____   _____
. . . .
_____   _____
_____   _____
. . . .
_____   _____

It's _____ outside.

Made in the Shade

Shade each box that has the word cold. Then match each number to the corresponding letter to fill in the blanks below.

5	cold	coal	coat	cod	colt
4	call	old	cold	cone	corn
3	gold	cloud	bold	sold	cold
2	fold	cold	once	old	call
1	all	close	cool	cold	told
	r	h	i	c	a

What has four legs but can't walk?

a __ __ __ __ __
     1   2   3   4   5

always

Trace the word **always** and say it aloud.

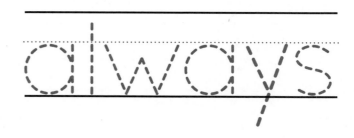

Practice writing the word **always**.

_____   _____

_____   _____

_____   _____

We _____ walk home together.

Word Tunnels

Connect the letters of the word **always** to make a tunnel. Use the number at the tunnel exit to complete the fun fact.

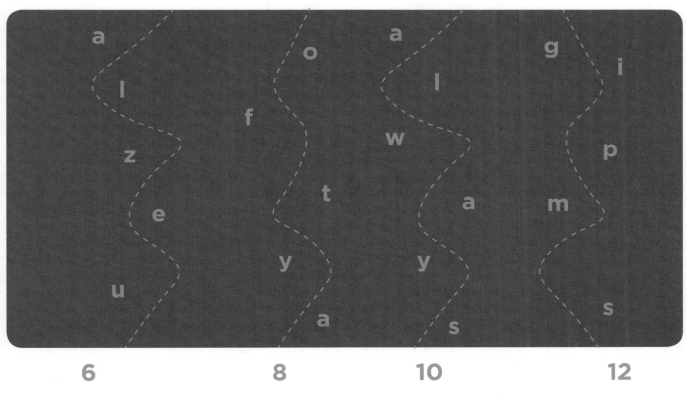

6   8   10   12

Most crabs have _____ legs.

Circle the shells that show the word **always**.

 anyway
 always
 anyway
 away
 always

off

Trace the word off and say it aloud.

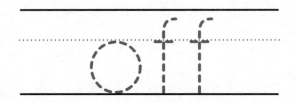

Practice writing the word off.

_____   _____
....
_____   _____
_____   _____
....
_____   _____

Turn _____ the TV.

Sight Word Slices

Draw a line from the word off in the middle of each pizza to the matching words on the edge of each pizza. See how many slices you make.

Pizza A

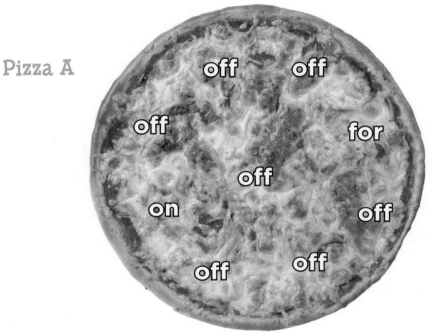

Pizza B

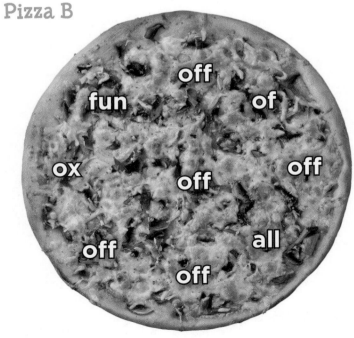

Which pizza has more slices?

_____

How many slices in all? _____

 **tell**

Trace the word tell and say it aloud.

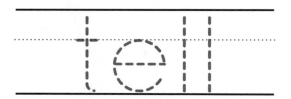

Practice writing the word tell.

_____   _____

....

_____   _____

....

_____   _____

I will _____ you about my day.

Postcard Puzzler

Circle the word **tell** each time it appears on the postcard. Write the number in the stamp in the corner. Find the matching number below to see where the postcard is from.

Dear Julie,

There is so much to tell you about this trip! The flight was very long. We spent the first week near the beach. I can't tell you how beautiful the reef was! Then we went to the "outback." I could tell right away it was going to be very different. It was a dry, hot desert. I will tell you all about the animals I saw when I get home! Please tell everyone hello from me.

Love,
Tess

Julie Green

27 Grand Street

Phoenix, AZ 85001

1. **Florida**

2. **California**

3. **France**

4. **Egypt**

5. **Australia**

6. **Japan**

 **upon**

Trace the word upon and say it aloud.

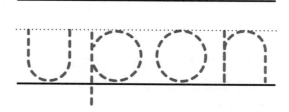

Practice writing the word upon.

The boat sailed _____ **the water.**

Riddle Row

Circle all rows and columns that have the word **upon** five times. Match the symbols with the letters outside the grid to solve the riddle.

	<	+	<	+	<	
+	up	on	pup	upon	one	w
<	not	cup	none	upon	no	o
+	pony	put	pound	upon	nut	y
<	upon	upon	upon	upon	upon	t
+	pun	pop	nope	upon	up	p
	a	g	n	e	l	

What do birds give out on Halloween?

___ w ___ ___ ___ s
  <   + + <

 **round** Trace the word round and say it aloud.

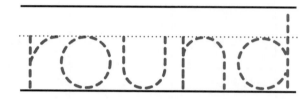

Practice writing the word round.

A circle is _____ .

Ladder Line Up

Underline round if it appears within the longer word. Circle the ladder that has an underlined word on the most steps.

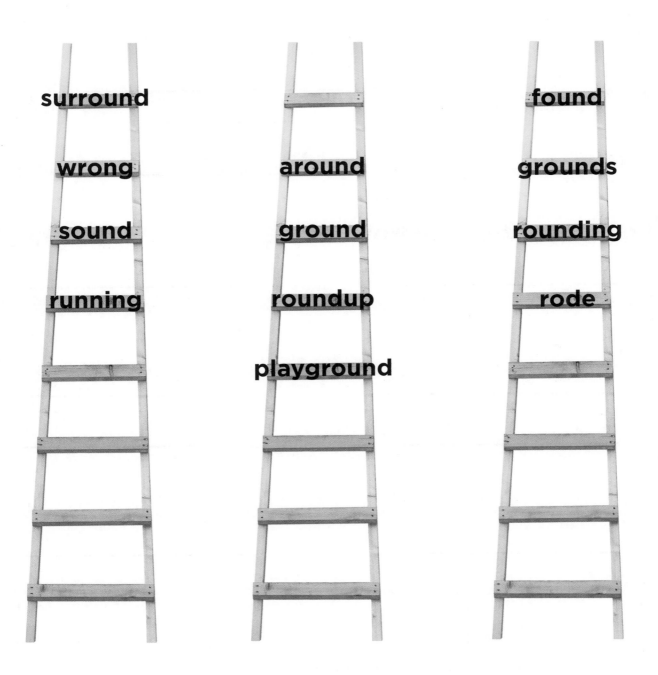

surround

wrong

sound

running

around

ground

roundup

playground

found

grounds

rounding

rode

Trace the word very and say it aloud.

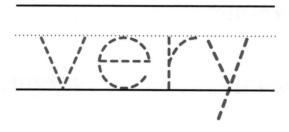

Practice writing the word very.

I am _____ happy.

Follow the Chain

Draw a circle every time you see the word very. If your circles make a chain, write the number of times the word very appears.

v e r y v e r y   _____

v e r y v e r y v e r y   _____

v e r y v e r y   _____

v e r y v e r y v e r y   _____

v e v y v e r y v r y y   _____

**best**

Trace the word **best** and say it aloud.

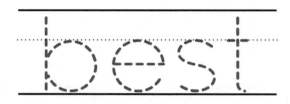

Practice writing the word **best**.

_____   _____

....

_____   _____

_____   _____

....

_____   _____

We had the _____ day!

Rhyme Score

Circle the word **best** each time it appears on the field. Underline any words that rhyme with best. Count the total for each and fill in the score board.

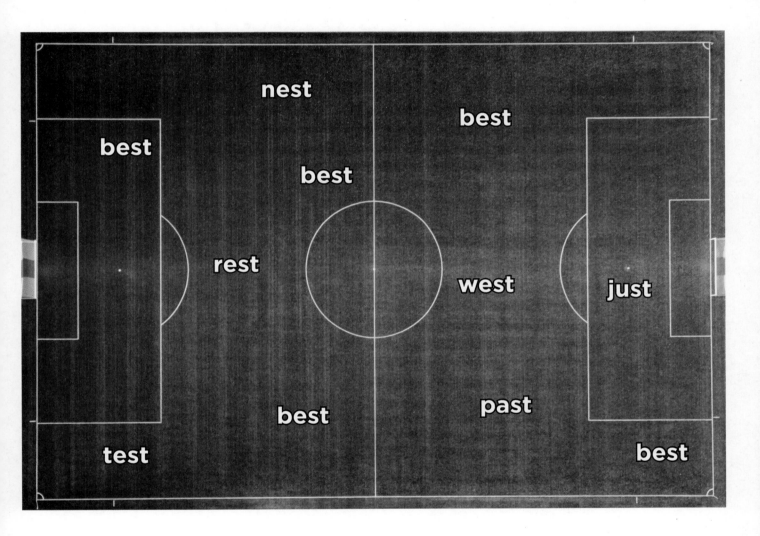

BEST

RHYMES WITH BEST

these

Trace the word these and say it aloud.

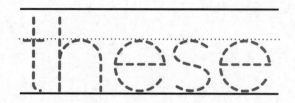

Practice writing the word these.

_____   _____

....

_____   _____

_____   _____

....

_____   _____

I like _____ shoes.

Three Ring Circus

Find the word **these** three times inside each ring and circle it.

this

these

those

geese

these

these

tease

his

these

these

these

the

these

them

these

he's

these

they

Trace the word sit and say it aloud.

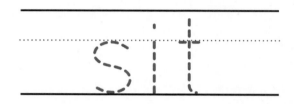

Practice writing the word sit.

_____   _____
....

_____   _____

_____   _____
....

_____   _____

We _____ at the table.

Play Along

Draw a circle around the word **sit** to make a music note. Follow the code for the circled notes to answer the joke.

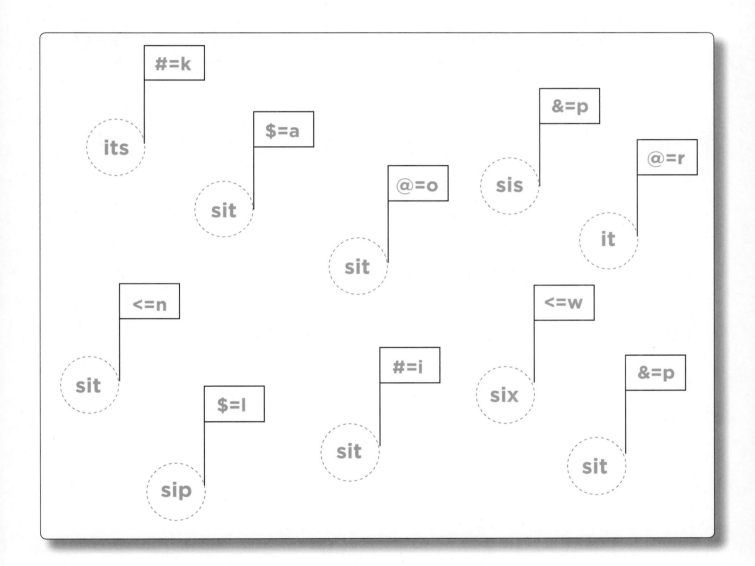

What has many keys but unlocks no doors?

___ ___ ___ ___ ___
 &   # $ <   @

357

REVIEW: The Bottom Line

Use the codes to help fill in the missing words to the story.

off	best	very	cold	always
▬▬▬	• • • • •	∿	══	▬ ▬ ▬

The _____ treat on a _____ hot day is _____ ice cream.
(• • • • •) (∿) (══)

I _____ cool _____ with a scoop of the _____ ice cream in
(▬ ▬ ▬) (▬▬▬) (• • • • •)

town. My _____ favorite flavor is vanilla. But I _____ try new
(∿) (▬ ▬ ▬)

flavors. _____ ice cream _____ makes me feel better!
(══) (▬ ▬ ▬)

How many times does each word appear in the story?

very _____   cold _____

best _____   off _____

always _____

REVIEW: Matching Caps

Draw a line to connect the matching sight words. Fill in the letter in the blue circle next to each cap to name the sport below.

1. five

2. tell

3. upon

4. round

5. these

6. sit

 upon — w

 sit — g

 round — i

 tell — o

 five — r

 these — n

In this sport, people race boats. It is also called "crew."

___ ___ ___ ___ ___ ___
1   2   3   4   5   6

Trace the word been and say it aloud.

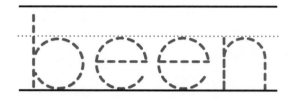

Practice writing the word been.

_____   _____

_____   _____

_____   _____

_____   _____

Have you _____ sick?

Button Up

Draw a circle around the word been to make buttons on the sweaters. Circle the sweater with more buttons.

been

been

bee

bean

been

beet

need

been

been

been

beep

been

Trace the word gave and say it aloud.

Practice writing the word gave.

_____   _____
....

_____   _____

_____   _____
....

_____   _____

My mom _____ me this.

Funny Food

Circle the word gave each time you see it. Write the total under each bag, and use the code to answer the joke.

gave
have
gave
gave
gave
give

_____ = o

save
gate
gave
gain
gave
pave

_____ = c

gave
gave
gave
game
gave
gave

_____ = e

love
give
get
gave
wave
are

_____ = n

gave
have
gave
ever
gave
gage

_____ = h

gave
gave
gave
gave
gave
gave

_____ = s

What do you call cheese that isn't yours?

____ a ____ ____ ____   ____ ____ ____ ____ ____ ____
1   2   3   4   2   3   5   5   6   5

Trace the word first and say it aloud.

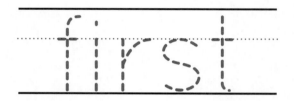

Practice writing the word first.

_____   _____

_____   _____

_____   _____

_____   _____

I was the _____ one there.

Check It Out

Put a check mark by the word first in the book titles. If the title does not have the word first, leave it blank.

The First Thanksgiving

My First Storybook

Find Your Dream

First Ladies

How to Win First Place

Furry Animals

Face Your Fears

Fast Cars

How many book titles have the word first?

_____

Trace the word wash and say it aloud.

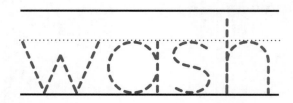

Practice writing the word wash.

We _____ our car.

Prize Tickets

Underline the word **wash** each time you see it on the ticket. Write the number on the line.

w a s h w a s h ___

W A S H W A S H ___

w a s w a s h s ___

w a s h a s h w ___

A W A S H A W ___

s w a h w a s h ___

Add up the numbers on all the tickets. _____

10   **2**   **5**   **2**   **1**

Circle the prizes you would choose with your tickets.

fast

Trace the word fast and say it aloud.

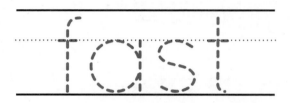

Practice writing the word fast.

_____   _____

_____   _____

_____   _____

This car goes _____.

Candy Code

Look at the letters inside each candy. If you can unscramble the letters to make the word fast, then write fast on the line and follow the code. If not, leave the line blank.

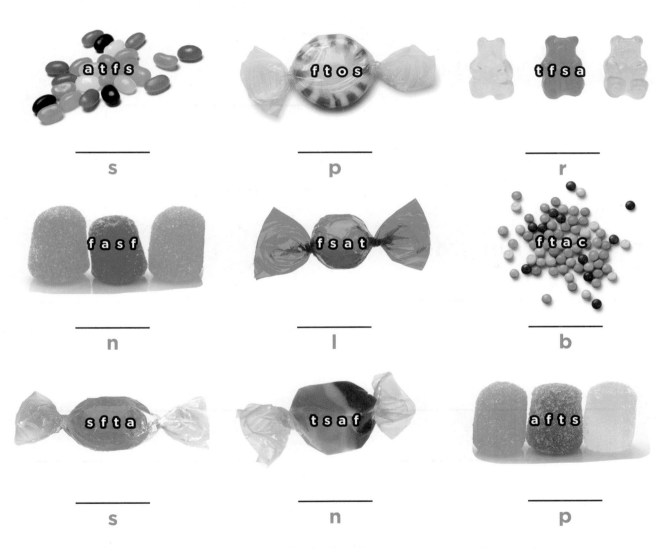

a t f s	f t o s	t f s a
_____	_____	_____
s	p	r
f a s f	f s a t	f t a c
_____	_____	_____
n	l	b
s f t a	t s a f	a f t s
_____	_____	_____
s	n	p

What candy topping is best on rainy days?

____ ____ ____ i ____ k ____ e ____

369

 **us**

Trace the word us and say it aloud.

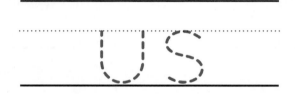

Practice writing the word us.

She always helps _____ .

Boxcar Race

Draw a box around the word **us** when you see it hiding inside another word. The car with more boxes wins the race.

crust

sung

buzz

pull

rust

cups

buns

focus

jump

---

rest

plus

bus

gust

sun

pups

just

must

dust

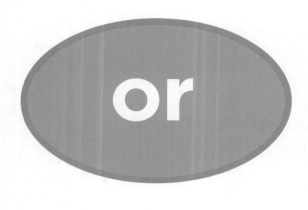

Trace the word or and say it aloud.

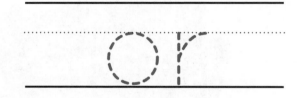

Practice writing the word or.

_____   _____
....

_____   _____

_____   _____
....

_____   _____

Do you want this one _____ that one?

Lucky Card

Color all the shapes that have the word or inside.

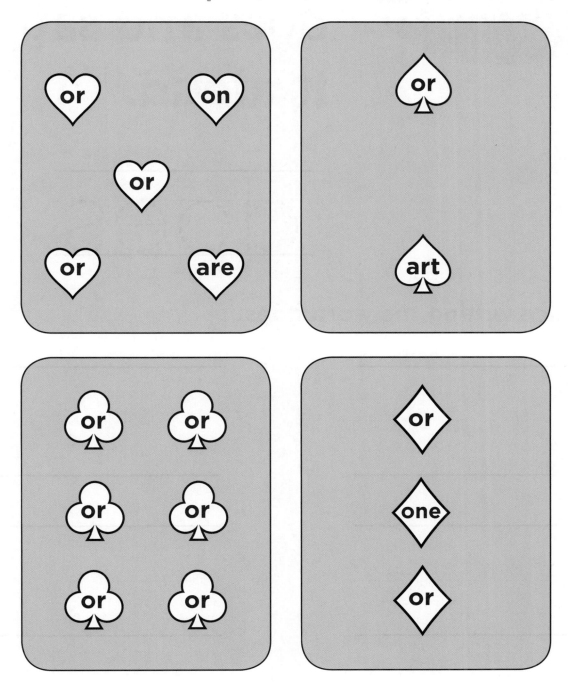

Circle the card suit that has all the shapes colored.

 **does**

Trace the word does and say it aloud.

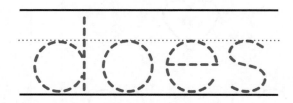

Practice writing the word **does**.

_____   _____

_____   _____

_____   _____

How _____ it work?

Around the Clock

Draw a line from the middle of the clock to the word **does**. Follow each line to fill in the correct letter below.

does

does   does

does   does

dose   does

does   does

does   goes

does

Why did the clock get in trouble?

___ ___ ___   ___ ___ ___ ___   ___ ___ ___ ___   ___ ___ ___
1   4   4   12 8   2   11   1   4   2   6   7   3   10

 **call**

Trace the word call and say it aloud.

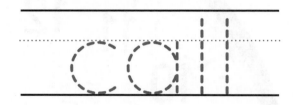

Practice writing the word call.

_____   _____

_____   _____

_____   _____

I _____ my mom.

Fishing for Rhymes

Draw a line from each fishing pole to the words that rhyme with call.

ball

halt

fall

walk

hall

sell

tall

hill

sale

mall

calm

wall

small

talk

bald

Which side caught more fish? _____

 **many**

Trace the word many and say it aloud.

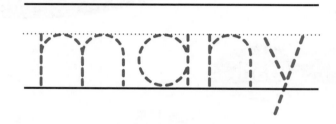

Practice writing the word many.

I have _____ friends.

Fun Fact

Ask an adult to read you the paragraph below. Then shade one box on the graph from the bottom up every time you see the word **many**.

3,000	many
2,500	many
2,000	many
1,500	many
1,000	many
500	many

Many people know that spiders have eight legs. But did you know that many spiders also have eight eyes? Why do spiders have so many eyes? They look for danger and keep spiders safe. Most spiders have four pairs of eyes. But spiders can have as many as twelve eyes. Some spiders have no eyes!

Use the number at the top of your bar to complete this fun fact:

A spider eats about _____ insects a year!

**green**

Trace the word green and say it aloud.

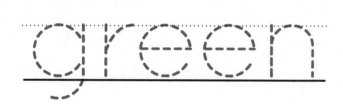

Practice writing the word green.

The leaf is _____.

Beautiful Bubbles

Cross out any bubble that does not have the word green.

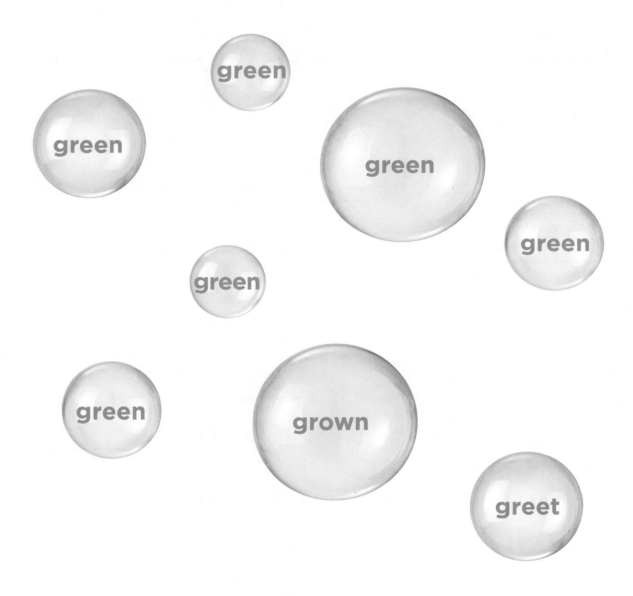

How many bubbles remain? _____

REVIEW: The Bottom Line

Use the codes to help fill in the missing words to the story.

us	many	gave	fast	first
▬▬	• • • • •	∿	═══	▬ ▬ ▬

On the _____ day of school, our teacher _____ _____
     ▬ ▬ ▬   ∿   ▬▬

name tags. The tags had our _____ and last names. There were
                            ▬ ▬ ▬

so _____ new students. She wanted to learn our names _____ .
    • • • • •   ═══

She also _____ _____ pencils and _____ books.
         ∿   ▬▬   • • • • •

The _____ book she _____ _____ was for reading.
     ▬ ▬ ▬   ∿   ▬▬

It had so _____ fun pictures. The day went by very _____ !
    • • • • •   ═══

How many times does each word appear in the story?

us	_____	fast	_____
many	_____	first	_____
gave	_____		

382

REVIEW: Matching Caps

Draw a line to connect the matching sight words. Fill in the letter in the blue circle next to each cap to name the sport below.

1. been

2. wash

3. or

4. does

5. call

6. green

 e

 r

 i

 b

 s

 f

In this game, players throw and catch flying discs.

___ ___ ___ ___ ___ ___ ___
 1   2   3   4   5   6   6

REVIEW: Word Search

Find the review words in the word search.

off   tell   upon   round   very   sit
or   does   call   green   us

```
P L S G R Y T J L U
A L I C U S I P L P
F G G W E E V D N A
V R U N D O O F F R
Y E D H O A S E M O
U E R X E P T I L U
S N B Y S O E E T N
G R N W F M L N Y D
F F P C A L L J V E
U P O N S T A O R L
```

REVIEW: The Lost Word

Look for each review word from **page 384** and circle it below. There is one word from the list that is missing.

Our class turtle wandered off! He does this sometimes. Keep an eye out for his round, green shell. He likes to sit in the sun. He is very special to us! If you see him, please tell a teacher or call our classroom.

Which review word is missing? _____

Crossword Clues

Complete each sentence with a review word from the box. Use the words to fill in the puzzle on the next page.

five   cold   always   best   these

gave   first   wash   fast   been   many

Across

2. I ate _____ bites.

6. We _____ help clean up.

7. Have you _____ there?

8. I will put _____ away.

9. Don't go so _____ .

Down

1. I _____ him my coat.

2. Ask your mom _____ .

3. The water is too _____ .

4. I have so _____ books.

5. We _____ the dishes.

7. You are my _____ friend.

Use the clues on page 386 to fill in the puzzle.

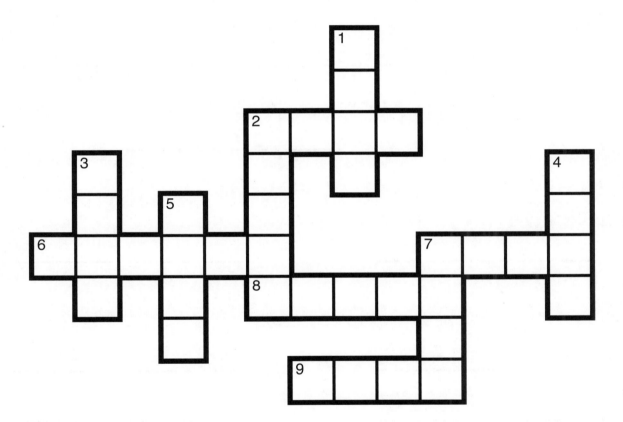

pull

Trace the word pull and say it aloud.

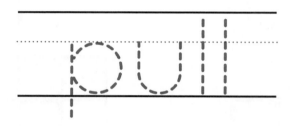

Practice writing the word pull.

We _____ on the rope.

Balloon Buddies

Draw a circle around the word pull to make
a balloon. Put an X through the other words.

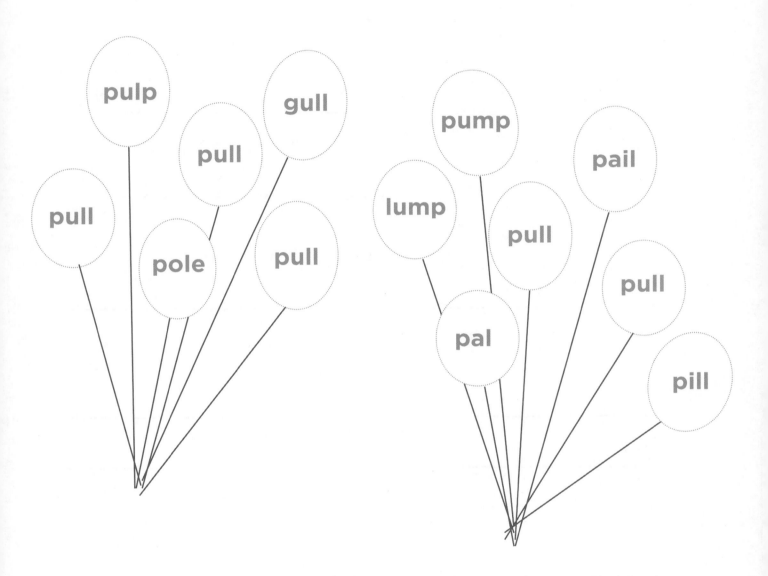

Count the balloons in each bunch.
Circle the bunch that has more balloons.

How many balloons are there altogether? _____

both

Trace the word both and say it aloud.

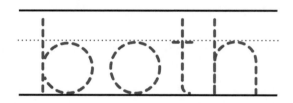

Practice writing the word both.

_____   _____

_____   _____

_____   _____

We are _____ in this class.

Made in the Shade

Shade each box that has the word both. Then match each number to the corresponding letter to fill in the blanks below.

5	best	both	those	bone	bet
4	the	with	both	bath	bold
3	born	path	boat	book	both
2	job	moth	bath	both	bow
1	both	bowl	bore	boy	but

c   e   n   r   a

What bird can pick up heavy things?

a ____ ____ ____ ____ ____

    1   2   3   4   5

 **around**

Trace the word around and say it aloud.

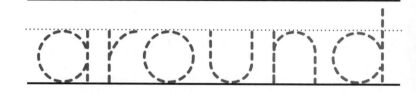

Practice writing the word around.

My dog runs _____ **in circles.**

Word Tunnels

Connect the letters of the word **around** to make a tunnel. Use the number at the tunnel exit to complete the fun fact.

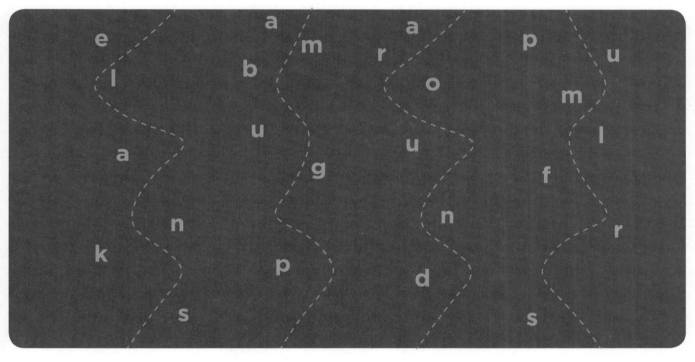

20   200   2,000   20,000

Crabs can lay up to _____ eggs.

Circle the shells that show the word **around**.

 ground  around  around  round  around

buy

Trace the word buy and say it aloud.

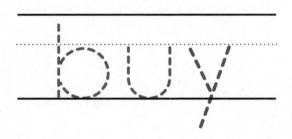

Practice writing the word buy.

I will _____ it at the store.

Sight Word Slices

Draw a line from the word buy in the middle of each pie to the matching words on the edge of each pie. See how many slices you make.

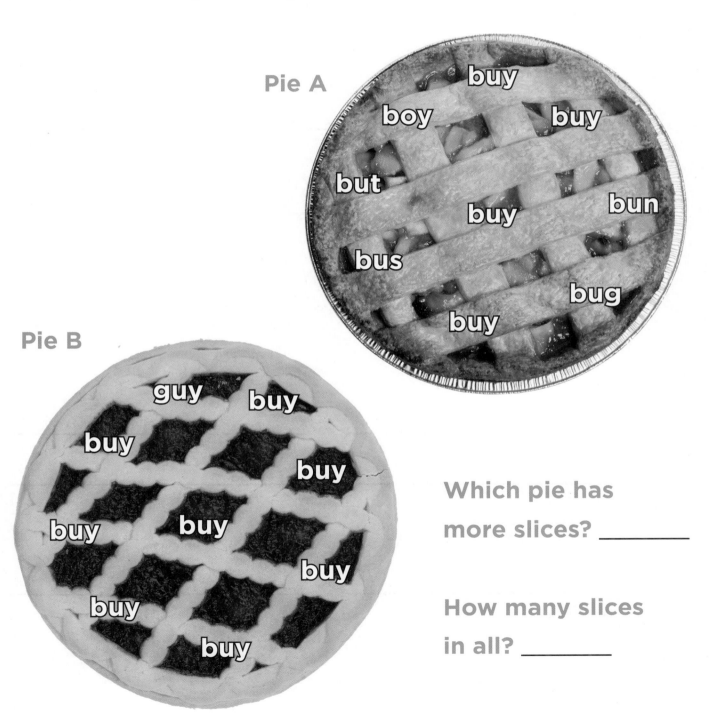

Pie A

buy

boy   buy

but

buy   bun

bus

bug

buy

Pie B

guy   buy

buy

buy

buy   buy

buy

buy

buy

Which pie has more slices? _____

How many slices in all? _____

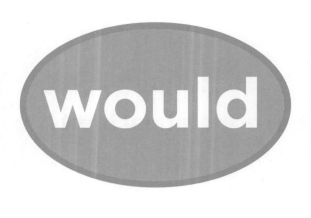 **would**

Trace the word would and say it aloud.

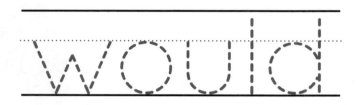

Practice writing the word would.

We _____ go with you.

Postcard Puzzler

Circle the word would each time it appears on the postcard. Write the number in the stamp in the corner. Find the matching number below to see where the postcard is from.

Dear Kari,

I am having a great time!
There are so may green trees
and forests here. That's why they
call this place the "Emerald City."
I would love to come back here
again. But next time I would bring
an umbrella. It rains a lot!

Love,
Helen

Kari Clark

3745 Central Ave.

Omaha, NE 68007

1. Chicago

2. Seattle

3. Las Vegas

4. Memphis

5. Dallas

6. Denver

their

Trace the word their and say it aloud.

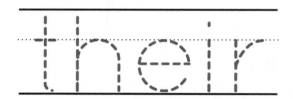

Practice writing the word **their**.

_____   _____
....

_____   _____

_____   _____
....

_____   _____

They took _____ shoes off.

Riddle Row

Circle all rows and columns that have the word **their** five times. Match the symbols with the letters outside the grid to solve the riddle.

	@	^	@	^	@	
@	their	the	their	tier	heir	d
^	their	their	their	their	their	v
@	their	they	their	their	the	g
^	their	their	they	there	their	k
@	their	their	here	their	them	w
	r	t	l	p	b	

What runs but cannot walk?

a __r__ i __v__ e __r__
   @   ^   @

Trace the word work and say it aloud.

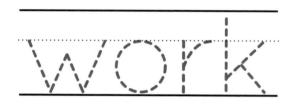

Practice writing the word work.

We _____ all day long.

Ladder Line Up

Underline work if it appears within the longer word. Circle the ladder that has an underlined word on the most steps.

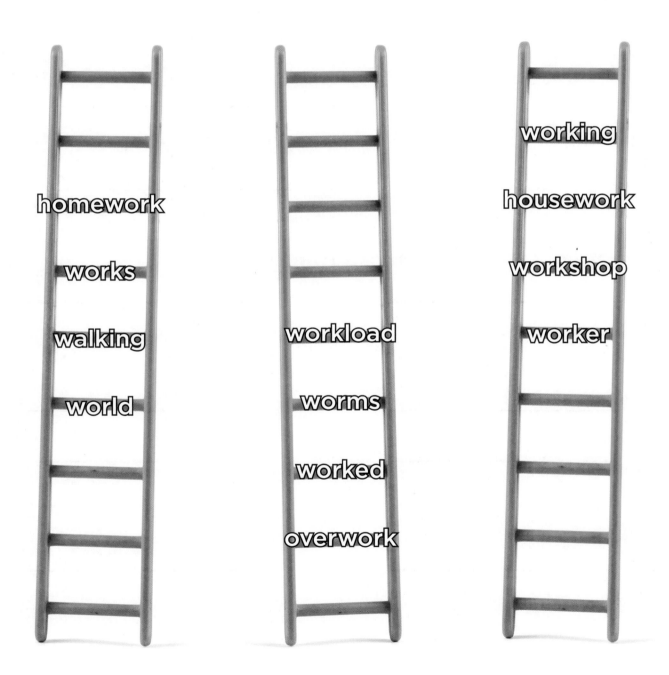

homework

works

walking

world

workload

worms

worked

overwork

working

housework

workshop

worker

made

Trace the word made and say it aloud.

Practice writing the word made.

I _____ lunch.

Follow the Chain

Draw a circle every time you see the word **made**.
If your circles make a chain, write the number of times
the word **made** appears.

m a d m a d e m   _____

m a d e m a d e   _____

m a d e m a d e m a d e   _____

m a d e m a d e   _____

m a d e m a d e m a d e   _____

**those**

Trace the word **those** and say it aloud.

Practice writing the word **those**.

_____   _____

_____   _____

_____   _____

I read all _____ books.

Rhyme Score

Circle the word **those** each time it appears on the field. Underline any words that rhyme with **those**. Count the total for each and fill in the score board.

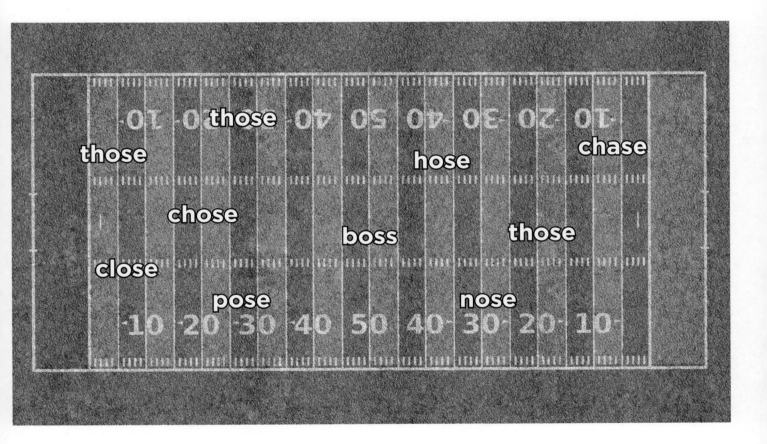

THOSE   RHYMES WITH THOSE

_____   _____

 **right**

Trace the word right and say it aloud.

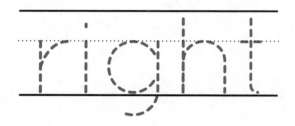

Practice writing the word right.

_____

....

_____

_____

....

_____

_____

....

_____

_____

_____

Go _____ on this street.

Three Ring Circus

Find the word **right** three times inside each ring and circle it.

write

right   right

right   light

ring

right

right

high

right   rice

night

right

height   might

right

bring

right

 **why**

Trace the word why and say it aloud.

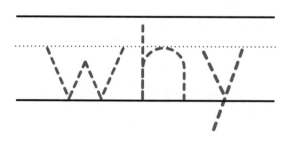

Practice writing the word why.

_____ did you do that?

Play Along

Draw a circle around the word **why** to make a music note. Follow the code for the circled notes to answer the joke.

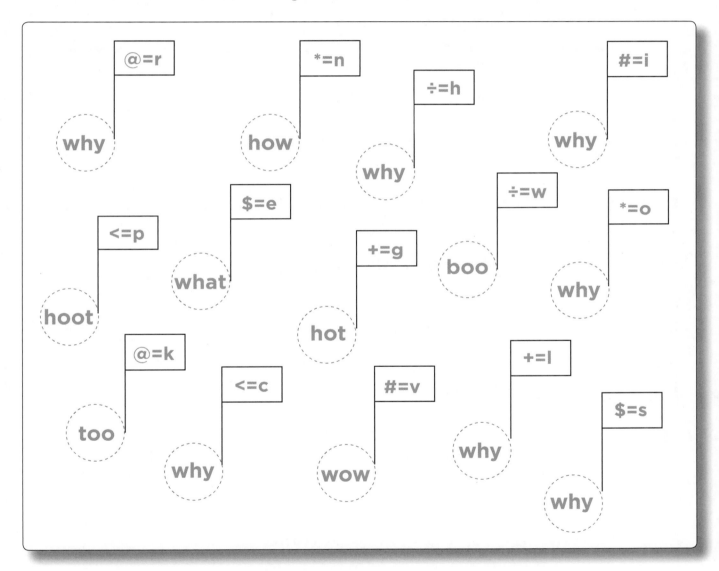

What has forty feet and sings?

the __ __ __ __ __ __ __ __ __ __ __ __ __

$\quad$ $ $\quad$ < $\quad$ ÷ $\quad$ * $\quad$ * $\quad$ + $\quad$ < $\quad$ ÷ $\quad$ * $\quad$ # $\quad$ @

REVIEW: The Bottom Line

Use the codes to help fill in the missing words to the story.

buy	would	made	work	around
▬▬	• • • • •	∿	══	▬ ▬ ▬

A lot of birds fly _____ our yard. I thought I _____ _____ a
     (▬ ▬ ▬)   (• • • • •) (══)

birdfeeder for them. I looked _____ at the store. But I didn't like any
                              (▬ ▬ ▬)

of them. So I _____ one instead! It was a lot of _____. I wanted to
              (∿)   (══)

make one that _____ feed a lot of birds. My hard _____ paid off.
              (• • • • •)   (══)

I _____ do it all again!
  (• • • • •)

How many times does each word appear in the story?

buy _____   work _____

would _____   around _____

made _____

REVIEW: Matching Caps

Draw a line to connect the matching sight words. Fill in the letter in the blue circle next to each cap to name the sport below.

1. pull

2. both

3. their

4. those

5. right

6. why

 m

 s

 n

 i

 g

 w

Some of the strokes in this water sport are "butterfly" and "freestyle."

__ __ __ __ __ __
1   2   3   4   4   3   5   6

Trace the word use and say it aloud.

Practice writing the word use.

_____ _____

....

_____ _____

_____ _____

....

_____ _____

You can _____ mine.

Button Up

Draw a circle around the word use to make buttons on the shirts. Circle the shirt with more buttons.

use

use

use

use

us

use

use

pup

use

pop

use

use

goes

Trace the word **goes** and say it aloud.

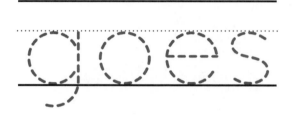

Practice writing the word goes.

_____   _____

_____   _____

_____   _____

_____   _____

She _____ to school early.

Funny Food

Circle the word **goes** each time you see it. Write the total under each can, and use the code to answer the joke.

Can 1:
goes
goes
goes
does
goes
goes

_____ = l

Can 2:
goose
ghost
gone
goes
guess
goes

_____ = e

Can 3:
goes
goes
goes
goes
goes
goes

_____ = r

Can 4:
gone
guest
goes
goal
gas
gust

_____ = u

Can 5:
goes
go
goes
goose
goes
goat

_____ = y

Can 6:
goes
goes
gold
gone
goes
goes

_____ = b

What is the saddest fruit?

___ ___ u ___ ___ ___ ___ ___ ___
4   5   2   4   2   6   6   3

wish

Trace the word wish and say it aloud.

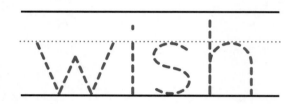

Practice writing the word wish.

I make a _____.

Check It Out

Put a check mark by the word wish in the book titles. If the title does not have the word wish, leave it blank.

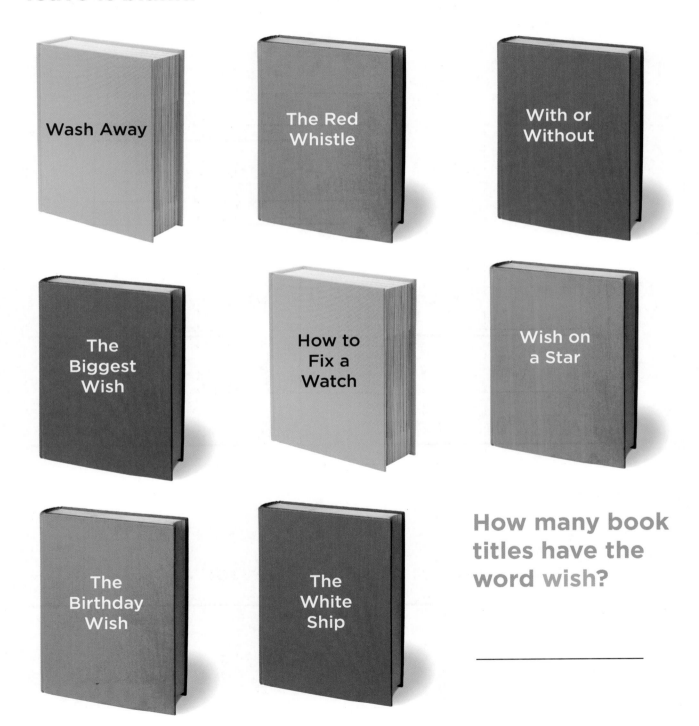

Wash Away

The Red Whistle

With or Without

The Biggest Wish

How to Fix a Watch

Wish on a Star

The Birthday Wish

The White Ship

How many book titles have the word wish?

_____

sing

Trace the word sing and say it aloud.

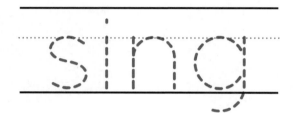

Practice writing the word sing.

We can _____ along.

Prize Tickets

Underline the word sing each time you see it on the ticket. Write the number on the line.

s i n g s i n g _____

S N G S I N G S _____

s i n g s n i g _____

s i m g s i n g _____

S I N G S I N G _____

s g s i n g i n _____

Add up the numbers on all the tickets. _____

10   2   5   2   1

Circle the prize or prizes you would choose with your tickets.

**read**

Trace the word read and say it aloud.

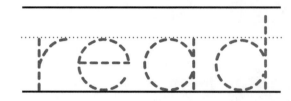

Practice writing the word read.

_____   _____

_____   _____

_____   _____

_____   _____

I _____ every day.

Candy Code

Look at the letters inside each candy. If you can unscramble the letters to make the word read, then write read on the line and follow the code. If not, leave it blank.

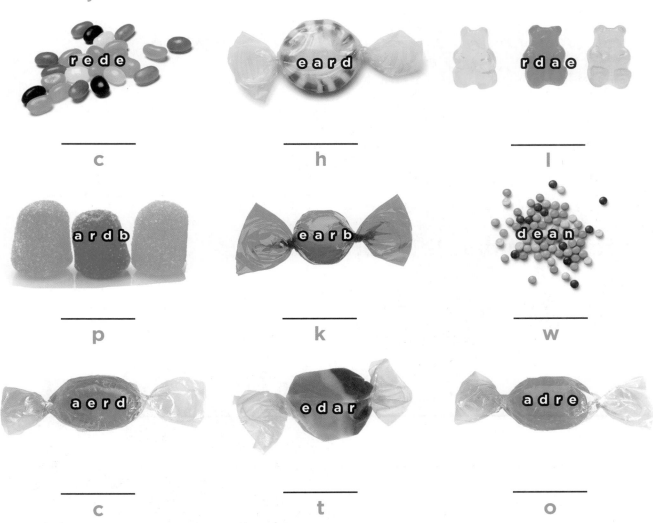

rede	eard	rdae
_____	_____	_____
c	h	l

ardb	earb	dean
_____	_____	_____
p	k	w

aerd	edar	adre
_____	_____	_____
c	t	o

Which candy is never on time?

_____ _____ _____ _____ _____ __ a __ e

 **sleep**

Trace the word sleep and say it aloud.

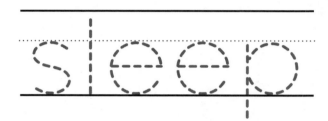

Practice writing the word sleep.

_____   _____

....

_____   _____

_____   _____

....

_____   _____

We _____ in our beds.

Boxcar Race

Draw a box around the word **sleep** when you see it hiding inside another word. The car with more boxes wins the race.

sloppy

slipping

sleepless

beeping

sleet

seats

sleepover

jeeps

sleeves

sledding

sleeping

sleeper

sleepwalk

asleep

slump

slapping

sleepy

sleeps

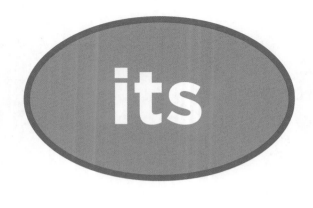

its

Trace the word its and say it aloud.

Practice writing the word its.

_____   _____

....

_____   _____

_____   _____

....

_____   _____

I like _____ color.

Lucky Card

Color all the shapes that have the word its inside.

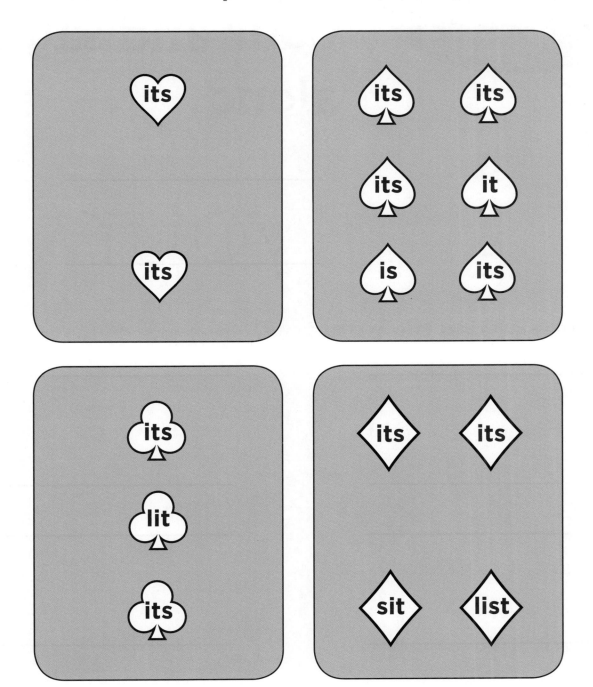

Circle the card suit that has all the shapes colored.

 **your**

Trace the word your and say it aloud.

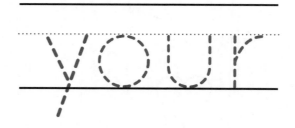

Practice writing the word your.

We like _____ **teacher.**

Around the Clock

Draw a line from the middle of the clock to the word your. Follow each line to fill in the correct letter below.

What time do ducks wake up?

a ___   ___ ___ e   ___ ___ a ___ ___
   4   4   1   7   12   10   8

o ___   ___ a ___ ___
   5   9   3   11

**found**

Trace the word found and say it aloud.

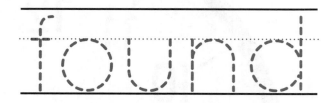

Practice writing the word found.

_____   _____

_____   _____

_____   _____

_____   _____

I _____ my book.

Fishing for Rhymes

Draw a line from each fishing pole to the words that rhyme with found.

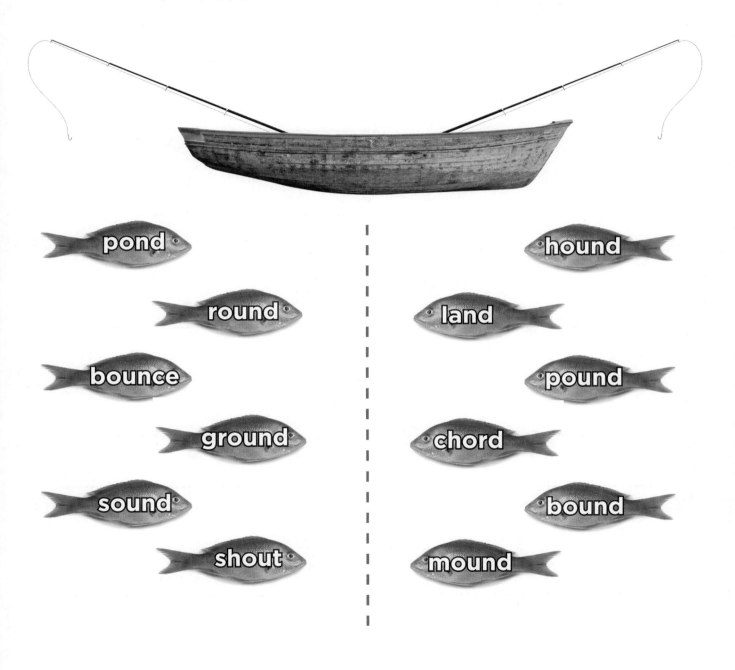

pond

hound

round

land

bounce

pound

ground

chord

sound

bound

shout

mound

Which side caught more fish? _____

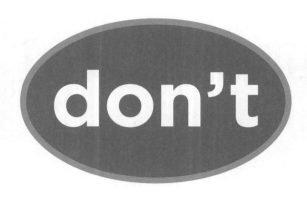

Trace the word don't and say it aloud.

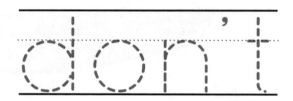

Practice writing the word don't.

_____   _____
....
_____   _____
_____   _____
....
_____   _____

We _____ have a pet.

Fun Fact

Ask an adult to read you the paragraph below. Then shade one box from the bottom up every time you see the word don't.

70	**don't**
60	**don't**
50	**don't**
40	**don't**
30	**don't**
20	**don't**
10	**don't**

Penguins are birds, but they don't fly. Their wings are more like flippers. They use their flippers to dive and swim in the water. They also slide on their bellies on the ice. They have feathers and fat to keep them warm. They build up fat so they can survive when they don't eat for three or four months!

Use the number at the top of your bar to complete this fun fact:

Penguins can stay under water for more than _____ minutes.

 **write**

Trace the word write and say it aloud.

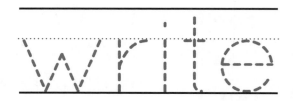

Practice writing the word write.

_____   _____

....

_____   _____

_____   _____

....

_____   _____

I _____ a letter.

Beautiful Bubbles

Cross out any bubble that does not have the word write.

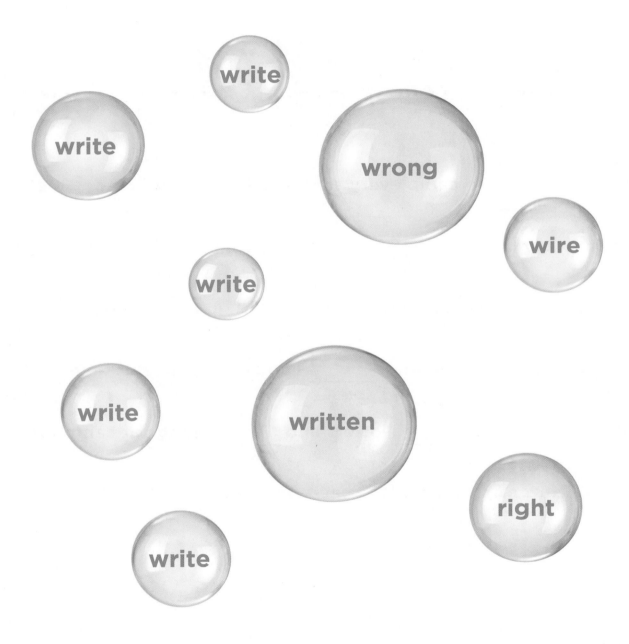

write

write

wrong

wire

write

write

written

right

write

How many bubbles remain? _____

REVIEW: The Bottom Line

Use the codes to help fill in the missing words to the story.

goes	sing	don't	wish	write
▬▬	•••••	～～	══	▬ ▬ ▬

My sister _____ to camp every summer. She likes to _____ me
        ══   ▬ ▬ ▬

letters. At camp, they _____ songs. Everyone _____ swimming and
                        •••••   ══

boating. I _____ I were older! Then I could go to camp too. I _____
            ══   ～～

think I can wait any longer. I _____ I could go now! But time _____ by
                                ══   ▬▬

quickly. Soon, I will _____ letters and _____ songs at camp too!
                       ▬ ▬ ▬   •••••

How many times does each word appear in the story?

goes _____   wish _____

sing _____   write _____

don't _____

434

REVIEW: Matching Caps

Draw a line to connect the matching sight words. Fill in the letter in the blue circle next to each cap to name the sport below.

1. use

2. read

3. sleep

4. its

5. your

6. found

its — e

found — l

use — b

read — a

sleep — s

your — b

In this sport, you are out if you get three strikes.

___ ___ ___ ___ ___ ___ ___ ___
1   2   3   4   5   2   6   6

REVIEW: Word Search

Find the review words in the word search.

around	buy	would	their	those
why	use	goes	your	found	don't

```
G  O  T  H  L  D  X  S  E  Y
A  E  I  R  G  R  W  P  Q  H
D  R  Y  N  S  F  Y  Z  C  J
O  T  O  B  W  O  U  L  D  R
N  H  U  U  H  U  I  T  M  H
T  E  R  Y  N  N  G  H  N  T
U  N  D  O  U  D  F  O  C  S
Y  T  H  E  I  R  O  S  E  U
W  O  G  S  U  E  L  E  D  S
U  F  W  H  Y  A  G  N  S  E
```

REVIEW: The Lost Word

Look for each review word from page 436 and circle it below. There is one word from the list that is missing.

Did you lose your lunchbox this year? Don't go buy a new one yet! Would you please check the Lost and Found in the cafeteria? Many students have left their lunchboxes around the cafeteria. All those lunchboxes are at the Lost and Found. Pick yours up soon. Why? Because at the end of the year, everything goes to a charity!

Which review word is missing? _____

Crossword Clues

Complete each sentence with a review word from the box. Use the words to fill in the puzzle on the next page.

> wish   made   sing   pull   read   right
> both   sleep   write   its   work

Across

2. We _____ at our desks.

3. I _____ for a new bike.

4. I put it in _____ box.

5. I like to _____ late.

7. I know the _____ way.

8. We _____ a cake.

Down

1. I like _____ books.

3. I _____ a note.

5. We _____ a song together.

6. We _____ the wagon.

7. Let's _____ the story.

Use the clues on page 438 to fill in the puzzle.

REVIEW: Sentence Sequence

Follow the code in the box to make sentences with sight words.

pull	cold	tell	made	both	first	wash	call
!	@	#	$	%	^	&	*

us	fast	very	those	don't	around
+	=	<	>	?	~

1. _____ _____ _____ .
    &&   >   ^

2. _____ _____ _____ !
    ?   #   +

3. _____ _____ _____ .
    *   +   ^

4. _____ _____ _____ .
    !   %   ~

5. _____ _____ _____ _____ _____ _____ .
    > $ +   %   <   @

6. _____ _____ _____ _____ .
    !   +   <   =

Some letters are short and some letters are tall.
Find the boxes that fit each word.

| work | goes | write | five | always | off | or |
| round | sing | green | sleep | its | use | right |

1.

2.

3.

4.

5.

6.

7.

8.

9.

10.

11.

12.

13.

14.

REVIEW: Four Squares

Find four sight words in each square. Draw a box around each correctly spelled word.

best	wish
werk	upon
read	does
your	allways
why	would
pul	found
sit	gave
buy	these
their	many
been	tel

REVIEW: Framed!

Cross out any words that are not spelled correctly.
You should have 22 correct sight words left. Color
the frame that has only correct words inside.

always
sing
ben
sleep
don't
very
gren
around
upan

us   goes
woold   meny
or   first
their   been
tell

right   does   made
pull   work   best
wash   call   round

REVIEW: In the End

Draw a line to the correct ending for each sight word. Then write the word on the line.

co   ny _____   wh s   _____   wri ld _____

ma ld _____   us e   _____   tho te _____

wi sh _____   it y   _____   wou se _____

up ad _____   fi ur _____

re ve _____   fa th _____

ga on _____   yo ve _____

                                    bo st _____

fou nd _____

gre se _____   s   uy _____

the en _____   o   ff _____

                                    b   it _____

Section 5

The sight words included in this section are:

about	eight	kind	shall
because	fall	laugh	show
before	far	light	six
better	full	long	small
bring	got	much	start
carry	grow	myself	ten
clean	hold	never	today
cut	hot	only	together
done	hurt	own	try
draw	if	pick	warm
drink	keep	seven	which

which

Trace the word which and say it aloud.

Practice writing the word which.

_____   _____

_____   _____

_____   _____

I know _____ way to go.

Balloon Buddies

Draw a circle around the word **which** to make a balloon. Put an X through the other words.

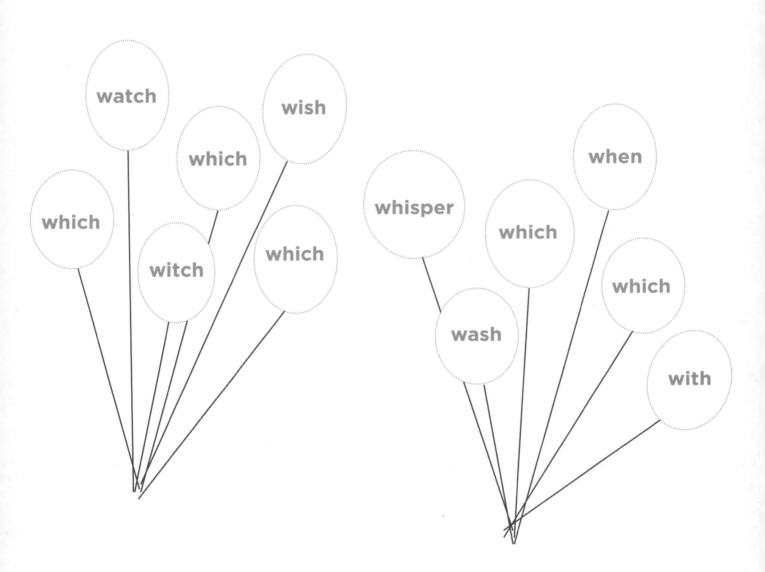

Count the balloons in each bunch.
Circle the bunch that has more balloons.

How many balloons are there altogether? _____

**fall**

Trace the word **fall** and say it aloud.

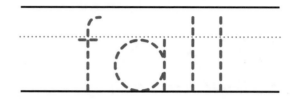

Practice writing the word fall.

_____   _____

_____   _____

_____   _____

_____   _____

Don't _____ into that hole.

Made in the Shade

Shade each box that has the word **fall**. Then match each number to the corresponding letter to fill in the blanks below.

5 fall	far	flaw	call	fill
4 flat	flag	fall	law	feel
3 fan	flop	hall	fell	fall
2 fault	fall	tall	fail	all
1 fair	ball	fat	fall	full

l   o   e   t   w

What gets wetter the more it dries?

____ ____ ____ ____ ____
 1   2   3   4   5

 **because**

Trace the word because and say it aloud.

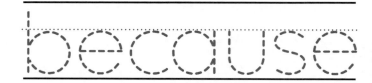

Practice writing the word because.

_____   _____

. . . .

_____   _____

_____   _____

. . . .

_____   _____

I went home _____ I'm sick.

Word Tunnels

Connect the letters of the word because to make a tunnel. Use the number at the tunnel exit to complete the fun fact.

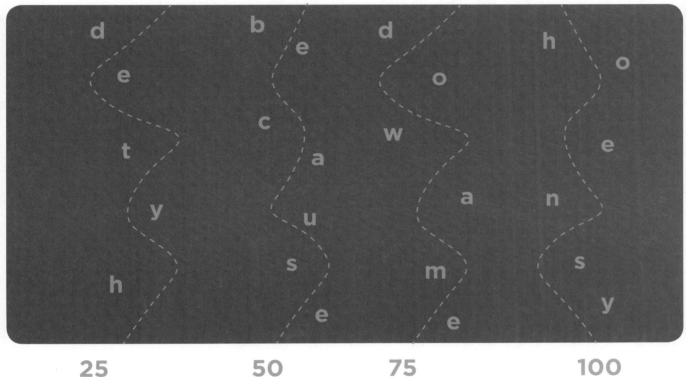

25   50   75   100

An ant can carry up to _____ times its body weight.

Circle the leaves that show the word because.

believe   cause   because   before   because

Trace the word ten and say it aloud.

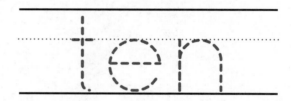

Practice writing the word ten.

_____   _____

_____   _____

_____   _____

_____   _____

Let's all count to _____ .

Sight Word Slices

Draw a line from the word ten in the middle of each pizza to the matching words on the edge of each pizza. See how many slices you make.

Pizza A

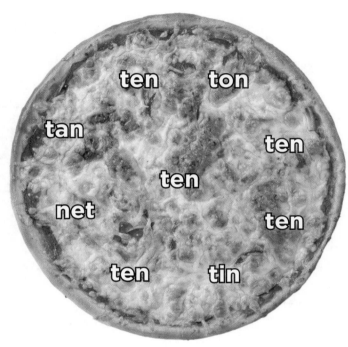

ten ton
tan
ten
ten
net
ten
ten tin

Pizza B

not
note teen
tea
ten
ten
tee
ten
ten

Which pizza has more slices?

_____

How many slices in all? _____

**today**

Trace the word today and say it aloud.

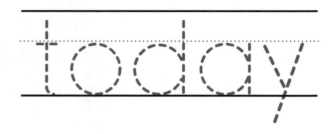

Practice writing the word today.

I have school _____ .

Postcard Puzzler

Circle the word **today** each time it appears on the postcard. Write the number in the stamp in the corner. Find the matching number below to see where the postcard is from.

Dear Sarah,

Today was a great day. I went to a museum, a palace, and a castle. But my favorite thing about today was visiting an old clock tower. It's called "Big Ben." I heard the bells of Big Ben chime today. I can't wait for another great day tomorrow!

Love,
Katie

Sarah Taylor

18 Pinecone Road

Boise, Idaho

1. Rome

2. Hong Kong

3. London

4. Seoul

5. Washington, DC

6. Tokyo

long

Trace the word long and say it aloud.

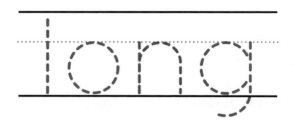

Practice writing the word long.

This rope is _____ .

Riddle Row

Circle all rows and columns that have the word long five times. Match the symbols with the letters outside the grid to solve the riddle.

	^	=	*	=	^	
=	lot	long	song	long	long	w
^	long	long	long	lung	long	f
*	lane	loan	long	long	long	g
^	long	low	look	gone	long	h
=	long	long	long	long	long	n
	b	t	m	l	p	

What has a head and tail but no legs?

a ____ e____ ____ y

^   =   =

 **hold**

Trace the word hold and say it aloud.

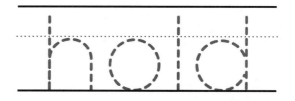

Practice writing the word hold.

_____   _____

_____   _____

_____   _____

_____   _____

Let's _____ hands.

Ladder Line Up

Underline hold if it appears within the longer word. Circle the ladder that has an underlined word on the most steps.

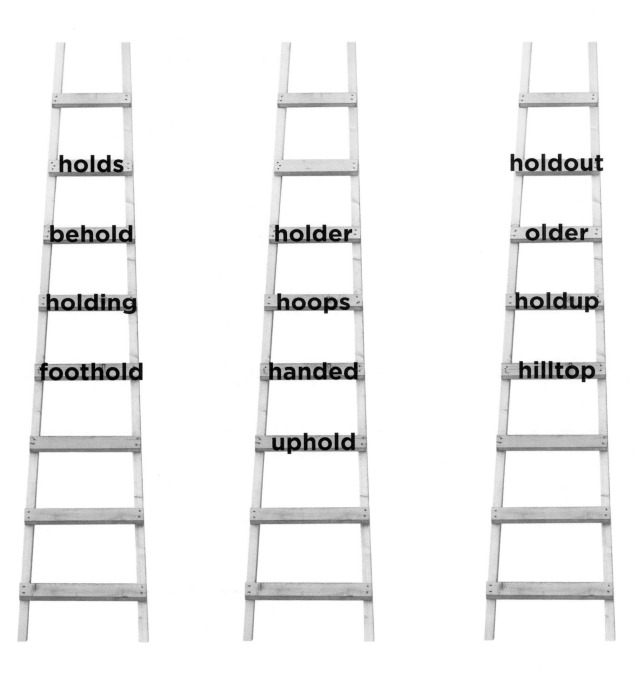

holds

behold

holding

foothold

holder

hoops

handed

uphold

holdout

older

holdup

hilltop

**cut**

Trace the word cut and say it aloud.

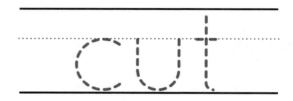

Practice writing the word cut.

I _____ the paper.

Follow the Chain

Draw a circle every time you see the word cut.
If your circles make a chain, write the number
of times the word cut appears.

c u t c u t c u t   _____

c u t c u t c u t c u t   _____

c u t c u t e c u t   _____

c u t c u t c u t   _____

c u t c u t c a t c u t   _____

Trace the word clean and say it aloud.

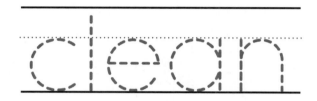

Practice writing the word clean.

_____   _____

....

_____   _____

_____   _____

....

_____   _____

I _____ my room.

Rhyme Score

Circle the word clean each time it appears on the field. Underline any words that rhyme with clean. Count the total for each and fill in the score board.

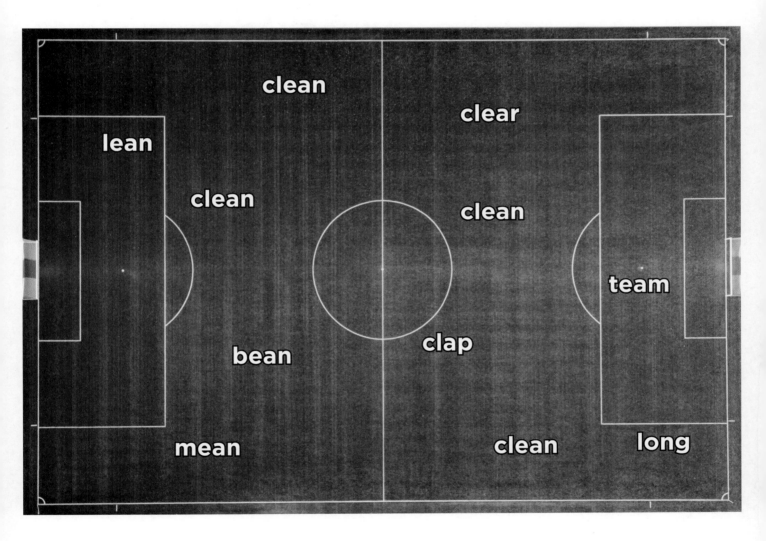

clean

clear

lean

clean

clean

bean

team

clap

mean

clean

long

CLEAN

RHYMES WITH CLEAN

_____

_____

before

Trace the word before and say it aloud.

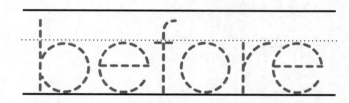

Practice writing the word before.

Can I come _____ ?

Three Ring Circus

Find the word **before** three times inside each ring and circle it.

begin

forty

before

believe

before

before

beneath

before

force

better

before

before

effort

first

before

before

before

four

 **got**

Trace the word got and say it aloud.

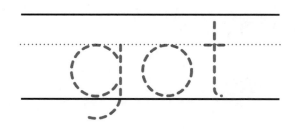

Practice writing the word got.

We _____ a new car.

Play Along

Draw a circle around the word **got** to make a music note. Follow the code for the circled notes to answer the joke.

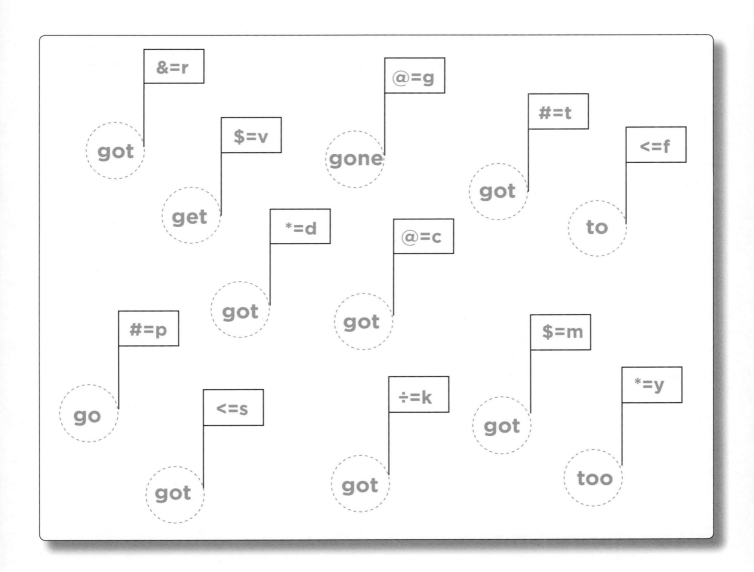

What do drummers bring to Thanksgiving dinner?

turkey ___ ___ u ___ ___ ___ i ___ ___ ___ ___

        *   & $ <   #   @   ÷   <

REVIEW: The Bottom Line

Use the codes to help fill in the missing words to the story.

got	long	cut	clean	today
▬▬▬	• • • • •	～～～	══	▬ ▬ ▬

_____ we _____ a lot of work done! We helped our
▬ ▬ ▬   ══

neighbor _____ her yard. We _____ to her house early.
              ══   ══

We _____ back the bushes. I used a _____ hose to water
   ～～～   • • • • •

everything. It was a _____ day. Her yard was so _____ when
                     • • • • •   ══

we were done. I feel really good about _____. We _____ her yard
                                       ▬ ▬ ▬   ══

so _____. _____ was a great day. I _____ to help someone.
   ══   ▬ ▬ ▬   ══

How many times does each word appear in the story?

got _____   clean _____

long _____   today _____

cut _____

REVIEW: Matching Caps

Draw a line to connect the matching sight words. Fill in the special letter from the cap to name the sport below.

1. which

2. fall

3. ten

4. because

5. hold

6. before

fall — i

which — d

hold — n

because — i

before — g

ten — v

In this sport, people do tricks in the air and land in the water.

___ ___ ___ ___ ___ ___
1   2   3   4   5   6

Trace the word hot and say it aloud.

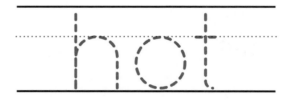

Practice writing the word hot.

_____   _____

_____   _____

_____   _____

The pan is _____ .

Button Up

Draw a circle around the word **hot** to make buttons on the sweaters. Circle the sweater with more buttons.

hot
hat
hot
hot
hot
hot

hot
hot
hut
hot
not
dot

full

Trace the word full and say it aloud.

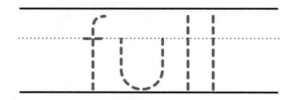

Practice writing the word **full**.

_____   _____
....

_____   _____

_____   _____
....

_____   _____

The box is _____.

Funny Food

Circle the word **full** each time you see it. Write the total under each can, and use the code to answer the joke.

full	fall	flu
full	full	full
full	fill	full
full	full	full
full	fun	fell
full	few	full

_____ = o   _____ = h   _____ = u

fold	full	dull
full	full	lull
fill	full	flew
flap	bull	full
fly	full	full
flat	full	full

_____ = r   _____ = t   _____ = y

What's the best thing to put into a pie?

___ ___ ___ ___   ___ _ e e ___ ___
 3   6   4   1   5   5   2

473

Trace the word about and say it aloud.

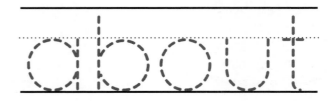

Practice writing the word about.

_____ _____

_____ _____

_____ _____

_____ _____

What is the movie _____?

Check It Out

Put a check mark by the word about in the book titles. If the title does not have the word about, leave it blank.

Above the Clouds

All About Dogs

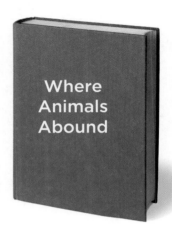

Where Animals Abound

Answers to your Questions

Learning About Numbers

Out and About

About, Over, and Under

Talking About Families

How many book titles have the word about?

_____

six

Trace the word six and say it aloud.

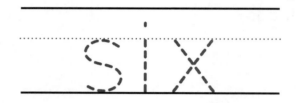

Practice writing the word six.

She is _____ years old.

Prize Tickets

Underline the word **six** each time you see it on the ticket. Write the number on the line.

s i x i x i s i x ___

I X S S I X X I S ___

s i x s i x s i x ___

s s x s i i s i x ___

S I X S I X S I X ___

x i s i x x x i ___

Add up the numbers on all the tickets. _____

11   2   5   2   1

Circle the prize that equals the number of underlined words.

Trace the word pick and say it aloud.

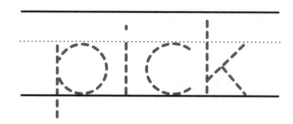

Practice writing the word pick.

_____   _____
....

_____   _____

_____   _____
....

_____   _____

Please _____ **what you want.**

Candy Code

Look at the letters inside each candy. If you can unscramble the letters to make the word pick, then write pick on the line and follow the code. If not, leave blank.

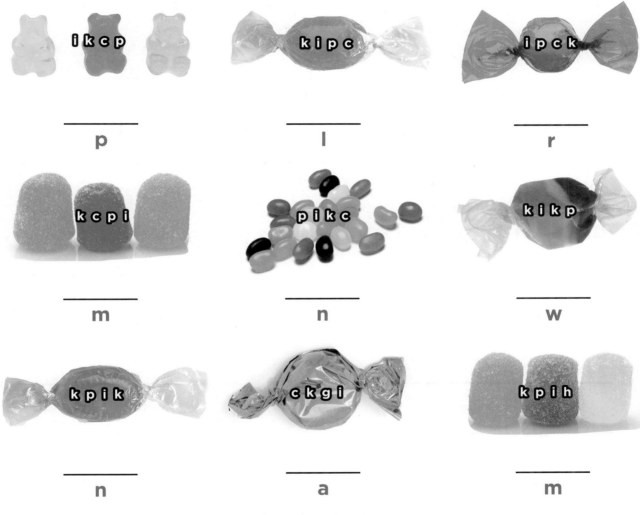

i k c p

k i p c

i p c k

_____
p

_____
l

_____
r

k c p i

p i k c

k i k p

_____
m

_____
n

_____
w

k p i k

c k g i

k p i h

_____
n

_____
a

_____
m

Which candy falls from trees?

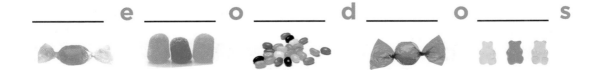

_____ _____ e   _____ _____ o   _____ d   _____ _____ o   _____ s

 **light**

Trace the word light and say it aloud.

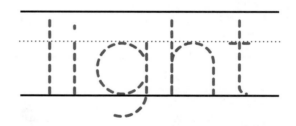

Practice writing the word light.

_____ _____

_____ _____

_____ _____

_____ _____

The _____ is bright.

Boxcar Race

Draw a box around the word light when you see it hiding inside another word. The car with more boxes wins the race.

lightly

bright   later

lifting   lighter

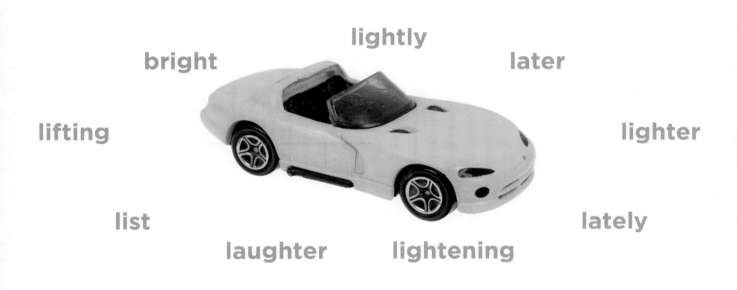

list   lately

laughter   lightening

---

slight

sunlight   twilight

flight

lighten   lines

right   delight
lively

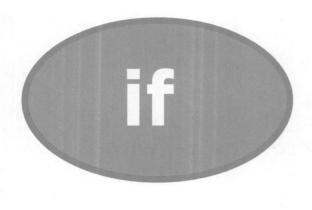 **if**

Trace the word if and say it aloud.

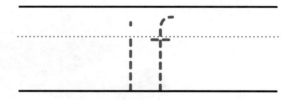

Practice writing the word if.

I don't know _____ I can go.

Lucky Card

Color all the shapes that have the word if inside.

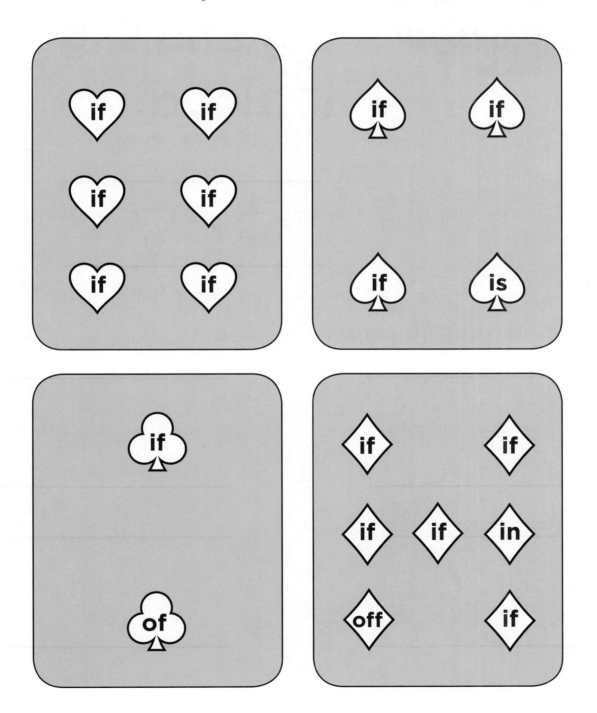

Circle the card suit that has all the shapes colored.

try

Trace the word try and say it aloud.

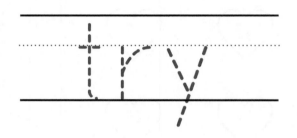

Practice writing the word try.

Always _____ your best.

Around the Clock

Draw a line from the middle of the clock to the word **try**. Follow each line to fill in the correct letter below.

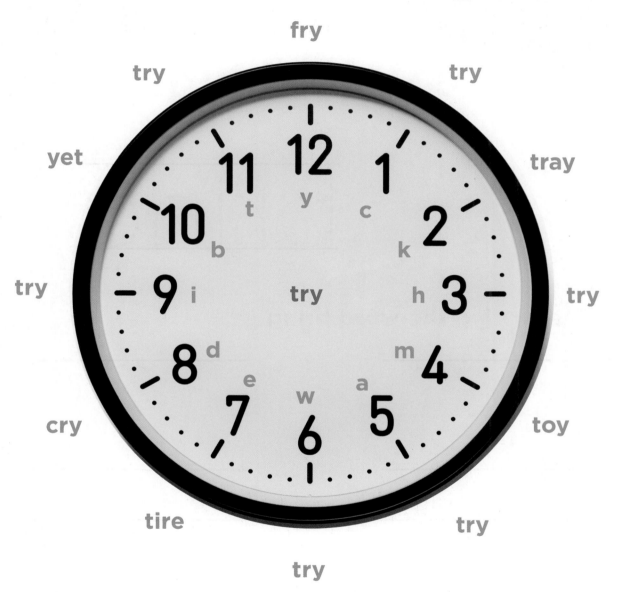

fry

try   try

yet   tray

try   try

cry   toy

tire   try

try

How does a witch tell time?

__	__	__	__		__		__	__	__	__	__
6	9	11	3		5		6	9	11	1	3

__	__	__	__	__
6	5	11	1	3

 **bring**

Trace the word bring and say it aloud.

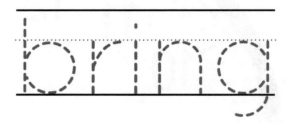

Practice writing the word bring.

_____   _____

....

_____   _____

_____   _____

....

_____   _____

Please _____ **a lunch.**

Fishing for Rhymes

Draw a line from each fishing pole to the words that rhyme with bring.

king

bright

ring

mint

sing

wing

sling

thing

swing

string

sting

strong

Which side caught more fish? _____

carry

Trace the word carry and say it aloud.

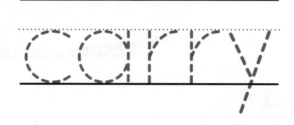

Practice writing the word carry.

_____   _____

_____   _____

_____   _____

_____   _____

I help _____ the box.

Fun Fact

Ask an adult to read you the paragraph below. Then shade one box on the graph from the bottom up every time you see the word carry.

70	carry
60	carry
50	carry
40	carry
30	carry
20	carry

Baby kangaroos are very small at birth. They are only about one inch long! Mother kangaroos carry their babies in a pouch. The pouch keeps them safe and warm. The baby kangaroos grow bigger in the pouch. After about ten months, they are ready to leave the pouch. Their mothers don't have to carry them anymore.

Use the number at the top of your bar to complete this fun fact:

Kangaroos can jump as far as _____ feet.

 **myself**

Trace the word **myself** and say it aloud.

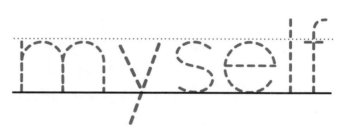

Practice writing the word myself.

_____   _____

_____   _____

_____   _____

I fell and hurt _____ .

Beautiful Bubbles

Cross out any bubble that does not have the word **myself**.

How many bubbles remain? _____

REVIEW: The Bottom Line

Use the codes to help fill in the missing words to the story.

hot	bring	pick	try	myself
——	•••••	~~~	═══	– – –

Everyone got to _____ something to _____ to the holiday
(~~~)   (•••••)

party. I wanted to _____ something sweet and _____. I decided
(~~~)   (——)

to _____ _____ chocolate. I wanted to _____ to make it _____.
(•••••)   (——)   (═══)   (– – –)

The _____ chocolate turned out great! Everyone wanted to
(——)

_____ it. I was proud of _____.
(═══)   (– – –)

How many times does each word appear in the story?

hot _____   try _____

bring _____   myself _____

pick _____

REVIEW: Matching Caps

Draw a line to connect the matching sight words. Fill in the letter in the blue circle next to each cap to name the sport below.

1. which

2. fall

3. because

4. ten

5. hold

6. before

 ten **l**

 which **s**

 hold **n**

 fall **a**

 before **g**

 because **i**

In this sport, people use the wind to race boats on the water.

__ __ __ __ __ __
1   2   3   4   3   5   6

REVIEW: Word Search

Find the review words in the word search.

today   clean   bring   before   if   about
try   full   fall   which   got

R A B H G L L C
T B E F O R E G
F O R O T D W C
U U D Y T R H L
L T O A R W I E
L A W H Y H C A
R B R I N G H N
Y V M F F A L L

REVIEW: The Lost Word

Look for each review word from page 494 and circle it below. There is one word from the list that is missing.

Help clean the school library today! If you've got books at home, bring them in before the end of the year. Talk to the librarian about any lost books. Let's try to make our bookshelves full again for next fall!

Which review word is missing? _____

Crossword Clues

Complete each sentence with a review word from the box.
Use the words to fill in the puzzle on the next page.

pick   ten   carry   six   long   myself

cut   hold   light   hot   because

Across

3. I _____ my bag.

4. We are happy _____ it's Friday.

6. Please _____ on tight.

8. The line is _____ .

9. It is _____ outside.

11. I _____ my finger.

Down

1. Always _____ up your toys.

2. I am happy with _____ .

5. There are _____ cookies.

7. The _____ helps us see.

10. We ran _____ laps.

Use the clues on page 496 to fill in the puzzle.

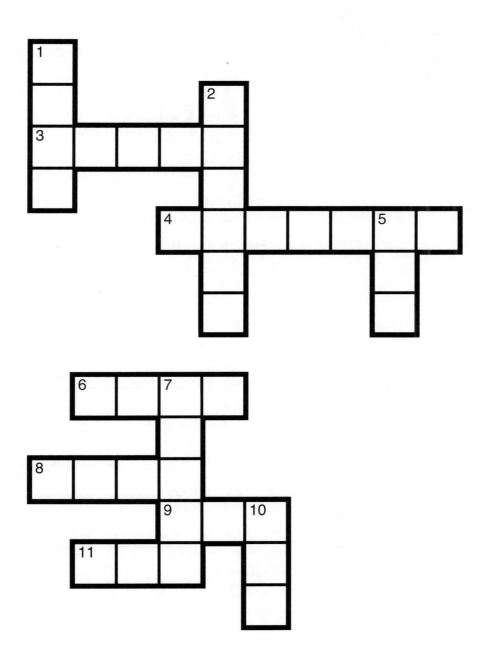

Trace the word seven and say it aloud.

_____

seven

Practice writing the word seven.

I see _____ birds.

Balloon Buddies

Draw a circle around the word seven to make a balloon.
Put an X through the other words.

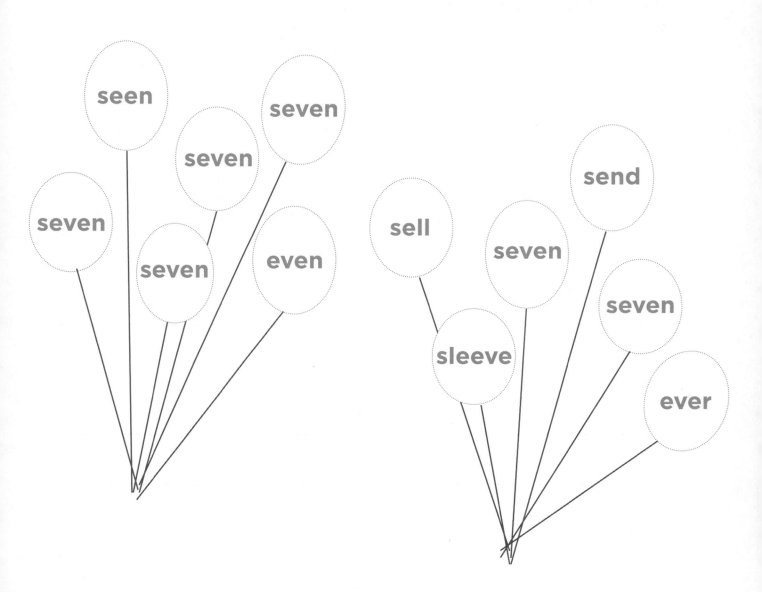

Count the balloons in each bunch.
Circle the bunch that has more balloons.

How many balloons are there altogether? _____

 **warm**

Trace the word warm and say it aloud.

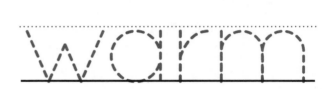

Practice writing the word warm.

Bring a _____ coat.

Made in the Shade

Shade each box that has the word **warm**.
Then match each number to the corresponding
letter to fill in the blanks below.

5 wow	arm	wart	worm	warm
4 wait	warm	with	yarn	war
3 harm	warp	farm	warm	walk
2 warm	want	war	were	arm
1 wave	worm	warm	wore	wall

w   m   s   i   s

What does a fish do in a school?

it ____ ____ ____ ____ ____
      1   2   3   4   5

together

Trace the word together and say it aloud.

together

Practice writing the word together.

Let's go to the park _____ .

Word Tunnels

Connect the letters of the word together to make a tunnel. Use the number at the tunnel exit to complete the fun fact.

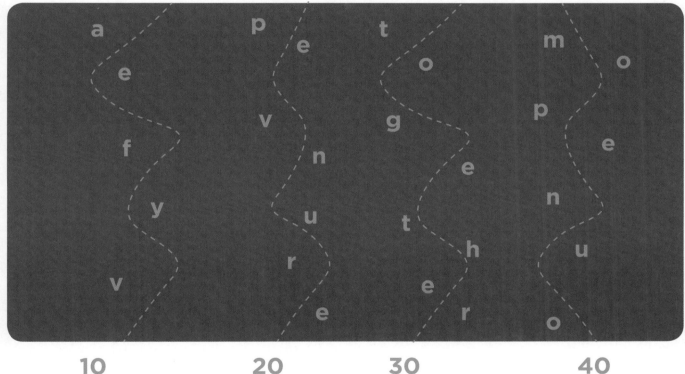

10   20   30   40

Some queen ants can live up to _____ years!

Circle the leaves that show the word together.

together   gather   together   together   today

Trace the word only and say it aloud.

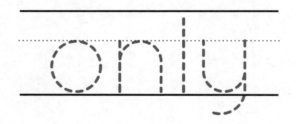

Practice writing the word only.

_____ _____

....

_____ _____

....

_____ _____

Please take _____ one.

Sight Word Slices

Draw a line from the word only in the middle of
each pie to the matching words on the edge
of each pie. See how many slices you make.

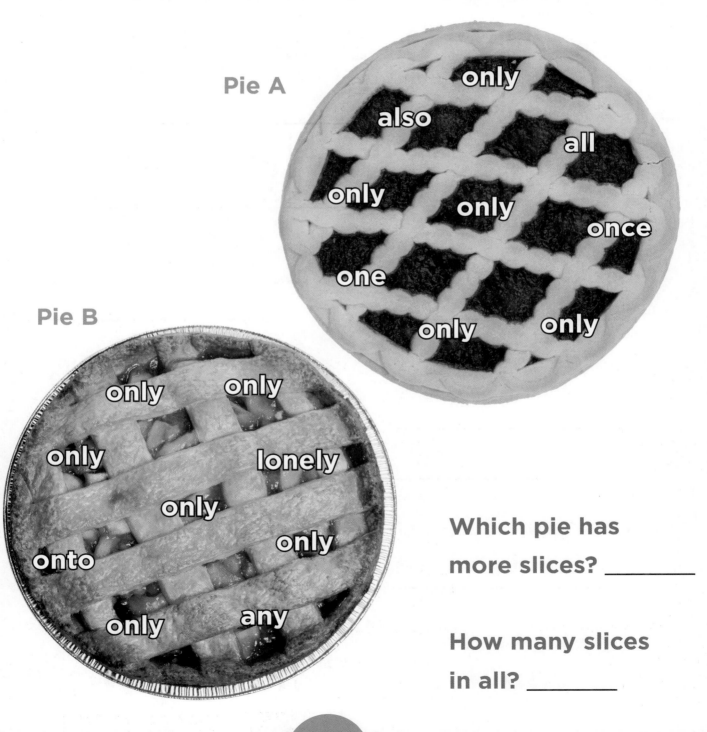

Pie A

only
also
all
only
only
once
one
only
only

Pie B

only
only
only
lonely
only
only
onto
only
any

Which pie has
more slices? _____

How many slices
in all? _____

 **done**

Trace the word done and say it aloud.

Practice writing the word done.

Are you _____ with your work?

Postcard Puzzler

Circle the word **done** each time it appears on the postcard. Write the number in the stamp in the corner. Find the matching number below to see where the postcard is from.

Dear Terry,

I have done so many things on this trip! I visited gardens, beaches, and forests. I've done a lot of fishing in the lakes here. The sun does not ever go down here during the summer. The day goes on and on! It is fun, but it can be hard to fall asleep when it's light outside. I will be home soon.

Best,
Chuck

Terry Jones

762 Center Street

Atlanta, GA   30301

1. China

2. Sweden

3. India

4. USA

5. Greece

6. Brazil

small

Trace the word small and say it aloud.

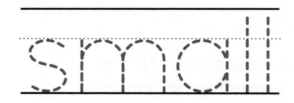

Practice writing the word small.

_____   _____

....

_____   _____

_____   _____

....

_____   _____

The bug is _____ .

Riddle Row

Circle all rows and columns that have the word small five times. Match the symbols with the letters outside the grid to solve the riddle.

	<	=	<	=	<	
<	smell	smart	small	sail	small	b
=	small	small	small	small	small	P
<	small	mile	small	small	salt	g
=	mall	small	small	sell	small	t
<	smile	small	small	small	silly	d
	w	f	t	v	r	

What did the hamburger name its daughter?

___ a ___ ___ y
=   <   <

 **grow**

Trace the word grow and say it aloud.

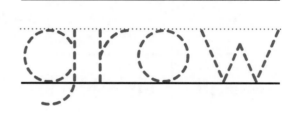

Practice writing the word grow.

The tree will _____ taller.

Ladder Line Up

Underline **grow** if it appears within the longer word.
Circle the ladder that has an underlined word
on the most steps.

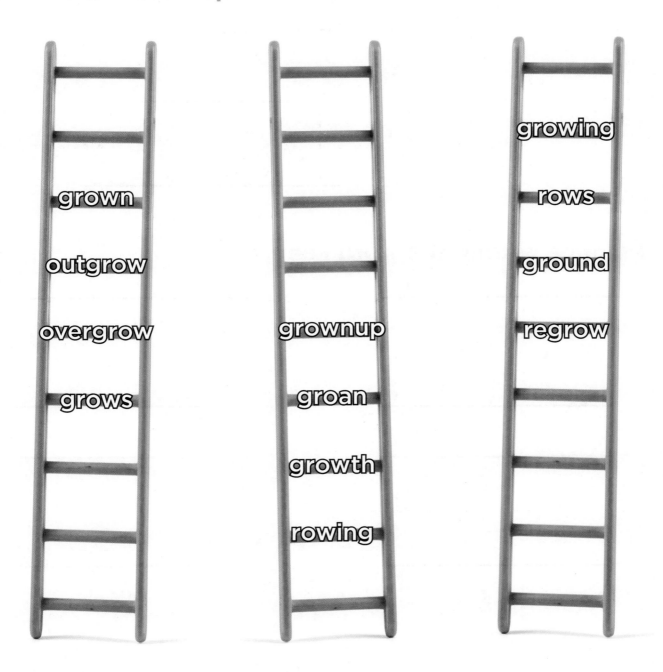

grown

outgrow

overgrow

grows

grownup

groan

growth

rowing

growing

rows

ground

regrow

 **keep**

Trace the word keep and say it aloud.

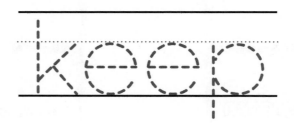

Practice writing the word keep.

I _____ it in my room.

Follow the Chain

Draw a circle every time you see the word **keep**.
If your circles make a chain, write the number of
times the word **keep** appears.

keepkeep _____

keepkeepkep _____

keepkeepkeep _____

keepkeep _____

keepkeepkeep _____

kind

Trace the word kind and say it aloud.

Practice writing the word kind.

_____   _____

_____   _____

_____   _____

She is very _____ to others.

Rhyme Score

Circle the word kind each time it appears on the field. Underline any words that rhyme with kind. Count the total for each and fill in the score board.

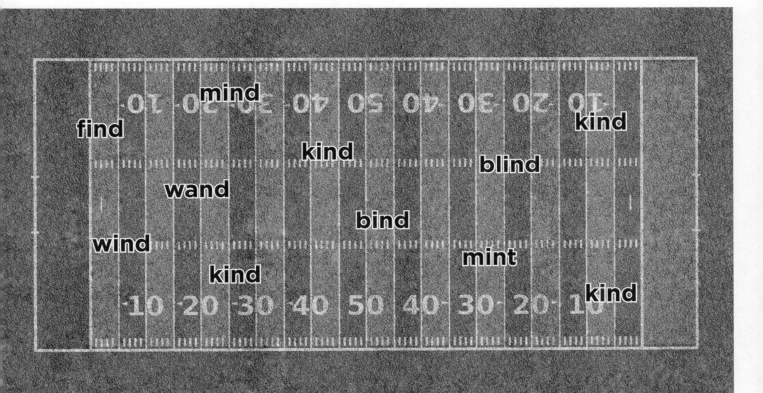

KIND

RHYMES WITH KIND

 **better**

Trace the word better and say it aloud.

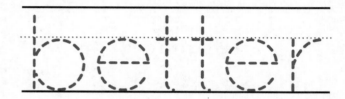

Practice writing the word better.

_____   _____

_____   _____

_____   _____

You will do _____ next time.

Three Ring Circus

Find the word **better** three times inside each ring and circle it.

batter

butter   better

better   better

bother

better

beetle   better

wetter   bottle

better

better

better   better

beat

betting

beets

Trace the word draw and say it aloud.

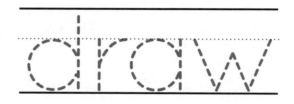

Practice writing the word draw.

_____   _____
....

_____   _____

_____   _____
....

_____   _____

Let's _____ a picture.

Play Along

Draw a circle around the word **draw** to make a music note. Follow the code for the circled notes to answer the joke.

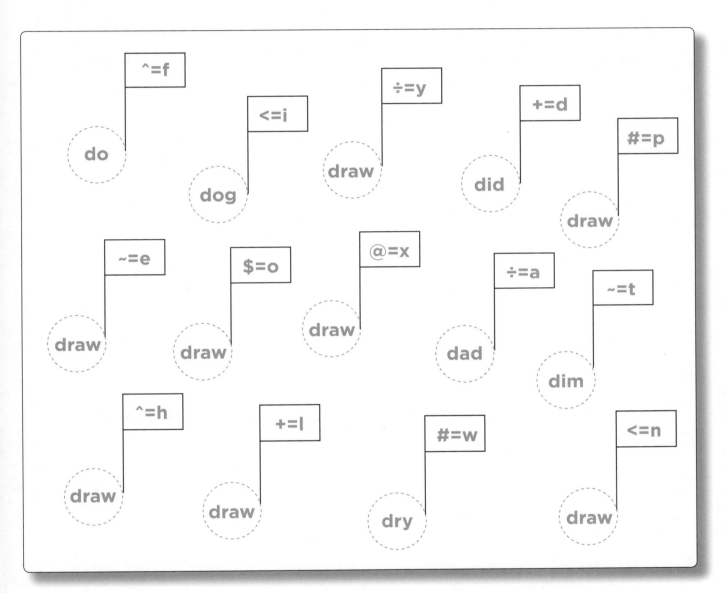

How do musicians call each other?

On the __ __ __ __   __ __ __ __ __

@   ÷   + $ #   ^ $ <   ~

REVIEW: The Bottom Line

Use the codes to help fill in the missing words to the story.

small	warm	grow	keep	together
——	•••••	∿	══	‑ ‑ ‑

Jane and Julia want to work _____ to _____ flowers. They find
                            ‑ ‑ ‑   ∿

a _____ spot in their yard that gets lot of _____ sunshine. They
    ══   •••••

plant the seeds _____ . If they _____ watering the _____
                ‑ ‑ ‑   ══   ——

seeds, they will _____ into beautiful flowers.
                  ∿

How many times does each word appear in the story?

small _____   keep _____

warm _____   together _____

grow _____

REVIEW: Matching Caps

Draw a line to connect the matching sight words.
Fill in the letter in the blue circle next to each cap to
name the sport below.

1. seven

2. only

3. done

4. kind

5. better

6. draw

 l

 b

 d

 a

 h

 n

This sport is also called "fieldball."

__ __ __ __ __ __ __ __
 1   2   3   4   5   2   6   6

 **own**

Trace the word own and say it aloud.

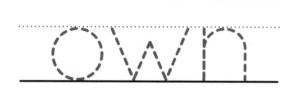

Practice writing the word own.

Bring your _____ ball.

Button Up

Draw a circle around the word own to make buttons on the shirts. Circle the shirt with more buttons.

owe

own

own

now

own

one

own

own

own

own

own

own

never

Trace the word never and say it aloud.

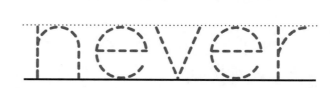

Practice writing the word never.

I have _____ been on a plane.

Funny Food

Circle the word **never** each time you see it. Write the total under each bag, and use the code to answer the joke.

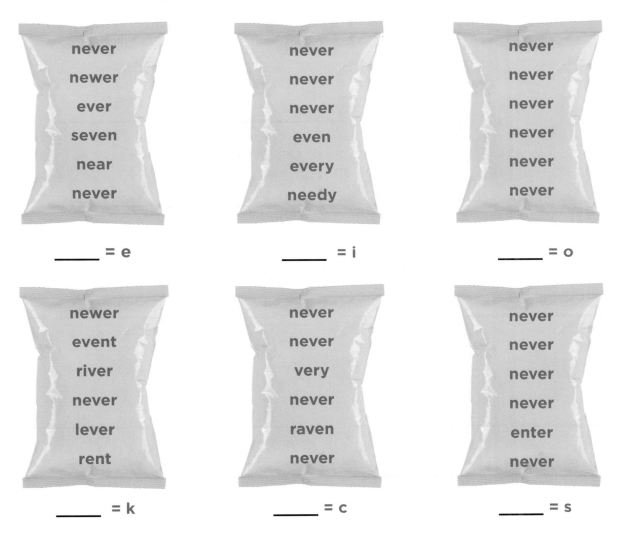

never	never	never
newer	never	never
ever	never	never
seven	even	never
near	every	never
never	needy	never
_____ = e	_____ = i	_____ = o

newer	never	never
event	never	never
river	very	never
never	never	never
lever	raven	enter
rent	never	never
_____ = k	_____ = c	_____ = s

What kind of keys can you eat?

____ ____ ____ ____ ____ ____ ____
4   6   6   1   3   2   5

 **laugh**

Trace the word laugh and say it aloud.

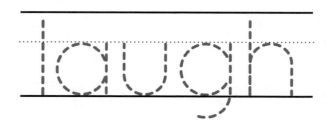

Practice writing the word laugh.

_____   _____

_____   _____

_____   _____

_____   _____

We _____ at the joke.

Check It Out

Put a check mark by the word laugh in the book titles. If the title does not have the word laugh, leave it blank.

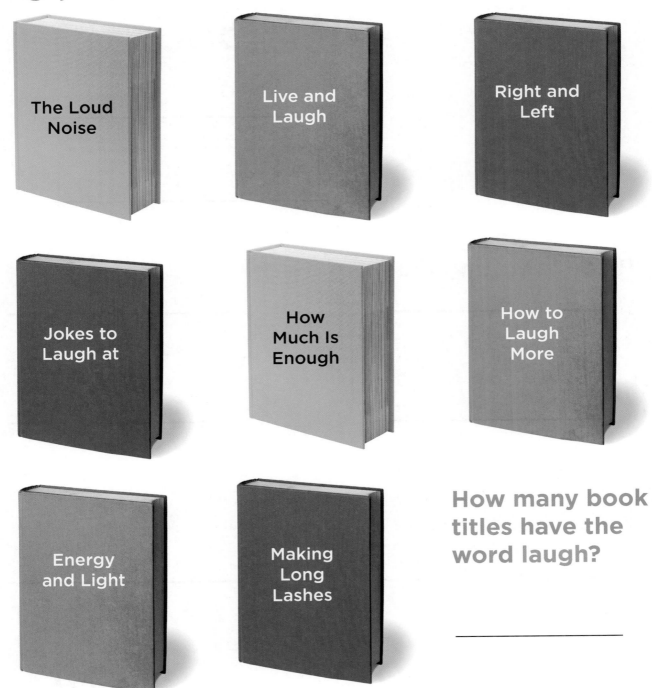

The Loud Noise

Live and Laugh

Right and Left

Jokes to Laugh at

How Much Is Enough

How to Laugh More

Energy and Light

Making Long Lashes

How many book titles have the word laugh?

_____

 **much**

Trace the word much and say it aloud.

much

Practice writing the word much.

_____   _____

....

_____   _____

_____   _____

....

_____   _____

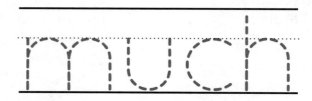 I ate too _____ food.

Prize Tickets

Underline the word **much** each time you see it on the ticket. Write the number on the line.

m u c h m u c h ___

M U T H M U C H ___

m h u m u c h m ___

m o u h c m u c ___

M U C H W A C H ___

h m u c h m u h ___

Add up the numbers on all the tickets. _____

10   **2**   **5**   **2**   **1**

Circle the prizes you would choose with your tickets.

Trace the word hurt and say it aloud.

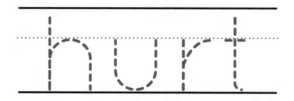

Practice writing the word hurt.

She _____ her toe.

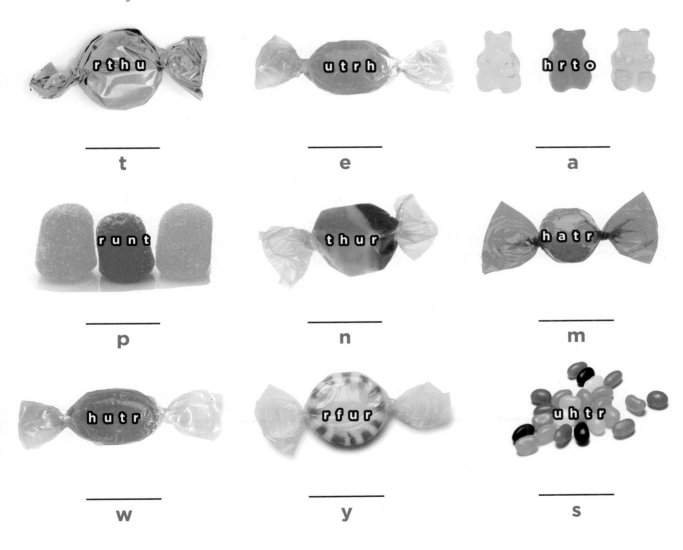

Candy Code

Look at the letters inside each candy. If you can unscramble the letters to make the word **hurt**, then write **hurt** on the line and follow the code. If not, leave the line blank.

rthu

utrh

hrto

_____
t

_____
e

_____
a

runt

thur

hatr

_____
p

_____
n

_____
m

hutr

rfur

uhtr

_____
w

_____
y

_____
s

What country does candy come from?

___ ___ ___ ___ ___ ___ ___

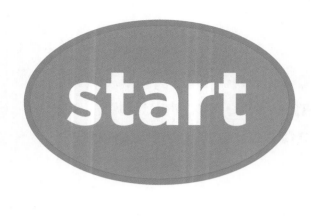

start

Trace the word start and say it aloud.

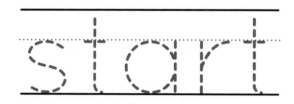

start

Practice writing the word start.

_____   _____

....

_____   _____

_____   _____

....

_____   _____

You may _____ the test.

Boxcar Race

Draw a box around the word start when you see it hiding inside another word. The car with more boxes wins the race.

stores   stamp

starts   starter

upstart   startled

restart   stars

stirring

---

tarts   started   stares

storing

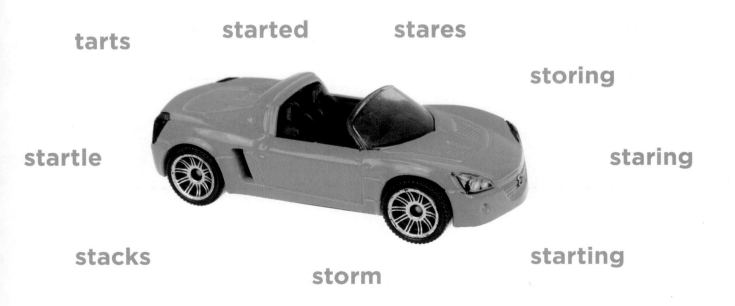

startle   staring

stacks   starting

storm

Trace the word far and say it aloud.

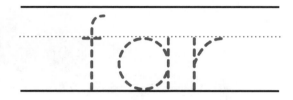

Practice writing the word far.

I walked very _____ .

Lucky Card

Color all the shapes that have the word far inside.

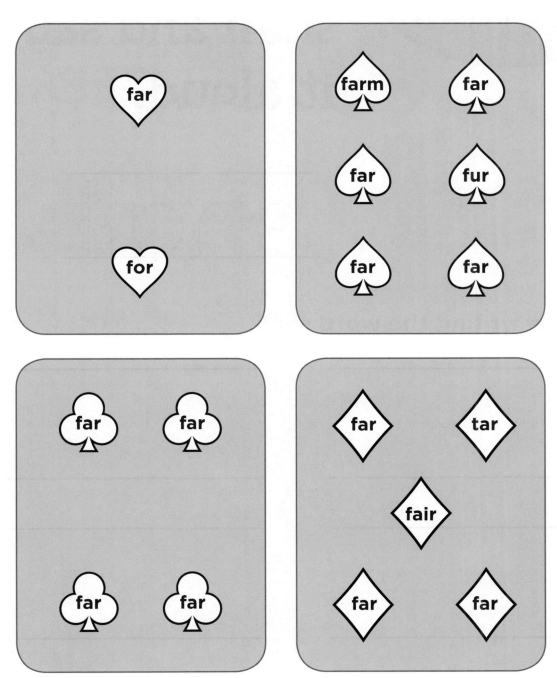

Trace the word shall and say it aloud.

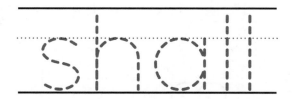

Practice writing the word shall.

_____   _____

_____   _____

_____   _____

_____   _____

What _____ we do today?

Around the Clock

Draw a line from the middle of the clock to the word **shall**. Follow each line to fill in the correct letter below.

Why did the clock slow down?

| 2 | 7 | | 1 | 4 | 7 | | 9 | | 7 | 2 | 11 | 10 | 12 | 7 |

Trace the word show and say it aloud.

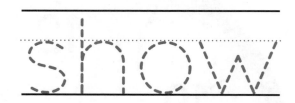

Practice writing the word show.

Please _____ **me the way.**

Fishing for Rhymes

Draw a line from each fishing pole to the words that rhyme with show.

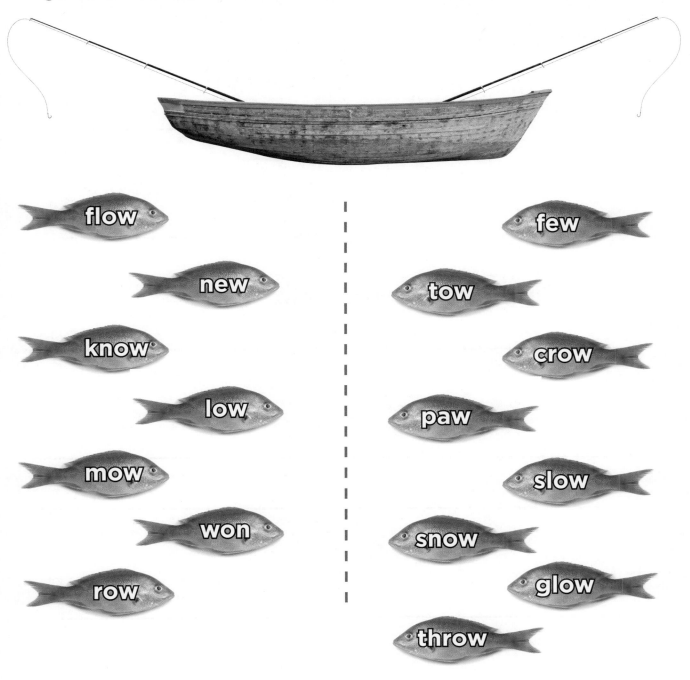

flow

new

know

low

mow

won

row

few

tow

crow

paw

slow

snow

glow

throw

Which side caught more fish? _____

 **drink**

Trace the word drink and say it aloud.

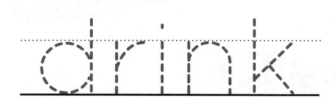

Practice writing the word drink.

Have a _____ of water.

Fun Fact

Ask an adult to read you the paragraph below. Then shade one box from the bottom up on the graph every time you see the word drink.

90	drink
80	drink
70	drink
60	drink
50	drink
40	drink
30	drink

Elephants drink a lot of water! Elephants use their trunks to help them drink. First, they suck up water with their trunks. Then, they curl their trunks down. The trunk sprays water like a hose into an elephant's mouth. This is how elephants drink water.

Use the number at the top of your bar to complete this fun fact:

Elephants drink up to _____ gallons of water a day.

 **eight**

Trace the word eight and say it aloud.

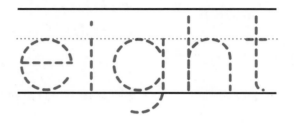

Practice writing the word eight.

I slept for _____ hours.

Beautiful Bubbles

Cross out any bubble that does not have the word **eight**.

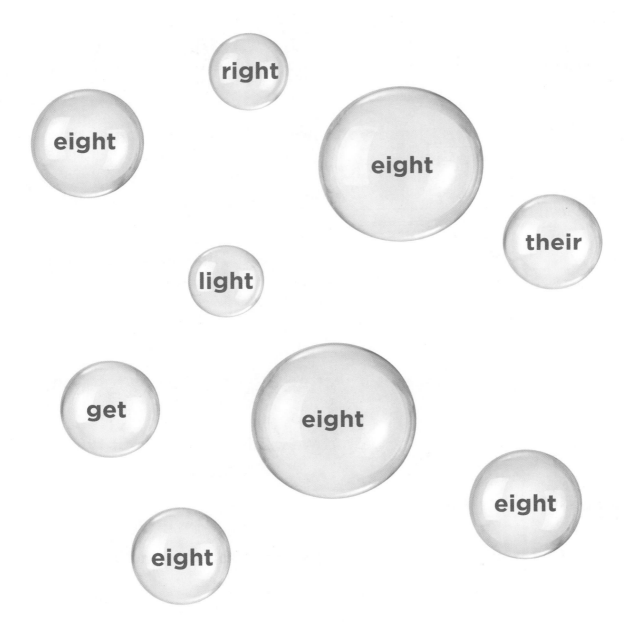

right

eight

eight

their

light

get

eight

eight

eight

How many bubbles remain? _____

REVIEW: The Bottom Line

Use the codes to help fill in the missing words to the story.

hurt	laugh	show	far	drink
———	• • • • •	~~~~	═══	– – –

Brad wanted to _____ everyone how fast he could run in the race.
(~~~~)

He hadn't gotten very _____ when he tripped and fell. Brad's knee
(═══)

was _____ . His pride was _____ , too. His friend Tracy wasn't
(———)   (———)

_____ behind him. She stopped and gave him a _____ . She
(═══)   (– – –)

wanted to _____ him that it was no big deal. Tracey told him a
(~~~~)

joke and made him _____ . Brad was still _____ , but he got up
(• • • • •)   (———)

and finished the race.

How many times does each word appear in the story?

hurt _____   far _____

laugh _____   drink _____

show _____

REVIEW: Matching Caps

Draw a line to connect the matching sight words.
Fill in the letter in the blue circle next to each cap
to name the sport below.

1. over

2. never

3. much

4. start

5. shall

6. eight

start — a

much — u

shall — s

eight — h

never — q

over — s

This sport shares its name with a vegetable!

__ __ __ __ __ __
1   2   3   4   5   6

REVIEW: Word Search

Find the review words in the word search.

seven   together   only   done   small
keep   kind   draw   much   show   eight

```
W E I G H T K I D T
N L T H Y R S T R U
K L O N L Y M H V J
E S G Q E G A U U K
D O E M X R L K C S
O S T V G J L E S H
N M H R E I G E P O
E R E V Q N H P K W
E D R A W I T V U Z
P W O Z N M K I N D
```

REVIEW: The Lost Word

Look for each review word from page 546 and circle it below. There is one word from the list that is missing.

Has anyone seen a small pencil case? I only keep seven or eight pencils together inside the case. I brought it to school to show my friends how I draw. When I was done, I left if behind. If you return it to me, I would appreciate it so much!

Which review word is missing? _____

Crossword Clues

Complete each sentence with a review word from the box. Use the words to fill in the puzzle on the next page.

warm   hurt   drink   start   better

shall   laugh   far   own   grow   never

Across

3. I _____ eat peanuts.

4. I have my _____ bike.

5. It time to _____ the game.

6. I live very _____ away.

7. I like to _____ milk.

8. The book makes me _____ .

10. My food is _____ .

Down

1. I feel _____ today.

2. Good food helps me _____ .

5. Where _____ we go?

9. He _____ my feelings.

Use the clues on page 548 to fill in the puzzle.

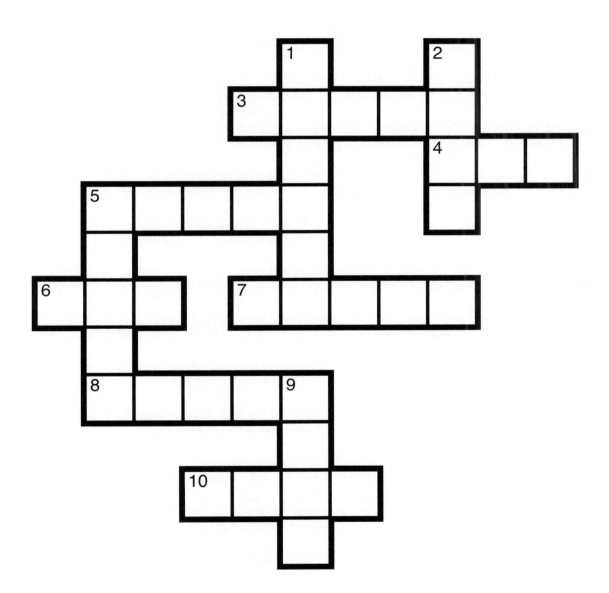

REVIEW: Sentence Sequence

Follow the code in the box to make sentences with sight words.

carry	better	keep	long	today	got	clean	together
!	@	#	$	%	^	&	*

before	because	bring	myself	light	warm
+	=	<	>	?	~

1. _____ it _____ .
       <   %

2. I _____ it _____ _____ it's _____ .
       !   >   =   ?

3. We _____ _____ _____ .
       &   @   *

4. It _____ _____ _____ .
       ^   ~   %

5. We _____ _____ _____ .
       #   ~   *

6. _____ _____ , it _____ _____ .
       + $ ^   ~

REVIEW: Wacky Word Boxes

Some letters are short and some letters are tall.
Find the boxes that fit each word.

only   seven   fall   if   much   pick   cut
own   laugh   hot   small   drink   done   which

1.

2.

3.

4.

5.

6.

7.

8.

9.

10.

11.

12.

13.

14.

REVIEW: Four Squares

Find four sight words in each square. Draw a box around each correctly spelled word.

start	hold
ten	hert
miself	about
show	never
eight	draw
hurt	full
shall	smal
try	six
becuz	grow
far	kind

REVIEW: Framed!

Cross out any words that are not spelled correctly. You should have 22 correct sight words left. Color the frame that has only correct words inside.

hurt
shall
fal
kut
about
pick
hot
draw
if

much   hold
tri   together
long   beter
cleen   before
        got

because   better   warm
start   myself   seven
eight   light   only

REVIEW: In the End

Draw a line to the correct ending for each sight word. Then write the word on the line.

ki ow _____   s wn _____   br day _____

sh aw _____   t ry _____   to ing _____

dr nd _____   o ix _____   wh ich _____

c ut _____   do ep _____

t ar _____   gr ll _____

f en _____   ke ne _____

                        fu ow _____

ca ean _____   nev nk _____

cl all _____   lau er _____

sm rry _____   dri gh _____

ANSWER KEY

Page 7

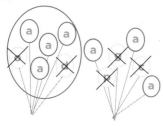

How many balloons are there altogether? __7__

Page 9

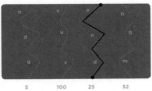

5	he	hen	thin	the	with
4	the	her	her	why	tee
3	to	tree	to	tee	the
2	this	the	she	that	than
1	it	then	the	his	tea
	i	h	C	e	i

What country makes you shiver?

__C__ __h__ __i__ __l__ __e__
 1   2   3   4   5

Page 11

   5   100   25   52

There are __25__ species of chipmunks!

Circle the nuts that show the word and.

Page 13

Which pizza has more slices? __B__

How many slices in all? __11__

Page 15

I am having so much fun! It rains a little bit in the morning. **I** go to the beach every day. Dad and **I** are visiting a volcano tomorrow. Dad says **I** have to wear sunblock. **I** miss you!

5. Hawaii

Page 17

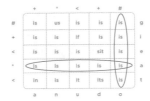

	+	*	<	+	#	
#	is	us	is	is	is	g
+	is	is	if	is	is	i
<	is	is	is	sit	is	e
+	is	is	is	is	is	a
<	in	is	it	its	is	t
	a	n	u	d	o	

Which two days other than Tuesday and Thursday start with a "T"?

__t__ __o__ __d__ __a__ __y__   __a__ __n__ __d__   __t__ __o__ __m__ __o__ __r__ __r__ __o__ __w__
 #   *   +   #   #   +

Page 19

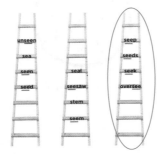

Page 21

   6
   7
   7
   8

Page 23

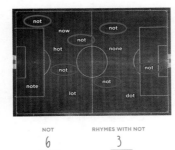

NOT   RHYMES WITH NOT
__6__   __3__

Page 25

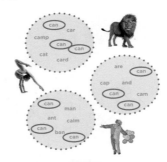

Page 27

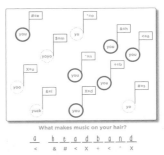

What makes music on your hair?

__a__ __h__ __e__ __a__ __d__ __b__ __a__ __n__ __d__
 <   &   #   <   X   +   <   "   X

Page 28

I went with my dad **to the** fair. We saw pigs **and** horses. **I** played lots of games. We ate hot dogs **and** popcorn. **I** wanted **to** buy cotton candy too. My dad **and I** rode **a** big slide together. It started **to** get dark. Some of **the** rides lit up! **I** stayed up late **to** watch **the** fireworks. Then it was time **to** go.

a	1
the	3
and	3
I	4
to	5

Page 29

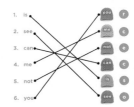

The field this sport is played on is called the "pitch."

__S__ __o__ __c__ __c__ __e__ __r__
 1   2   3   4   5   6

Page 31

Page 33

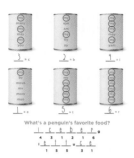

3 = c   2 = b   4 = i

1 = e   5 = t   6 = r

What's a penguin's favorite food?

I c e b e r g
4   3   1   2   1   6

l e t t u c e
1   5   5   3   1

Page 35

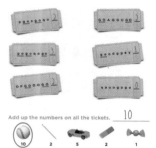

How many book titles have the word for? **5**

Page 37

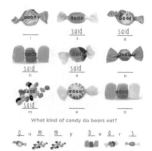

Add up the numbers on all the tickets. **10**

10   2   5   2   1

Page 39

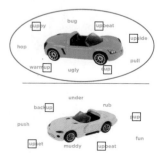

said   said
l   s   g

said   said
b   a   p

said
m   e   n

What kind of candy do bears eat?

g u m m y   b e a r s

Page 41

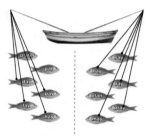

puppy, bug, upbeat, upside, hop, warmup, ugly, pull, cup

under, backup, rub, push, up, upset, muddy, upbeat, fun

Page 43

Circle the card suit that has all the shapes colored. ◇ ♡ ♧ △

Page 45

big, beg, big, big, big, big, dig, bag, big, big, pig

Why was the clock in the corner?

It was I n   a   t i m e   o u t
10 7   4   2 10 8 6   11 12 2

Page 47

plate, pat, day, pay, lay, hay, say, bay, ray, plan, pray, may

Which side caught more fish? **right**

Page 49

70 run
60 run
50 run
40 run
30 run
20 run
10 run

Cheetahs can run very fast! How do they run so fast? Their long legs help them run. Cheetah's bodies are light. This helps them run faster than other animals. Their claws grip the ground as they run. Cheetahs like to run away instead of fighting.

Use the number at the top of your bar to complete this fun fact:

Cheetahs can run about **60** miles per hour.

Page 51

How many bubbles remain? **4**

Page 52

My dog Sparky is really **big**. Sparky likes to **run** and **play** outside. He can **run** fast and catch a ball in his mouth. **We** go on walks and **play** at the park. Sometimes, Sparky chews on **my** shoes. **My** mom doesn't like that. On weekends, Sparky gets on **my** **big** bed and **we** take a nap. Sparky is **my** best friend.

my	5
big	2
run	2
we	2
play	2

Page 53

1. it
2. go
3. said
4. here
5. for
6. up

here a, for t, it k, go a, up e, said r

In this sport, you wear a colored belt to show what level you are.

k a r a t e
1 2 3 4 5 6

Page 54

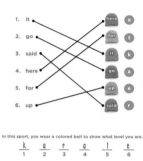

C F N (M E) J F Y
N (I) D W T (A N D)
O (S) T U K (Y) D T
(A) R V W B (O) Q C
U (C A N T (U P) X
T Y B U (M) J K O
(B I G) N (Y) T (I) U
X T H D (F O R) Y

Page 55

Stormy **is** lost!
Can **you** help **me** find **my** cat, Stormy?
She **is** **big** **and** gray.
I have **a** reward **for** anyone who **can** help!

Which review word is missing? **up**

Page 56

Across

2. We live <u>here</u>.
5. Do <u>not</u> run.
7. Let's <u>play</u> outside.
9. <u>The</u> game is today.
10. We <u>go</u> to school.

Down

1. I <u>see</u> a rainbow.
3. We <u>run</u> in the race.
4. Today, <u>it</u> is sunny.
6. He <u>said</u> his name.
8. <u>We</u> are at home.
9. You can go <u>to</u> the park.

Page 57

Page 59

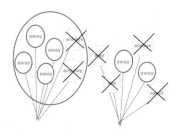

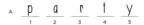

How many balloons are there altogether? ___6___

Page 61

What kind of tea should you give a large group?

A <u>p</u> <u>a</u> <u>r</u> <u>t</u> <u>y</u>
 1   2   3   4   5

Page 63

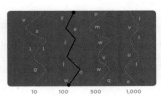

Chipmunks gather about __100__ acorns a day!
Circle the nuts that show the word yellow.

Page 65

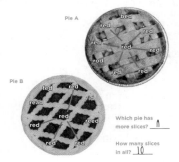

Which pie has more slices? __A__

How many slices in all? __10__

Page 67

Dear Brad,
This has been the best **two** weeks! We take the subway to all kinds of places. We are only **two** stops away from a great museum. We are close to Central Park too. I saw **two** musicals on Broadway. The time is flying by. I will be home in **two** days. See you soon!

~Peter

4. New York City

Page 69

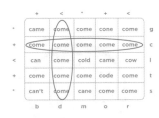

What has thirteen hearts?

A <u>c</u> <u>a</u> <u>r</u> <u>d</u> <u>d</u> <u>e</u> <u>c</u> <u>k</u>.

Page 71

Page 73

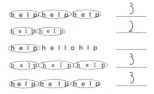

help help help — 3
help help — 2
help hello hlp — 3
help help help — 3
help help help — 3

Page 75

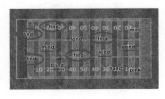

FIND — 5
RHYMES WITH FIND — 4

Page 77

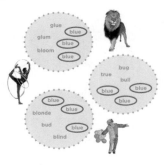

Page 79

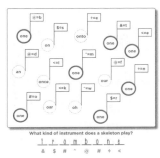

What kind of instrument does a skeleton play?

<u>t</u> <u>r</u> <u>o</u> <u>m</u> <u>b</u> <u>o</u> <u>n</u> <u>e</u>
& $ # ^ @ # ÷ <

Page 80

I got **two red** balloons at the fair. One balloon blew **away** in the wind. I wanted to **find** my balloon! Far **away**, I saw a something **red**. But it was just a ball. I saw lots of **red** things, but not my balloon. I needed **help** to **find** my balloon. I asked my **two** friends to **help** me. We were able to **find** it in a tree. Now, I have **two red** balloons again!

away — 2
help — 2
find — 3
two — 3
red — 4

Page 81

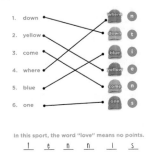

In this sport, the word "love" means no points.

<u>t</u> <u>e</u> <u>n</u> <u>n</u> <u>i</u> <u>s</u>

Page 83

Page 85

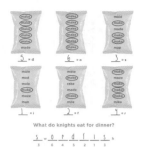

5 = d   6 = o   3 = s

main   male   mad   male   maze   man
mad   rake   made   mile   mile

1 = i   2 = f   4 = r

What do knights eat for dinner?

S _ o _ r _ d _ f _ i _ s h
3   6   4   5   2   1   1

Page 87

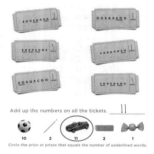

✓ The Little Cabin   ✓ Little Boy Blue   The Magic Letter

✓ Projects for Little Hands   No More Litter   ✓ A Little Bit of Sunshine

The Light in the Forest   ✓ A Little Sugar on Top

How many book titles have the word little?

5

Page 89

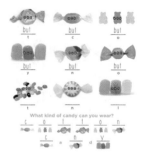

Add up the numbers on all the tickets.   11

soccer ball 10   pencil 2   car 11   chocolate bar 3   bowtie 1

Circle the prize or prizes that equals the number of underlined words.

Page 91

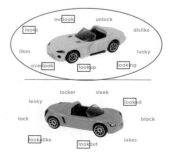

but t   but c   but o

but y   but n   but o

_ t _   _ n _   _ l _

What kind of candy can you wear?

c _ o _ t _ t _ o _ n
c _ n _ d _ y

Page 93

outlook   unlock
looks   dislike
likes   lucky
overlook   lookup   looking

locker   sleek
leaky   looked
lock   block
looklike   lookout   lakes

Page 95

Circle the card suit that has all the shapes colored.   ◇ ♡ ♡ ♧ (spade)

Page 97

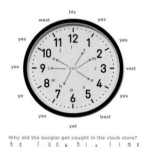

his
west   yes
yes   yes
yes   vest
ye   yes
yes   best
yet

Why did the burglar get caught in the clock store?

h e _ t o o k _ h i s _ t i m e
7   4   1   10 10   7   9   1   9   2   4

Page 99

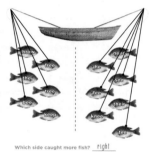

throw   near
free   she
the   see
tree   tee
bee   their
keep   knee
tee

Which side caught more fish?   right

Page 101

35 jump
30 jump
25 jump
20 jump
15 jump
10 jump
5 jump

Many kinds of frogs can leap and jump. When they are in danger, they can just jump away. Often times, they land in the water to hide. Their webbed feet push off the ground. Frogs close their eyes when they jump! This protects their eyes. Not all frogs can jump. Some walk or hop instead.

Use the number at the top of your bar to complete this fun fact:

Some frogs can jump   20   times their body length.

Page 103

funny
funny   funny
funny   funny
funny   funny
funny

How many bubbles remain?   4

Page 104

I like to draw **funny** pictures **in** my notebooks. **On** the front of my notebook I put my name **in** big letters. First, I **make** the outline **in** pencil. Then I color it **in** with markers or crayons. I like to sit **on** my bed to **make** these **funny** pictures. Once, I drew a monster with **three** heads! I have filled **three** notebooks already. Soon I will start **on** my fourth notebook and **make** more **funny** pictures.

three   2
make   3
in   4
on   3
funny   3

Page 105

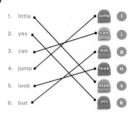

1. little
2. yes
3. can
4. jump
5. look
6. but

jump i
can i
but g
look n
little s
yes k

This sport can be done on the water or on the snow.

s _ k _ i _ i _ n _ g
1   2   3   4   5   6

Page 106

K K H K B T W F J Z
L H Q A N W R I J V
O C B B U M O N D C
O R F L Y A S D N H
K E V U E V V F I E
V D W E H E T O Z L
N Y H Q H T W O M P
Y R E Q U L L G Y S
M B R A W A Y S F B
E I E J I F B U T B

Page 107

Please **help** me **find** my **red** hat! It blew **away** **in** the wind, and I don't know **where** it ended up. It has **two** **blue** flowers **on** it. Please **look** **in** your neighborhood for my **red** hat!

Which review word is missing?   **but**

Page 108

Across

1. I can **jump** over the rocks.
4. Count to **three**.
6. The lemon is **yellow**.
7. The joke is **funny**.
9. It is **so** cold today.
11. Please **come** with me.

Down

2. I **make** my lunch each day.
3. The baby is **little**.
5. We go **down** the slide.
8. Please say **yes**.
10. There is only **one** left.

Page 109

Crossword:
- 1 (down) JUMP
- 3 (down) LITTLE
- 4 (across) THREE
- 5 (down) DOWN
- 6 (across) YELLOW
- 7 (across) FUNNY
- 9 (down/across) YES
- 8 ON
- 10 COME

Page 110

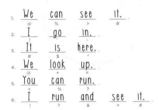

1. We can see it.
2. I go in.
3. It is here.
4. We look up.
5. You can run.
6. I run and see it.

Page 111

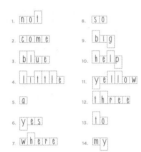

1. not
2. come
3. blue
4. little
5. a
6. yes
7. where
8. so
9. big
10. help
11. yellow
12. three
13. to
14. my

Page 112

the / away
ott / find
down / said
jump / help
on / make

me / amd
for / one
two / play
red / funny
kan / but

Page 113

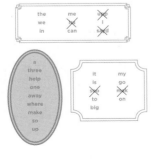

the | me | ~~up~~
we | can | I
in | ~~can~~ | said

a / three / help / one / away / where / make / so / up

it | my
is | go
~~up~~ | ~~mak~~
to | on
big

Page 114

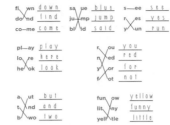

fl—wn → down
do—nd → find
co—me → come

sa—ue → blue
ju—mp → jump
bl—id → said

s—ee → see
r—es → yes
y—un → run

pl—ay → play
lo—re → here
he—ok → look

r—ou → you
n—ed → red
y—or → for
f—ot → not

a—ut → but
t—nd → and
b—wo → two

fun—ow → yellow
lit—ny → funny
yell—tle → little

Page 117

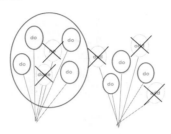

do, do, do, done, do, do, do, do

How many balloons are there altogether? 7

Page 119

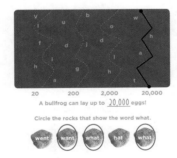

5	like	lick	life	lake	lie
4	lake	lock	like	lime	lie
3	lie	bike	luck	lit	like
2	line	like	lie	lack	lick
1	lick	life	line	like	live

p | u | t | i | l

What flower grows best between your nose and chin?

t u l i p
1 2 3 4 5

Page 121

20 | 200 | 2,000 | 20,000

A bullfrog can lay up to 20,000 eggs!

Circle the rocks that show the word what.
went | want | what | hat | what

Page 123

Pizza A
salt, said, say, sap, say, save, say, zap, say

Pizza B
soy, say, say, and, say, yes, say, say

Which pizza has more slices? B

How many slices in all? 8

Page 125

Dear Luke,

I went **with** my cousins to the most amazing place! There are beautiful layers of rocks all around. We hiked **with** a guide down into the deep canyon. I brought lots of water **with** me. But I forgot to bring my camera **with** me. I hope you can come back here **with** me some day.

Love,
Dan

5. Grand Canyon

Page 127

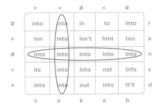

	<	+	#	<	#	
#	into	into	in	to	into	r
+	inn	into	isn't	hint	too	a
#	into	into	into	into	into	n
<	its	into	into	not	info	s
+	into	into	out	into	it'll	d
	v	o	k	e	b	

What do you call a man with a nose but no body?

n o b 0 d y   n 0 s e
+ +   # +

Page 129

Ladder 1: before, begin, maybe, being, behave, webbing
Ladder 2: below, born
Ladder 3: bone, beside, become, deep

Page 131

- (at)(at)(at) t(at)(at)
- (at)(at)(at)(at)(at) → 6
- (at)(at)(at)(at)(at)(at) → 7
- (at)(at)(at)(at)(at) → 5
- (at)(at)(at)(at) → 4

Page 133

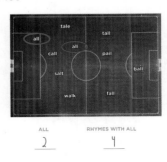

tale, tall, all, call, all, pail, salt, ball, walk, fall

ALL: 2
RHYMES WITH ALL: 4

Page 135

Page 137

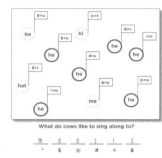

What do cows like to sing along to?

m o o s i c
* $ @ # < &

Page 138

Today I went swimming with my brother **at** the pool. I jumped <u>**into**</u> the water first. <u>**He**</u> waited **at** the side for a while. Then **he** jumped <u>**into**</u> the pool **with** a big noodle. I swam <u>**all**</u> the way across the pool. <u>**He**</u> waited **at** the shallow end. We swam <u>**all**</u> day. Then we changed into dry clothes and walked <u>**all**</u> the way home.

How many times does each word appear in the story?

he	3
into	2
all	3
at	3
with	1

Page 139

This sport can be played on ice, a field, or a roller rink.

h o c k e y
1 2 3 4 5 6

Page 141

Page 143

3 = a   1 = n   4 = o

5 = s   6 = t   2 = d

What kind of nut has a hole?

a d o n u t
5   2 4 1 3 6

Page 145

How many book titles have the word good?

6

Page 147

Add up the numbers on all the tickets. 8

10   2   5   2   1

Circle the prize or prizes that equals the number of underlined words.

Prizes circled will vary.

Page 149

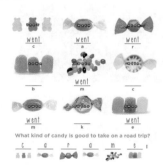

What kind of candy is good to take on a road trip?

c a r a m e l

Page 151

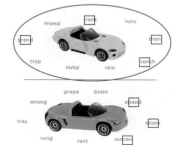

Page 153

Circle the card suit that has all the shapes colored. ◇ ♡ ♠ ♣

Page 155

Why did the boy throw the clock in the trash?

t o   w a s t e   t i m e
8 3   11 1 2 8 5   8 7 10 5

Page 157

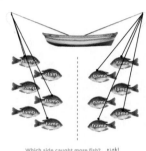

Which side caught more fish? **pink!**

Page 159

Owls have feathers that help them blend in. Their feathers might be <u>brown</u>, gray, or white. They make nests in the <u>brown</u> tree trunks and branches. Barns also make good homes for owls. Owls can hide in logs, grass, or bushes. They have good eyesight. Owls with <u>brown</u> or black eyes like to hunt at night.

Use the number at the top of your bar to complete this fun fact:

Owls have 3 eyelids.

Page 161

How many bubbles remain? 5

Page 162

My sister **ran** in a race today. I **went** to watch her run. It **was** a relay race. **She went** first. **She ran** around the track once. When **she came** back to the starting line, another runner **was** waiting. Each person on the team **ran** when her turn **came**. They all **ran** so fast! Their team **came** in first. It **was** a great race!

went	2
was	3
ran	4
came	3
she	3

Page 163

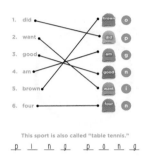

This sport is also called "table tennis."

p i n g   p o n g

Page 164

Page 165

My dog **ran into** the woods **four** days ago! **He** has **brown** fur **with** white spots. I **am** so worried, and I **want** to find him. **He** is a **good** dog. If you see him, call me **at** 555-7456. Thank you!

Which review word is missing?   **do**

Page 166

Across

2. She **was** there early.
4. I **like** pizza.
6. **What** is your name?
9. My mom **came** to get me.

Down

1. We **did** our homework.
2. I **went** to the game.
3. Can you **say** it?
5. I think **she** is funny!
7. It is **too** cold outside.
8. I want to **be** an artist.
10. I was **all** alone.

Page 167

Page 169

How many balloons are there altogether?   6

Page 171

How do you cut the sea in half?

With a   S   e   a   S   a   w
         1   2   3   4   3   5

Page 173

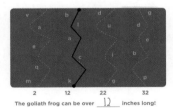

The goliath frog can be over   12   inches long!

Circle the rocks that show the word black.

Page 175

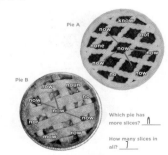

Which pie has more slices?   A

How many slices in all?   7

Page 177

Dear Laura,
This city is amazing! Today, I **saw** famous paintings at a museum. I also **saw** some very old churches and the Eiffel Tower. Last night, we **saw** an opera! The food here is wonderful. Some people **say** this is "The City of Lights." I'll see you soon when I get home.

3. Paris

Page 179

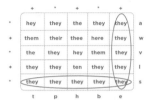

What kind of shoes do spies wear?

S   n   e   ak   e   r   S

Page 181

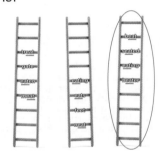

Page 183

w i l l	w i l l	w i l l		3
w i l l	w i l l	w i l l	w l l	3
w i l l	w i l l	w i l l		3
w i l l	w l l	w i l l	w i l l	
w i l l	w i l l			2

Page 185

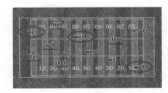

| WELL | RHYMES WITH WELL |
| 3 | 5 |

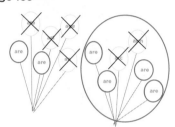
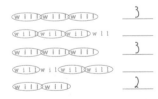

Page 187

hair, hive, have, here, hand, have, favor, have, ever, have, hard, hare, has, have, cave, heave, have, dove, wave, have, ham

Page 189

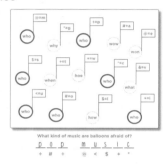

What kind of music are balloons afraid of?

p o p   m u s i c
+ # ÷   @ < $ + *

Page 190

Black bears **are** not always **black**! **They** can have **black**, brown, or even white fur. **Black** bears live in forests, and **they** like to be near trees and rivers. Their claws **are** sharp. This helps them climb trees **well** and catch fish to **eat**. **Black** bears also **eat** berries, plants, and grass. **They are** amazing animals!

eat	2
well	1
they	3
are	3
black	5

Page 191

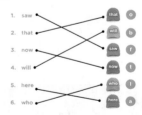

1. saw — saw / f
2. that — that / o
3. now — now / t
4. will — will / b
5. here — here / a
6. who — who / l

In this sport, players try to get the ball to the "end zone."

f o o t b a l l

Page 193

Page 195

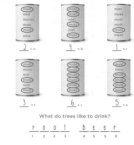

2 = o   4 = b   1 = r

3 = t   6 = e   5 = e

What do trees like to drink?

r o o t   b e e r
1 2 2 2   4 5 5 6

Page 197

How many book titles have the word **white**?

4

Page 199

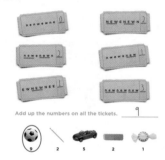

Add up the numbers on all the tickets.   9

9   2   5   2   1

Page 201

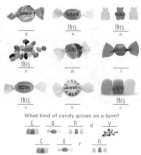

this, this, this, this, this

What kind of candy grows on a farm?

c a n d y

c o r n

Page 203

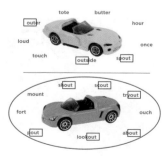

tote, butter, outer, hour, loud, once, touch, outside, spout

shout, scout, mount, tryout, fort, ouch, pout, lookout, about

Page 205

Circle the card suit that has all the shapes colored. ◇ ♡ △ ♧

Page 207

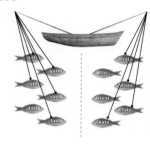

What did the clock hands say when they passed each other?

w a t c h   o u t
5 1 6 n 7   9 3 4

Page 209

Which side caught more fish? left

Page 211

70	there
60	there
50	there
40	there
30	there
20	there
10	there

<u>There</u> are not many giant pandas left in the wild. Pandas live in the mountains of China. They like the bamboo trees <u>there</u>. But bamboo forests can get cut down. Pandas lose their homes and their food. <u>There</u> are many people trying to help save pandas. These people protect the bamboo forests. Is <u>there</u> something you can do to help too?

Use the number at the top of your bar to complete this fun fact:

Giant pandas eat 20 to __40__ pounds of bamboo a day.

Page 213

soon, soon, soon, soon, soon, soon

How many bubbles remain? 4

Page 214

I went to a **new** camp **this** summer. As **soon** as I got **there**, I went to my cabin. I made a lot of **new** friends **there**. **Our** cabin was **new** and very clean. **There** was a lake with canoes near **our** cabin. **This** was **our** favorite part of camp! I hope to see my friends again **soon**. I want to go to **this** summer camp again next year.

new	3
this	3
our	3
there	3
soon	2

Page 215

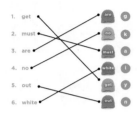

1. get — a
2. must — get
3. are — g
4. no — white
5. out — n
6. white — are

This name of this sport means "hunter's boat."

k a y a k i n g
4 2 1 2 4 6 5 3

Page 216

Page 217

Who can help me find my **black** backpack? It is a **new** backpack with white **stripes**. I left it **out** on the grass after school. Now, it's not **there**. I **must** find it **soon**! If you find it, you **will** **get** a reward!

Which review word is missing?   saw

Page 218

Across
2. I like **this** one here.
4. We **ate** it all up!
5. We washed **our** car.
6. It's time for dinner **now**.
8. Let's **eat** lunch outside.

Down
1. Where is **that** book I was reading?
3. We **have** a pet dog.
4. They **are** sisters.
6. There is **no** food inside.
7. She does not feel **well**.
9. I hope **they** get home soon.

Page 219

Page 220

1. She will have that.
2. What did they eat?
3. He was out there.
4. They want that.
5. That was good.
6. He will eat that.

Page 221

1. ate
2. all
3. say
4. get
5. black
6. no
7. must
8. who
9. came
10. this
11. with
12. white
13. do
14. four

Page 222

whot	be
at	went
too	eat
new	are
soon	our
ran	like
now	wint
blak	am
well	brown
are	into

Page 223

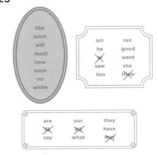

Page 224

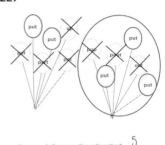

d×e — be   o×d — did   th×ur — four
b×o — do   w×as — was   fo×is — this
a–t — at   a×ut — out   we–ll — well

a×ow — now   ca×at — that
n×ll — all   in×th — with
e–at — eat   th×me — came
            wi×to — into

a×et — get   br×ack — black
w×ho — who   bl×ere — there
g×te — ate   th×own — brown

Page 227

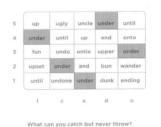

How many balloons are there altogether? 5

Page 229

5	up	ugly	uncle	under	until
4	under	until	up	end	onto
3	fun	undo	untie	upper	under
2	upset	under	and	bun	wander
1	until	undone	under	dunk	ending
	l	c	a	d	o

What can you catch but never throw?

a   c   o   l   d
1   2   3   4   5

Page 231

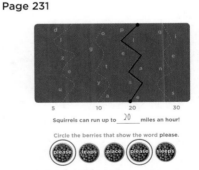

Squirrels can run up to 20 miles an hour!

Circle the berries that show the word please.

please   leaps   place   please   sleeps

Page 233

Pizza A

Pizza B

Which pizza has more slices? A

How many slices in all? 8

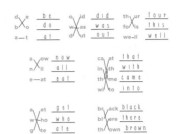

Page 235

Dear Lauren,
I love camping! This place is so **pretty**. We go hiking in the mountains every day. Then I watch the sunset. I can see all the **pretty** stars at night. We went to see a geyser today. Hot water shoots out of the ground. It's **pretty** amazing. It's called "Old Faithful." I'll be home soon!

     Love,
     Rita

3. Yellowstone

Page 237

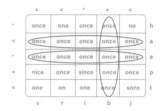

Who can shave all day and still have a beard?

_a_ _b_ _a_ _r_ _b_ _e_ _r_
< + < + ˚

Page 239

Page 241

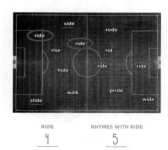

4
3
3
4

Page 243

RIDE   RHYMES WITH RIDE
4   5

Page 245

Page 247

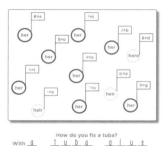

How do you fix a tuba?
With _a_   _t_ _u_ _b_ _a_   _g_ _l_ _u_ _e_
   <   ˚ $ / <   X ÷ ˚ #

Page 248

Once I found a nest **under** an **old** bridge. The nest **had** a bird in it. I wondered if the bird **had some** babies in the nest too. I **had** to wait quietly for a long time. **Once** the bird flew away, I saw **some** small baby birds in the nest! They were probably a few weeks **old**. The mother bird came back with **some** food for the babies. I **had** so much fun watching these birds **under** the bridge!

once   2
old   2
had   4
some   3
under   2

Page 249

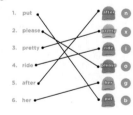

This sport is played in a ring and has "rounds."
_b_ _o_ _x_ _i_ _n_ _g_
1   2   3   4   5   6

Page 251

Page 253

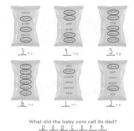

3 = c   4 = o   5 = p
6 = n   1 = o   2 = o

What did the baby corn call its dad?
_p_ _o_ _p_ _c_ _o_ _r_ _n_

Page 255

How many book titles have the word from?
4

Page 257

Add up the numbers on all the tickets. 11
11   2   5   2   1

Page 259

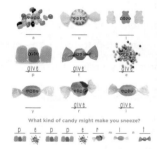

give   _give_   _give_
p   t   e

give   _give_   _give_
y   r   l

What kind of candy might make you sneeze?
_p_ _e_ _p_ _p_ _e_ _r_ _m_ _i_ _n_ _t_

Page 261

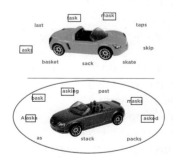

Page 263

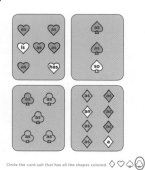

Circle the card suit that has all the shapes colored. ◇ ♡ ♠ (♣)

Page 265

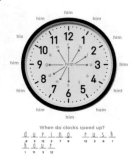

When do clocks speed up?
d u r i n g   r u s h
8 12 7 9   12 5 8 1
h o u r
1 11 3 12

Page 267

Which side caught more fish? right

Page 269

24	has
21	has
18	has
15	has
12	has
9	has
6	has

Koala bears live in eucalyptus trees. A koala has sharp claws to grip the branches. Eucalyptus leaves are the main food for a koala. This leaf has a strong smell, like a cough drop. A koala bear has the same smell because it eats so many leaves! The number of trees has gone down over the years. So, it's harder for a koala to find a home and food. Everyone has to work together to protect the trees and the koalas.

Use the number at the top of your bar to complete this fun fact:

A koala can sleep up to 18 hours a day.

Page 271

How many bubbles remain? 4

Page 272

I am **going** to my friend's birthday party. I'm **going** to get a gift **from** the store as soon as it is **open**. I want to **give** **him** a baseball. Another friend is **going** to **give** **him** a glove. We are **going** to **give** them together. They will be **from** both of us. We hope he will **open** our gift first! We really want **him** to like it.

give	3
from	2
open	2
him	3
going	4

Page 273

1. fly
2. how
3. ask
4. as
5. stop
6. has

In a marathon, people do this for over 26 miles.
r u n n i n g

Page 274

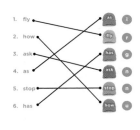

T G I V E P U T
P O K M A F N U
L I P U E R D N
E N L S T O L D
A G U B R M R E
S O M E T I V R
E H A S F A S K
S A F T E R O M

Page 275

Please help me find my **old** baseball mitt! I **put** it **under** the bench **after** the game. This mitt was a gift **from** my dad. I am **going** to **give** it to my brother. Please **ask** around and see if anyone on that team **has** seen it!

Which review word is missing?   **some**

Page 276

Across
1. How can I help you?
3. Clap your hands only once.
4. Please stop that now.
6. That dress is so pretty.
8. I had a cold last week.

Down
1. I like her picture!
2. He is as tall as you.
3. Please open the window.
5. We will fly on a plane.
7. I ride the train every day.
8. Let's sing a song to him.

Page 277

Page 279

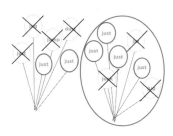

How many balloons are there altogether? 6

Page 281

5	then	them	their	hen	ten
4	the	they	them	these	met
3	them	ten	the	mesh	than
2	there	these	they	them	hem
1	hem	then	tent	there	them

o   d   u   l   c

What do you call a sheep with no head and no legs?

a c l o u d
   1 2 3 4 5

Page 283

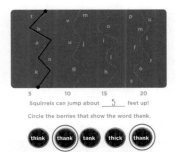

5   10   15   20

Squirrels can jump about 5 feet up!

Circle the berries that show the word thank.

think   (thank)   tank   thick   (thank)

Page 285

Which pie has more slices? B

How many slices in all? 7

Page 287

Dear Tom,
I wish you <u>were</u> here! My parents <u>were</u> right about going on a cruise. It's amazing. Yesterday we saw big, icy glaciers. Big chunks of ice <u>were</u> breaking off and splashing into the water. Today our ship stopped in Skagway. We <u>were</u> going to ride a train into the mountains. But instead, we went on a wildlife tour. We saw bears! There <u>were</u> also tons of bald eagles. I'm so glad I came!
　　　　Love,
　　　　Rudy

5. Alaska

Page 289

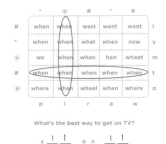

What's the best way to get on TV?

s <u>t</u> <u>a</u> <u>r</u>　o n　<u>a</u> <u>i</u>
　@　# 　　　@　#

Page 291

Page 293

3
3
4

Page 295

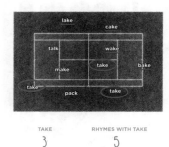

TAKE　　　RHYMES WITH TAKE
　3　　　　　5

Page 297

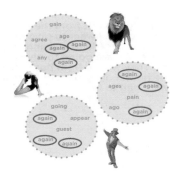

Page 299

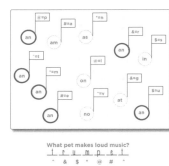

What pet makes loud music?
t r u m p e t
^　&　$　*　@　#　^

Page 300

Our neighbors <u>were</u> moving away. I decided to <u>take</u> some boxes <u>over</u> to <u>them</u>. Pretty soon, all those boxes <u>were</u> full. So I brought boxes from home <u>again</u>. We helped <u>them take</u> the boxes to the truck. We <u>were</u> sad to say goodbye. I hope we see our neighbors <u>again</u>. I'd like to <u>take</u> a trip to visit <u>them</u>.

over　1
take　3
again　2
were　3
them　3

Page 301

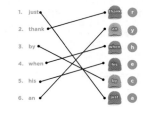

In this sport, people use a bow to shoot arrows at targets.
a r c h e r y
1　2　3　4　5　2　6

Page 303

Page 305

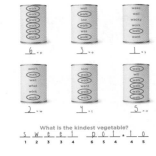

6 = p　　3 = o　　1 = s

2 = w　　4 = t　　5 = e

What is the kindest vegetable?
s w e e t　　p o t a t o
1　2　3　3　4　　6　5　4　　4　5

Page 307

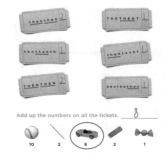

How many book titles have the word live?
4

Page 309

Add up the numbers on all the tickets. 8

10　　2　　8　　2　　1

Page 311

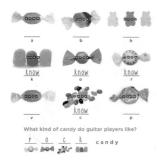

a　　　b　　　h

know　　know　　know
k　　　o　　　r

know
v　　　c　　　p

What kind of candy do guitar players like?
r o c k　candy

Page 313

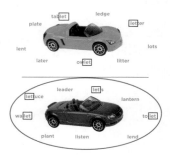

Page 315

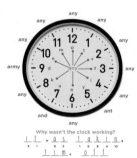

Circle the card suit that has all the shapes colored. ◇ ♡ ♠ ♣

Page 317

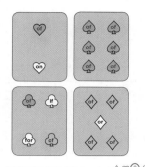

Why wasn't the clock working?
I t   w a s   t a k i n g
t i m e   o f f

Page 319

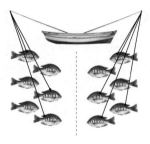

Which side caught more fish? right

Page 321

20,000	could
1,600	could
1,200	could
800	could
400	could

Imagine you are in the dark. Could you still find something to eat? A bat could! Bats send out a sound wave. They listen for an echo to bounce back. The echo helps bats find food in the dark. This is called echolocation. It could even work to help bats find tiny insects!

Use the number at the top of your bar to complete this fun fact:

Bats can eat up to 1,200 mosquitoes per hour!

Page 323

How many bubbles remain? 5

Page 324

I **walk** home from school **every** day. I **know** the way. I always **think** about my day as I **walk**. When I get home, I **know** I need to do my homework. **Then** I have a snack. I **know** how to make **every** snack in our cookbook. **Then**, I play outside with my friends. I **think** I **know every** kid on my street!

walk	2
then	2
think	2
every	3
know	4

Page 325

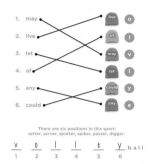

1. may
2. live
3. let
4. of
5. any
6. could

There are six positions in this sport: setter, server, spotter, spiker, passer, digger.

v o l l e y ball
1 2 3 4 5 6

Page 326

```
E T L N O W U N V C
W E E R B C G X O F
L E T K N O W D L M
O T H Y I U V Z I T
T H E N D L O D W H
Y I U C L T B R E
K N F K W O H W L M
B K P N K V L A J K
Y N W E R E M Y A I
R I F D Y R I F N P
```

Page 327

Do you **know** where the school Lost and Found is? It is **over by** the lunch area. If you **think** your things **were** lost at school, **then** please tell **an** aide. The aides **let** students check the Lost and Found before school. You **could** also ask **them** for help after school.

Which review word is missing? of

Page 328

Across

4. We **live** in that house.
5. **Thank** you so much!
6. I know **when** the show starts.
8. We **may** read or draw.
10. I **just** got home.

Down

1. We **walk** across the street.
2. I want to play **again**.
3. Check **every** name on the list.
7. He eats **his** lunch.
9. You may choose **any** book.
11. Let's **take** the ball to the park.

Page 329

Page 330

1. Please put them by her.
2. Ask him again.
3. Please give her some.
4. Please ride after him.
5. Put some over by them.
6. Please take them again.

Page 331

1. under
2. had
3. once
4. walk
5. know
6. just
7. stop
8. let
9. may
10. of
11. think
12. live
13. open
14. his

Page 332

fly / could
thank / pretty
plees / old
when / has
going / wen

every / were
from / then
any / an
as / wons

Page 333

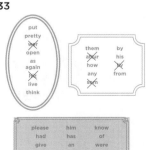

put, pretty, ~~win~~, open, as, again, ~~am~~, live, think

them, by, ~~afour~~, his, how, any, ~~seen~~, from

please, him, know, had, has, of, give, an, were

Page 334

st~~i~~de → ride	tha~~n~~nk → thank	a~~n~~ly → fly
ri~~g~~me → some	und~~l~~ld → could	m~~n~~ay → may
so~~l~~op → stop	cou~~n~~er → under	f~~l~~sk → ask

ov~~n~~lk → walk	th~~n~~ke → take
wh~~l~~er → over	ta~~n~~ce → once
wa~~l~~en → when	on~~n~~en → then
	ju~~n~~st → just

o~~n~~er → her	af~~n~~ery → every
h~~l~~ld → old	go~~n~~ter → after
l~~n~~et → let	ev~~n~~ing → going

Page 337

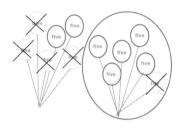

How many balloons are there altogether? __7__

Page 339

5	cold	coal	coat	cod	colt
4	call	old	cold	cone	corn
3	gold	cloud	bold	sold	cold
2	fold	cold	once	old	call
1	all	close	cool	cold	told
	r	h	i	c	a

What has four legs but can't walk?

a __c__ __h__ __a__ __i__ __r__
  1   2   3   4   5

Page 341

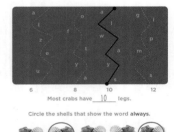

Most crabs have __10__ legs.

Circle the shells that show the word **always**.

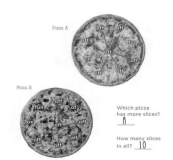

Page 343

Which pizza has more slices? __A__

How many slices in all? __10__

Page 345

Dear Julie,
There is so much to **tell** you about this trip! The flight was very long. We spent the first week near the beach. I can't **tell** you how beautiful the reef was! Then we went to the "outback." I could **tell** right away it was going to be very different. It was a dry, hot desert. I will **tell** you all about the animals I saw when I get home! Please **tell** everyone hello from me.

Love,
Tess

5. Australia

Page 347

+	up	on	pup	upon	one	w
<	not	cup	none	upon	no	o
+	pony	put	pound	upon	nut	y
<	upon	upon	upon	upon	upon	t
+	pun	pop	nope	upon	up	p
	a	g	n	e	l	

What do birds give out on Halloween?

__t__ __w__ __e__ __e__ __t__ s
 <   +   +   <

Page 349

surround / wrong / sound / running

around / ground / roundup / playground

found / grounds / rounding / rode

Page 351

very very → 2
very very very → 3
very very → 2
very very very → 3

v e v y **very** v r y y → ___

Page 353

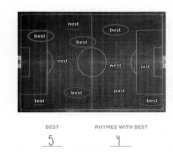

BEST	RHYMES WITH BEST
5	4

Page 355

Page 357

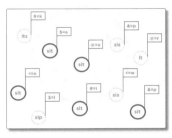

What has many keys but unlocks no doors?

__p__ __i__ __a__ __n__ __o__
 &   # $ <   @

Page 358

The **best** treat on a **very** hot day is **cold** ice cream. I **always** cool **off** with a scoop of the **best** ice cream in town. My **very** favorite flavor is vanilla. But I **always** try new flavors. **Cold** ice cream **always** makes me feel better!

very	2
best	2
always	3
cold	2
off	1

Page 359

1. five
2. tell
3. upon
4. round
5. these
6. sit

In this sport, people race boats. It is also called "crew."

__r__ __o__ __w__ __i__ __n__ __g__
 1   2   3   4   5   6

Page 361

Page 363

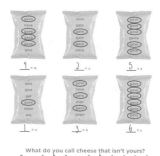

What do you call cheese that isn't yours?

n a c h o   c h e e s e
1 2 3 4   2 3 5 6 5

Page 365

How many book titles have the word first?

4

Page 367

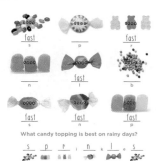

Add up the numbers on all the tickets. 8

10   5   2   1

Prizes circled will vary.

Page 369

fast
s

fast
p

fast
r

fast
n

fast
t

fast
b

fast
s

fast
n

fast
p

What candy topping is best on rainy days?

s p r i n k l e s

Page 371

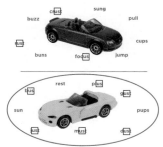

crush   sung
buzz   pull
bus   cups
buns   focus   jump

rest   plus
bus   bus
sun   pups
bus   mus   crus

Page 373

Circle the card suit that has all the shapes colored. ◇ ♡ ♧ 🂡

Page 375

Why did the clock get in trouble?

t o o   m u c h   t o c k - i n g
1 4 4   12 2 11   1 4 2 6   7 3 10

Page 377

Which side caught more fish? left

Page 379

3,000	many
2,500	many
2,000	many
1,500	many
1,000	many
500	many

Many people know that spiders have eight legs. But did you know that many spiders also have eight eyes? Why do spiders have so many eyes? They look for danger and keep spiders safe. Most spiders have four pairs of eyes. But spiders can have as many as twelve eyes. Some spiders have no eyes!

Use the number at the top of your bar to complete this fun fact:

A spider eats about 2,000 insects a year!

Page 381

How many bubbles remain? 6

Page 382

On the **first** day of school, our teacher **gave us** name tags. The tags had our **first** and last names. There were so **many** new students. She wanted to learn our names **fast**. She also **gave us** pencils and **many** books. The **first** book she **gave us** was for reading. It had so **many** fun pictures. The day went by very **fast**!

us	3
many	3
gave	3
fast	2
first	3

Page 383

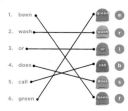

In this game, players throw and catch flying discs.

f r i s b e e
1 2 3 4 5 6 6

Page 384

Page 385

Our class turtle wandered **off**! He **does** this sometimes. Keep an eye out for his **round**, **green** shell. He likes to **sit** in the sun. He is **very** special to **us**! If you see him, please **tell** a teacher **or call** our classroom.

Which review word is missing? **upon**

Page 386

Across

2. I ate <u>five</u> bites.

6. We <u>always</u> help clean up.

7. Have you <u>been</u> there?

8. I will put <u>these</u> away.

9. Don't go so <u>fast</u>.

Down

1. I <u>gave</u> him my coat.

2. Ask your mom <u>first</u>.

3. The water is too <u>cold</u>.

4. I have so <u>many</u> books.

5. We <u>wash</u> the dishes.

7. You are my <u>best</u> friend.

Page 387

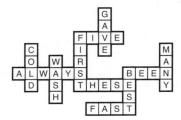

Page 389

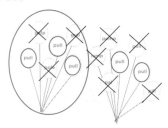

How many balloons are there altogether? __5__

Page 391

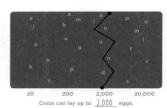

	c	e	n	r	a
5	best	**both**	those	bone	bet
4	the	with	**both**	bath	bold
3	born	path	boat	book	**both**
2	job	moth	bath	**both**	bow
1	**both**	bowl	bore	boy	but

What bird can pick up heavy things?

a __C__ __r__ __a__ __n__ __e__
   1   2   3   4   5

Page 393

20   200   **2,000**   20,000

Crabs can lay up to __2,000__ eggs.

Circle the shells that show the word **around**.

Page 395

Which pie has more slices? __B__

How many slices in all? __10__

Page 397

Dear Kari,
I am having a great time! There are so may green trees and forests here. That's why they call this place the "Emerald City." I **would** love to come back here again. But next time I **would** bring an umbrella. It rains a lot!

Love,
Helen

2. Seattle

Page 399

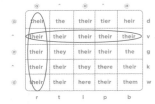

What runs but cannot walk?

a __r__ __i__ __v__ __e__ __r__
   @   ^   @

Page 401

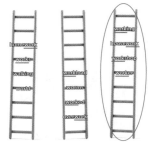

Page 403

m a d (m a d e) m

(m a d e) (m a d e)   __2__

(m a d e) (m a d e) (m a d e)   __3__

(m a d e) (m a d e)   __2__

(m a d e) (m a d e) (m a d e)   __3__

Page 405

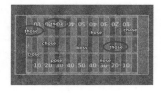

THOSE   RHYMES WITH THOSE

__3__   __5__

Page 407

Page 409

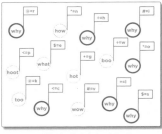

What has forty feet and sings?

the __S__ __C__ __H__ __O__ __O__ __L__ __C__ __H__ __O__ __I__ __R__
   $ < ÷ * * +   < ÷ * # @

Page 410

A lot of birds fly **around** our yard. I thought I **would** **buy** a birdfeeder for them. I looked **around** at the store. But I didn't like any of them. So I **made** one instead! It was a lot of **work**. I wanted to make one that **would** feed a lot of birds. My hard **work** paid off. I **would** do it all again!

buy	1
would	3
made	1
work	2
around	2

Page 411

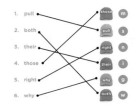

Some of the strokes in this water sport are "butterfly" and "freestyle."

__S__ __W__ __I__ __M__ __M__ __I__ __N__ __G__
1 2 3 4 5 6

Page 413

Page 415

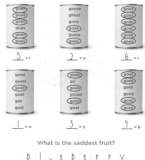

__5__ = i   __2__ = e   __6__ = r

__1__ = u   __3__ = y   __4__ = b

What is the saddest fruit?

__b__ __l__ __u__ __e__ __b__ __e__ __r__ __r__ __y__
4 5   2 4 2 6 6 3

Page 417

How many book titles have the word wish?

3

Page 419

Add up the numbers on all the tickets. 8

10   2   5   2   1

Page 421

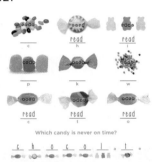

Which candy is never on time?

c h o c o l a t e

Page 423

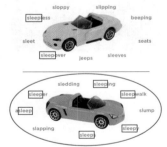

Page 426

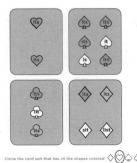

Circle the card suit that has all the shapes colored. ◇ ♡ ♧ ♧

Page 427

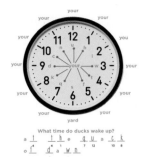

What time do ducks wake up?

a t   t h e   q u a c k
   4 5   7   8   10 8
o f   d a w n
      10 8

Page 429

Which side caught more fish? right

Page 431

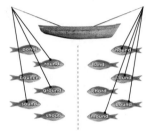

70	don't
60	don't
50	don't
40	don't
30	don't
20	don't
10	don't

Penguins are birds, but they don't fly. Their wings are more like flippers. They use their flippers to dive and swim in the water. They also slide on their bellies on the ice. They have feathers and fat to keep them warm. They build up fat so they can survive when they don't eat for three or four months!

Use the number at the top of your bar to complete this fun fact:

Penguins can stay under water for more than 20 minutes.

Page 433

How many bubbles remain? 5

Page 434

My sister **goes** to camp every summer. She likes to **write** me letters. At camp, they sing songs. Everyone **goes** swimming and boating. I **wish** I was older! Then I could go to camp too. I **don't** think I can wait any longer. I **wish** I could go now! But time **goes** by quickly. Soon, I will **write** letters and sing songs at camp too!

goes	3
sing	2
don't	1
wish	2
write	2

Page 435

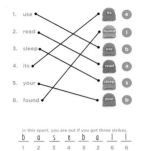

1. use
2. read
3. sleep
4. its
5. your
6. found

its — e
found — i
use — b
read — a
sleep — s
your — b

In this sport, you are out if you get three strikes.

b a s e b a l l
1 2 3 4 5 2 6 6

Page 436

```
G O T H L D X S E Y
A E I R G R W P Q H
D R Y N S F Y Z C J
D O N T O B W O U L D R
O N T H E U U H U I T M H
T E R Y N N G H N T
U N D O U D F O C S
Y T H E I R O S E U
W O G S U E L E D S
U F W H Y A G N S E
```

Page 437

Did you lose **your** lunchbox this year? **Don't** go **buy** a new one yet! **Would** you please check the Lost and **Found** in the cafeteria? Many students have left **their** lunchboxes **around** the cafeteria. All **those** lunchboxes are at the Lost and **Found**. Pick yours up soon. **Why**? Because at the end of the year, everything **goes** to a charity!

Which review word is missing?   use

Page 438

Across
2. We work at our desks.
3. I wish for a new bike.
4. I put it in its box.
5. I like to sleep late.
7. I know the right way.
8. We made a cake.

Down
1. I like both books.
3. I write a note.
5. We sing a song together.
6. We pull the wagon.
7. Let's read the story.

Page 439

Page 440

1. Wash those first.
2. Don't tell us.
3. Call us first.
4. Pull both around.
5. Those made us both very cold.
6. Please take them again.

Page 441

1. five
2. green
3. always
4. night
5. off
6. sing
7. use
8. goes
9. or
10. sleep
11. work
12. its
13. round
14. write

Page 442

best	wish
werk	upon
read	does
your	allways
why	would
pul	found
sit	gave
buy	these
their	many
been	tel

Page 443

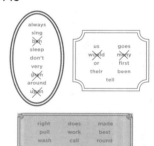

Page 444

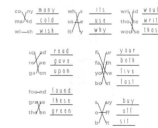

Page 447

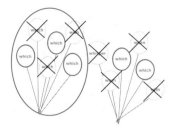

How many balloons are there altogether? 5

Page 449

	l	o	e	t	w
5	fall	far	flaw	call	fill
4	flat	flag	fail	law	feel
3	fan	flop	hall	fell	fail
2	fault	fall	tail	fail	all
1	fair	ball	fat	fall	full

What gets wetter the more it dries?

t o w e l
1 2 3 4 5

Page 451

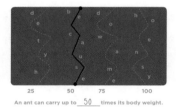

An ant can carry up to 50 times its body weight.

Circle the leaves that show the word because.

Page 453

Which pizza has more slices? A

How many slices in all? 7

Page 455

Dear Sarah,
Today was a great day. I went to a museum, a palace, and a castle. But my favorite thing about today was visiting an old clock tower. It's called "Big Ben." I heard the bells of Big Ben chime today. I can't wait for another great day tomorrow!

Love,
Katie

3. London

Page 457

lot	long	song	long	long	w
long	long	long	lung	long	f
lane	loan	long	long	long	g
long	low	look	gone	long	h
long	long	long	long	long	n
b	t	m	l	p	

What has a head and tail but no legs?

a p e n n y

Page 459

Page 461

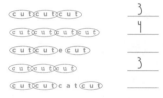

Page 463

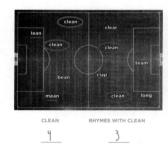

CLEAN   RHYMES WITH CLEAN

4   3

Page 465

Page 467

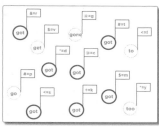

What do drummers bring to Thanksgiving dinner?
turkey d r u m s t i c k s
* & $ < # @ ÷ <

Page 468

__Today__ we __got__ a lot of work done! We helped our neighbor __clean__ her yard. We __got__ to her house early. We __cut__ back the bushes. I used a __long__ hose to water everything. It was a __long__ day. Her yard was so __clean__ when we were done. I feel really good about __today__. We __got__ her yard so __clean__. __Today__ was a great day. I __got__ to help someone.

got   3
long   2
cut   1
clean   3
today   3

Page 469

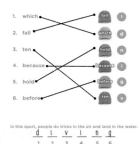

In this sport, people do tricks in the air and land in the water.
d i v i n g
1 2 3 4 5 6

Page 471

Page 473

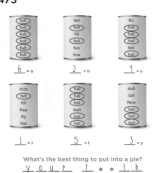

What's the best thing to put into a pie?
y o u r   t e e t h
3 6 4 1   5   5 2

Page 475

How many book titles have the word about?
5

Page 477

Add up the numbers on all the tickets. 11

11   2   5   2   1

Page 479

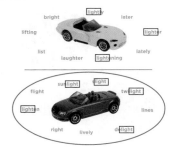

pick   pick   pick
p   l   r

pick   pick   pick
m   n   w

pick   pick   pick
n   a   m

Which candy falls from trees?

l e m o n   d r o p s

Page 481

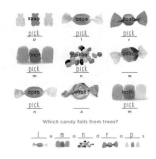

bright   later
lifting   lighter
list   lately
    laughter lightening

    sunlight light
flight   twilight
lighten   lines
    right   lively delight

Page 483

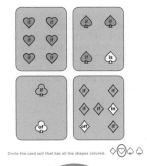

Circle the card suit that has all the shapes colored. ◇♡♧♤

Page 485

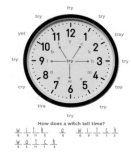

How does a watch tell time?
W i t h   a   w i t c h
6 9 11 3   6   9 11 3

w a t c h
6 5 11 3

Page 487

Which side caught more fish? right

Page 489

70 carry
60 carry
50 carry
40 carry
30 carry
20 carry

Baby kangaroos are very small at birth. They are only about one inch long! Mother kangaroos __carry__ their babies in a pouch. The pouch keeps them safe and warm. The baby kangaroos grow bigger in the pouch. After about ten months, they are ready to leave the pouch. Their mothers don't have to __carry__ them anymore.

Use the number at the top of your bar to complete this fun fact:

Kangaroos can jump as far as __30__ feet.

Page 491

How many bubbles remain? 7

Page 492

Everyone got to __pick__ something to __bring__ to the holiday party. I wanted to __pick__ something sweet and __hot__. I decided to __bring__ __hot__ chocolate. I wanted to __try__ to make it __myself__. The __hot__ chocolate turned out great! Everyone wanted to __try__ it. I was proud of __myself__.

hot   3
bring   2
pick   2
try   2
myself   2

Page 493

1. which
2. fall
3. because
4. ten
5. hold
6. before

ten — i
which — s
hold — n
fall — a
before — g
because — i

In this sport, people use the wind to race boats on the water.

s a i l i n g
1 2 3 4 5 6

Page 494

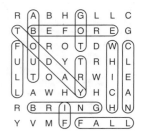

R A B H G L L C
T B E F O R E G
F O R O T D W C
U U D Y T R H L
L T O A R W I E
L A W H Y H C A
R B R I N G H N
Y V M F F A L L

Page 495

Help <u>clean</u> the school library <u>today</u>! If you've <u>got</u> books at home, <u>bring</u> them in <u>before</u> the end of the year. Talk to the librarian <u>about</u> any lost books. Let's <u>try</u> to make our bookshelves <u>full</u> again for next <u>fall</u>!

Which review word is missing?   which

Page 496

Across
2. I <u>carry</u> my bag.
4. We are happy <u>because</u> it's Friday.
6. Please <u>hold</u> on tight.
8. The line is <u>long.</u>
9. It is <u>hot</u> outside.
11. I <u>cut</u> my finger.

Down
1. Always <u>pick</u> up your toys.
3. I am happy with <u>myself</u>.
5. There are <u>six</u> cookies.
7. The <u>light</u> helps us see.
10. We ran <u>ten</u> laps.

Page 497

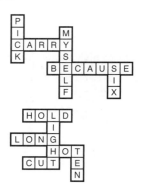

Page 499

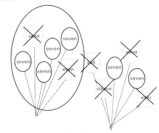

How many balloons are there altogether? 6

Page 501

5	wow	arm	wart	worm	warm
4	wait	warm	with	yarn	war
3	harm	warp	farm	warm	walk
2	warm	want	war	were	arm
1	wave	worm	warm	wore	wall

w   m   s   i   s

What does a fish do in a school?

it S W I M S
   1 2 3 4 5

Page 503

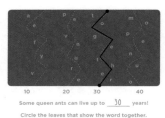

10   20   30   40

Some queen ants can live up to 30 years!

Circle the leaves that show the word together.

together gather together together today

Page 505

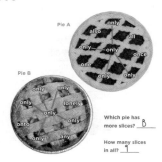

Pie A
Pie B

Which pie has more slices? B
How many slices in all? 9

Page 507

Dear Terry,
I have **done** so many things on this trip! I visited gardens, beaches, and forests. I've **done** a lot of fishing in the lakes here. The sun does not ever go down here during the summer. The day goes on and on! It is fun, but it can be hard to fall asleep when it's light outside. I will be home soon.

Best,
Chuck

2. Sweden

Page 509

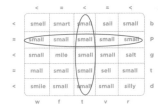

	<	=	<	=	<	
<	smell	smart	small	sail	small	b
=	small	small	small	small	small	P
<	small	mile	small	small	salt	g
=	mall	small	small	sell	small	t
<	smile	small	small	small	silly	d
	w	f	t	v	r	

What did the hamburger name its daughter?

p a t t y

Page 511

Page 513

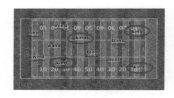

k e e p k e e p — 2
k e e p k e e p k e p —
k e e p k e e p k e e p — 3
k e e p k e e p — 2
k e e p k e e p k e e p — 3

Page 515

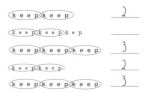

KIND   RHYMES WITH KIND
 4   5

Page 517

Page 519

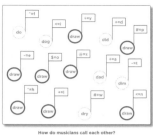

How do musicians call each other?

On the x y l o p h o n e
@ ÷ + $ _ # ^ $ < -

Page 520

Jane and Julia want to work **together** to **grow** flowers. They find a **small** spot in their yard that gets lot of **warm** sunshine. They plant the seeds **together**. If they **keep** watering the **small** seeds, they will **grow** into beautiful flowers.

small	2
warm	1
grow	2
keep	1
together	2

Page 521

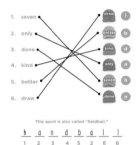

1. seven
2. only
3. done
4. kind
5. better
6. draw

draw — l
better — b
kind — d
only — a
seven — h
done — n

This sport is also called "fieldball."

h a n d b a l l
1 2 3 4 5 2 6 6

Page 523

Page 525

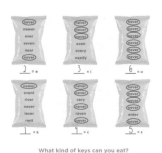

2 = e   3 = i   6 = o
1 = k   4 = c   5 = s

What kind of keys can you eat?

c o o k i e s
4 6 6 1 3 2 5

Page 527

The Loud Noise
Live and Laugh ✓
Right and Left
Jokes to Laugh at
How Much Is Enough
How to Laugh More
Energy and Light
Making Long Lashes

How many book titles have the word laugh?

3

Page 529

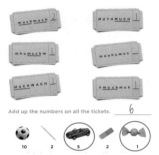

muchmuch 2
NUTHMUCH 1
mhumuchm 1
mouhcmuc 1
MUCHWACH 1
hmuchmuh 1

Add up the numbers on all the tickets. 6

10   2   5   2   1

Page 531

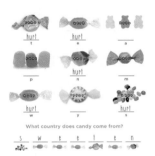

hurt — t   hurt — e   ___ — a
___ — p   hurt — n   ___ — m
hurt — w   ___ — y   hurt — s

What country does candy come from?

S w e e t e n

Page 533

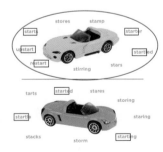

stores   stamp
start   starter
upstart   started
restart   stars
stirring

tarts   stares
started
storing
starting   staring
stacks   storm
starting

Page 535

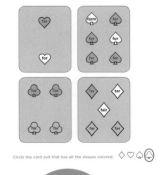

Circle the card suit that has all the shapes colored. ◇ ♡ ♧ (♧)

Page 537

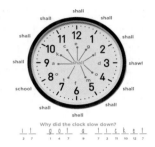

Why did the clock slow down?

I t   g o t   a   t i c k e t
2 7   1 4 7   9   7 2 11 10 12 7

Page 539

flow   stew
new   crow
know   tow
low   paw
mow   slow
won   snow
row   glow
throw

Which side caught more fish? right

Page 541

90	drink
80	drink
70	drink
60	drink
50	drink
40	drink
30	drink

Elephants <u>drink</u> a lot of water! Elephants use their trunks to help them <u>drink</u>. First, they suck up water with their trunks. Then, they curl their trunks down. The trunk sprays water like a hose into an elephant's mouth. This is how elephants <u>drink</u> water.

Use the number at the top of your bar to complete this fun fact:

Elephants drink up to 50 gallons of water a day.

Page 543

eight   ~~right~~   eight
~~light~~   ~~their~~
~~get~~   eight   eight
eight

How many bubbles remain? 5

Page 544

Brad wanted to <u>**show**</u> everyone how fast he could run in the race. He hadn't gotten very <u>**far**</u> when he tripped and fell. Brad's knee was <u>**hurt**</u>. His pride was <u>**hurt**</u>, too. His friend Tracey wasn't <u>**far**</u> behind him. She stopped and gave him a <u>**drink**</u>. She wanted to <u>**show**</u> him that it was no big deal. Tracey told him a joke and made him <u>**laugh**</u>. Brad was still <u>**hurt**</u>, he got up and finished the race.

hurt   3
laugh   1
show   2
far   2
drink   1

Page 545

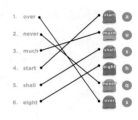

This sport shares its name with a vegetable!

S q u a s h
1 2 3 4 5 6

Page 546

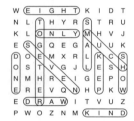

Page 547

Has anyone seen a <u>**small**</u> pencil case? I <u>**only**</u> <u>**keep**</u> <u>**seven**</u> or <u>**eight**</u> pencils <u>**together**</u> inside the case. I brought it to school to <u>**show**</u> my friends how I <u>**draw**</u>. When I was <u>**done**</u>, I left if behind. I would appreciate any help so <u>**much**</u>!

Which review word is missing?   kind

Page 548

Across

3. I <u>never</u> eat peanuts.

4. I have my <u>own</u> bike.

5. It time to <u>start</u> the game.

6. I live very <u>far</u> away.

7. I like to <u>drink</u> milk.

8. The book makes me <u>laugh</u>.

10. My food is <u>warm</u>.

Down

1. I feel <u>better</u> today.

2. Good food helps me <u>grow</u>.

5. Where <u>shall</u> we go?

9. He <u>hurt</u> my feelings.

Page 549

Page 550

1. <u>Bring</u> it <u>today</u>.

2. I <u>carry</u> it <u>myself</u> <u>because</u> it's <u>light</u>.

3. We <u>clean</u> <u>better</u> <u>together</u>.

4. It <u>got</u> <u>warm</u> <u>today</u>.

5. We <u>keep</u> <u>warm</u> <u>together</u>.

6. <u>Before</u> <u>long</u>, it <u>got</u> <u>warm</u>.

Page 551

1. fall
2. cut
3. hot
4. which
5. small
6. pick
7. done
8. drink
9. only
10. seven
11. own
12. if
13. much
14. laugh

Page 552

start   hold
ten   hert
miself   about
show   never
eight   draw

hurt   full
shall   smal
try   six
becuz   grow
far   kind

Page 553

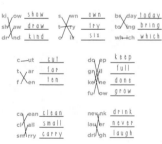

hurt
shall
✗
✗
about
pick
hot
draw
if

much   hold
✗   together
long   ✗ver
clean   before
✗   got

because   better   warm
start   myself   seven
eight   light   only

Page 554

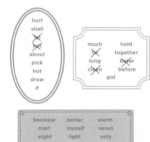

ki_ow show   s_wn own   br_day today
sh_aw draw   t__ty try   to_ing bring
dr_nd kind   _ix six   wh_ch which

c_ut cut   do_ep keep
t_ar far   gn_ll full
f_en ten   ke_ne done
                 fu_ow grow

ca_ean clean   nev_nk drink
cl_all small   lau_er never
sm_rry carry   dri_gh laugh